THE BUSH IS SWEET

Identity, Power and Development
among WoDaaBe Fulani in Niger

KRISTÍN LOFTSDÓTTIR

NORDISKA AFRIKAINSTITUTET, UPPSALA 2008

Indexing terms:
Ethnic groups
Pastoralists
Cultural identity
Ethnicity
Traditional culture
Social change
Social and cultural anthropology
Fula
Niger

Photos: Kristín Loftsdóttir
Maps: Guðmundur Ó. Ingvarsson
Language checking: Elaine Almén
Index: Rohan Bolton
Layout: ilo grafisk form
ISBN 978-91-7106-617-6
© The author and Nordiska Afrikainstitutet 2008
Printed in Sweden by GML Print on Demand AB, Stockholm 2008

CONTENTS

ACKOWLEDGEMENTS 7

INTRODUCTION 9
WoDaaBe 11
Ethnographer 14
Doing Fieldwork 15
Theoretical Influences 16
Organization of the Book 22

CHAPTER 1: THE EVER CHANGING WORLD 24
Creating the Developing World 27
Pastoral People and Development 30
Niger and Development 33
The Importance of Land 37
In Conclusion 40

CHAPTER 2: A GLOBAL WORLD OF IMAGES 42
Categorizing the World 43
Representations of Indigenous People 46
Imagining the Fulani 48
In Conclusion 55

CHAPTER 3: AT HOME IN THE BUSH 57
The Ecology of the Bush 59
WoDaaBe Homes 61
Living in a *Wuro* 63

CHAPTER 4: ANIMALS IN WODAABE ECONOMIC AND SOCIAL LIFE 67
Djelgul, the Symbol of Ownership 69
The Affection for and Economics of Cows 71
Social Life and Livestock 72

CHAPTER 5: THE COLD AND THE HOT SEASON 75
A Letter to a Place Far Away 87

CHAPTER 6: WODAABE ETHNIC IDENTITY 90
Mbodagansi 92
Today and the Past: The Council of Elders 98

CHAPTER 7: GENDER AND POWER 101
Construction of Gender 102
Gender Relations 103
Tegal Marriage and the Lineage 106
The *BoofiiDo* 108
Resistance and Agency 111

CHAPTER 8: THE RAIN STARTS TO FALL 114

CHAPTER 9: THE BORDER TOWN 129

CHAPTER 10: WORKING IN THE CITY 137
Migrant Work in the Past 141
Migrant Work Today 143
Relations with the Bush 146

CHAPTER 11: THE MAKERS OF HANDICRAFTS 149
Shame and Survival 154
Ethnic Relations in Niamey 156

CHAPTER 12: JUMARE'S ACCIDENT 160

CHAPTER 13: GENDERED LIVES 167
Working in the City 170

CHAPTER 14: DANCING IN NIAMEY 178
Going to the Dance 179
Classification of Dance Permances among the WoDaaBe 184
Diversity and Fractions within Unity 185

CHAPTER 15: DESIRE AND IDENTITY 191
The Dances 192

CHAPTER 16: LIVED RELATIONS 200
WoDaaBe Agency 202
WoDaaBe and Development 203
The Handicraft Work 207
Relations of Power 208
Desires and Power 211

CHAPTER 17: DEVELOPMENT AND IDENTITY: CREATING SUBJECTS 214
Creating the WoDaaBe Subject 215

CONCLUDING REMARKS 222

APPENDIX I 227
Transforming Experience into a Text 227

APPENDIX II 232
Intersubjectivity 232

APPENDIX III 234
Earlier Research on WoDaaBe 234

References 236

Index 258

WoDaaBe main lineage organization as seen from Gojanko'en individuals

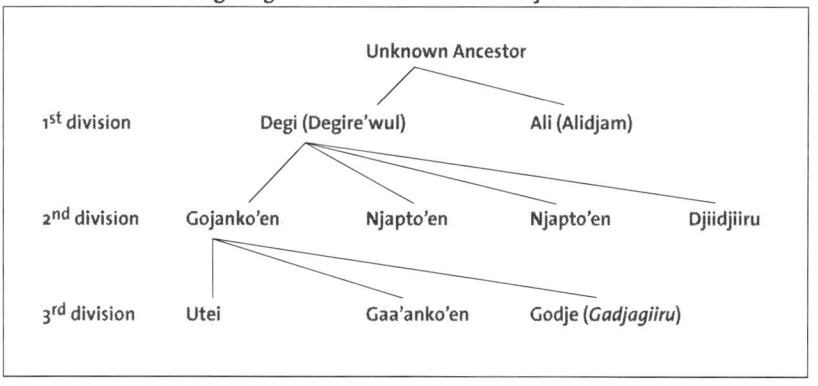

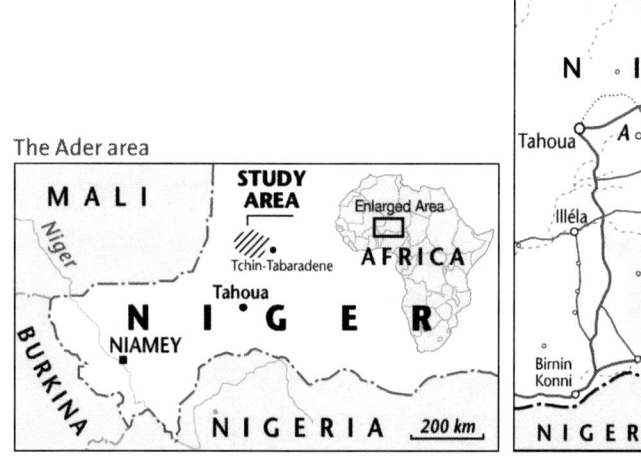

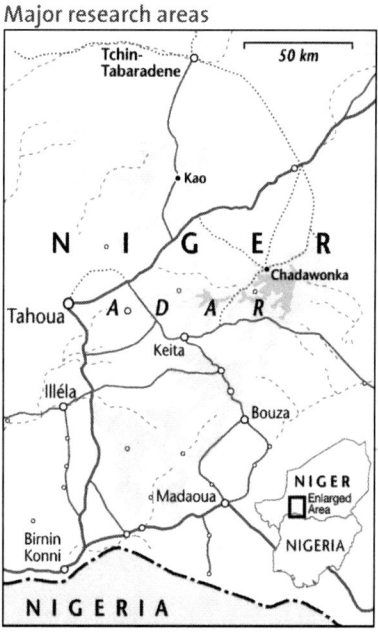

		Unknown Ancestor		
1st division	Degi (Degire'wul)		Ali (Alidjam)	
2nd division	Gojanko'en	Njapto'en	Njapto'en	Djiidjiiru
3rd division	Utei	Gaa'anko'en	Godje (*Gadjagiiru*)	

The Ader area

Major research areas

GLOSSARY

Anasara	white person, person from the West, a Christian.
ArDo	the lineage chief.
Dabbunde	the time of the season when it is cold and, windy and with regular sandstorms.
DuDal	the cattle coral. It is made during the rainy season by lighting a fire for the cattle to free them from the mosquitoes.
BoofiiDo	a womaen becomes a *boofiiDo* bofido when pregnant with their her first child and is still defined as *boofiiDo* bofido two or three years after giving birth to the child.
CeeDu	the hot season.
Gonsul	aA general term over migration movements.
HaBBanaaji	cattle loans.
Yaawol	a season of prosperity and pleasure.
KooBgal	Marriage within the lineage. The parents organize this type of marriage for their children usually when the children are young.
KoDei	desire, greed.
Kokke	The time of the season when the first rain starts to fall.
LaamiiDo	the highest indigenous authority of the WoDaaBe. A *laamiiDo* can be an authority over several lineages. The chiefs (ardo) of different WoDaaBe lineages have to report to the *laamiiDo*.
Mbodagansi	a core concept in characterizing WoDaaBe identity, embracing various aspects of what it means to be WoDaaBe.
Munyal	patience, tolerance, one of the major characteristics that the WoDaaBe value and see as characterizing themselves.
Ndunngu	time of the season the season when there is a lot of grass.
Pulaaku	a core concept in characterizing the Fulani identity, referring to moral virtues and behaviour.
Semaru	a person with whom one is engaged in a sexual relationship. WoDaaBe cannot generally marry their *semaru*, which who are usually found within the same lineage group.
SemtuDum	shame, respect, one of the characteristics that the WoDaaBe value greatly and see as characterizing themselves.
Si'ire	town.
Surbaajo	girl, young woman.
Suudu (pl. *cuuDi*)	house-units constituting the WoDaaBe *wuro* or home.
Teegal	marriage between people from different lineages or lineage fractions. It is forbidden between members of the same lineage.
Wuro (pl. *gure*)	a term over for house, hut, village, or town. A WoDaaBe *wuro* is composed by of several smaller units called *cuudi* (sing. *suudu*).

ACKNOWLEDGEMENTS

I would like to thank all those who helped and took care of me during my research and who patiently tolerated my limitations during my fieldwork in Niger. Especially, I want to thank the people in the Gojanko'en lineage group I stayed with most. To Gaa'i, Ganjado, Girgi, Ibanou, Dro, Mawde, Ganay'i, Tumbido, Budjo, Baya, Madika, Dembe and many others who generously gave me their time and more importantly, a part of themselves, I want to say: *Mi yetti, mi yetti gore gore gore, wana dum seda. Mi yetti amina on'on. Allah wadan barki* (I thank you, I thank you so much for your friendship. May God help you). In Niger, I met kindness and assistance from various other individuals. I want especially to mention Idrissa Yansambou, Directeur des Archives Nationales Niamey; Moussa Abdou Akoda at Prefecture Tahoua, M. Bagoudou Maidaji at the Ministry of Herding and Agriculture, Maïkorema Zakari, Directeur de l'IRSH (*Institut de Recherche en Sciences Humaines*); Gambo Boukary, Maidaji Maiguida, Madame Idrissa neé Salmou Salifouse at IRSH, as well as other individuals connected to these above mentioned institutions. Also, I would like to thank Serhirou Boubacar, Bill Phelan, Boubacar Hassane, Raquel Christine de Sousa, Keith E. Syler, Basonka, Bob Winterbottom, Lisbet Holtedahl, Mahmoudou Djingui and Thomas Painter who in different ways gave assistance or advice to the dissertation research.

My gratitude also goes to others who were crucial to this project in a more indirect way, my husband and better half, Már Wolfgang Mixa, who helped me through this long journey with patience and love; my parents, Loftur Magnússon and Erla G. Sigurðardóttir for their support and enthusiasm for the research as well for providing endless hours of baby-sitting of my three small children during the writing of this book. My thanks extend as well to my siblings, Ásta, Jónína Dögg and Magnús, and other family members who wrote to me during fieldwork time and kept me a part of their lives during my long absence from Iceland. I also want to thank my friend, Árni Víkingur Sveinsson, who assisted with bringing this work to life from its beginning.

My students at the University of Iceland, Helga Björnsdóttir and Jo Tore Berg, were persistent in encouraging me to publish this book, and I wish to thank Jo for critical comments that he made on the manuscript.

The book is based on my dissertation (2000) which I defended at the University of Arizona in the fall of 1999. To my mentors, Thomas K. Park, Richard Henderson, Helen Henderson, Ana María Alonso and Hermann K. Bleibtreu, I want to express gratitude for various kinds of assistance in relation to my research, critical comments and encouragement. Richard Henderson and Helen Henderson also opened their homes to me and later to my family, providing shelter, love and support from my first day in Tucson. Thomas K. Park, my main advisor, provided extensive support and challenges for me during my student years, encouraging me to continue my studies, never questioning my abilities.

The ethnographic research conducted in Niger from August 1996 until the end of June 1998, was made possible with funding from the Nordic Africa Institute and Rotary International. Funding from the Jón Þórarinsson Educational Fund, given by Flensborg College made exploratory research in Niger in 1996 possible. I am very grateful to these institutions for giving me the opportunity to conduct this research. Furthermore, I received scholarships from the Nordic Africa Institute to stay there as a student and then later as a guest researcher when writing up results and analyzing the data, benefiting from kind advice, stimulating discussions with various individuals associated with the Institute who are too numerous to be mentioned but include Mette Bovin, Harri Englund, Ebrima Sall and Bawa Yamba. I also want to mention the generous assistance that I have received over the years in regard to various issues from Karin Andersson Schiebe, Nina Frödin and Susanne Linderos at the Nordic Africa Institute.

INTRODUCTION

I am the white anthropologist. At this moment that is who I am. A white person with a pen in my hand, papers in my lap, in an ambiguous power relationship with those I am working with. My assistant, Akali, is afraid to join the group I am talking to because he also stands in a specific power relationship with these individuals. They are a group of elderly men. He is young; they are old. Power is no less a part of his life than it is of mine.

I feel shy; perhaps I have started to absorb the WoDaaBe[1] sense of shame in crossing boundaries of age and gender. The men are sitting beneath a cluster of trees. It is late in the day, the sun still high in the sky. These men are approaching the later stages of their lives, the youngest being Kala'i, who I guess is in his early seventies. The others are much older. One of the men, whom I call Ardo, is a chief. Two of the men I do not know very well, the fifth is from another lineage group. I sit in the corner of the straw mat, having been given permission to join them and talk. The issues we are discussing concern power, the lack of power and the identity of the WoDaaBe as a group. We have discussed these issues many times before – the lack of rain, the insecurity of the area, the leaving of young people to go and search for work in the city. They are relevant now as always, a new year is starting and everyone fears it will be more difficult than this passing year. The rain came late and some lost a number of their few animals. What will the next year bring? These problems and issues strike at the heart of what it means to be a WoDaaBe, the desire to exist as a group, to be engaged in herding.

Ardo is speaking, "What we want is prosperity for our area, we want prosperity and peace. If it rains, we will prosper. If it rains we will gain well being.

---

[1] In transcription I have tried to follow the recommendations made by the experts of the Congress for the Unification of Alphabets of the National Languages of West Africa in 1966, organized by UNESCO. The capitalized B and D refer to the glottalized or injective consonants in the Fulfulde language (see Pelletier and Skinner 1981:3). Riesman calls these sounds "injective" consonants (Riesman 1977:xxi). The glottal stop is indicated by an apostrophe.

We will herd our animals, we will live with the bush with our animals. But if it does not rain, we will not gain prosperity. Then all kinds of problems will arise."

Another man says, "I have no millet, no milking cows, no well to fetch water."

There is silence. Then Ardo speaks again firmly but gently. "What we want now is help, assistance. Help with getting peace in this area, with water and animals. May God show me the day when we get this."

Kala'i turns towards me smiling, asking me to find him a well to give his animals water so he does not have to retreat to the city. "People of the city do not migrate, my cows would suffer from hunger." He is teasing when he speaks of his retreat to the city, because he has always been a herder. His voice carries the passion he has for his cows. He has told me many times how important they are for him and his family, for the WoDaaBe. He is the one who has taught me a simple truth: that the well-being of animals ensures the well-being of people.

I have seen the problems they are discussing. I came to Niger to find out whether the WoDaaBe were something other than the painted people living in harmony and peace I had observed previously in the popular press. What I encountered was desperation, fear of losing one's cows, waiting for rain and the frustration that every year seems to bring too little rain. Their lives are, however, not simply a struggle for basic survival, but embody all spectra of human creativity, dynamics and interactions of power.

The constant interplays of power that are part of my everyday existence, probably stimulated my interest in analyzing power as it operates in the many phases of WoDaaBe lives. Power became important as a research topic because it was so relevant in my relationships there and, obviously, also in their lives. My interest grew around the historical reasons for the powerlessness that the WoDaaBe find themselves in today, as well as WoDaaBe identity in a world of development and globalization.

I think of words that were said to me in the city Niamey, where rules can be bent more easily than in the bush. These words were spoken in anger and frustration at exactly the same situation that these men are discussing here.

> You should not forget that I am someone, that I am somebody. My life is perhaps not very fine, I never went to school, I am a black man, I do not own anything; I realize that I don't know anything like your people, but I am still someone. You should remember that I am somebody just like you. Just as you, I have some things that I love and some things I don't like (from my personal notebook).

The man who spoke these words is a WoDaaBe migrant worker. The situation in the bush had brought him to migrant work many years ago, and since then his life has been a struggle in attempting to rebuild his herd but also perhaps also to try to "make it" in a new world of urban jewelry selling. He has learned that those who are able to make white friends are the ones who are more likely to make a living from their work in the city. These relationships are not of equals, and the fact that the WoDaaBe place value on not expressing their feelings demonstrates the speaker's sense of powerlessness and frustration.

Identities and power are never static or singular. This applies to me as well as those around me. I see that my discussion with the elderly men has ended, they asking me politely if this is all and my role changes suddenly from being the white anthropologist into that of a "Young Woman at Kala'i's House." I thank them for their information and discussion, and start gathering my things together. The old men observe me in a different way and those who do not know me start asking Kala'i about me. "So, she speaks Fulfulde", one says, and Kala'i nods. "Yes, she speaks Fulfulde now." "Mariyama", he turns toward me, "what is the name for this?" He points at an object nearby. His voice is different from before, softer and he speaks slower. He is proud of me, I think, and wants to show how well I have been brought up. He points to the different things around us and I slowly name everything, like an obedient child. The men clearly enjoy this demonstration of my abilities, smiling kindly to me. They also use a different tone of voice speaking to me, and like Kala'i, see me now as Mariyama. The anthropologist only momentarily rose to the surface.

WoDaaBe

A majority of WoDaaBe live in Niger, even though some WoDaaBe groups can be found in neighboring countries. Most scholarly work identifies WoDaaBe as a subsection of the Fulani,[2] who are scattered over large parts of West Africa and have traditionally subsisted on pastoralism. WoDaaBe are,

---

[2] I was unfortunately not able to find accurate information regarding the numbers of WoDaaBe in Niger. I heard the estimation 100,000 while in Niger. Carol Beckwith estimated in 1983 that they were 45,000. The Fulani are estimated as 10 percent of Niger's population (Lund 1997:14), WoDaaBe probably being included in this number.

furthermore, often characterized in older sources as the "purest" form of Fulani culture, due to their close attachment to herding and nomadism. Even though WoDaaBe assign primary importance to livestock herding as a way of life, they have occasionally cultivated fields as a fallback activity, usually aiming at rebuilding the herd. Like probably all other social and cultural groups, the WoDaaBe have in recent years increasingly been brought into a global context even though never removed from West African dynamic and political spheres. Books and articles have been produced for mass markets, involving narratives about WoDaaBe, and their images are used on products for global markets. At the same time as the WoDaaBe have become more integrated into a global world, they have been increasingly marginalized within it. They find themselves in drier areas than before, with smaller spaces of land to utilize and their traditional alternative fallback activities are becoming more limited. The droughts of 1968–1974 and 1984 led to great livestock losses in resource poor Niger, which in spite of various development assistance projects continues to be identified as one of the poorest few countries of the world. Many WoDaaBe have turned to migrant labor in order to reconstruct their herds and to provide for their extended families remaining in the bush. Many are not able to return to the pastoral economy, whereas the benefits of migrant labor are in most cases meager. My discussion focuses on how identity is negotiated in these circumstances, in interactions among the WoDaaBe themselves and in relationships with non-WoDaaBe. I seek to understand identity by situating it within relations of power on a global scale, placing the current WoDaaBe situation within a broad field of national and international politics of development and commercialization which bring real individuals from different parts of the world into contact.

Research on development and identity has a tendency to take place in separate streams of discourses; research on identity is usually informed by theoretical insights such as post-colonialism while development issues are analyzed from an applied angle almost as if this something we call development was separated from issues of identity and power. Development is a part of people's everyday lives in Niger – it is "there", both visually and ideologically – featuring highly in many people's hopes and desires for the future. I see development as a global phenomenon, stressing ethnic and cultural aspects of WoDaaBe lives in the context of their attempts to improve their lives by getting "development" and marketing their products in the city. I use my own ethnographic experience to give insight into WoDaaBe contemporary life in the bush and in the city, as well as to discuss more abstract relations of power between Westerners and WoDaaBe that underline both development issues and WoDaaBe global market relations. In a sense this is an ethnography of an interconnected world, showing how the local and global, or even different types of locality are interwoven in complex and sometimes unexpected ways.

I demonstrate increased WoDaaBe popularity in recent decades in the commercial mass media, with them being featured in high profile magazines and "coffee-table" books. This association of objects with a specific identity can be seen as a part of a general trend of transformation of so called indigenous people into commodities valued in the Western world. Popular representations contribute toward increased interest in WoDaaBe objects among Westerners, who are the main consumer of these craft products. My discussion outlines how globalization affects the WoDaaBe through this popularization of images and through international development. Many WoDaaBe manipulate their recent popularity in the global mass produced media by creating tourist friendly artifacts, which are popular within the development community in Niger. The artisanry production involves relationships which are complicated and ambiguous, interweaving various themes of power, desire and objectification. WoDaaBe involvement with the production and selling of handicrafts and with development signals a somewhat problematic relationship with predominantly white people, white Westerners, being seen as a way to prosperity and riches. WoDaaBe see their occupation in the city generally as a temporary phase in their lives. Some individuals express a deep nostalgic desire to return to the bush while in the city, but once in the bush they experience life there as difficult and monotonous, thus indicating the contradictory and complex effects of migrant work on people's lives. WoDaaBe migrant workers' self-identification with pastoral life is also reflected in how they situate their work in the city as a form of risk management, identifying it with other strategies that WoDaaBe have used in the past to rebuild their stock of animals. Instead of being associated with sedentary life in cities, migrant work can be seen as a new way of using mobility thus negotiating pastoral identities with the city life that migrant work requires

The discussion also points out that while the city brings WoDaaBe into contact with an increased number of ethnicities, city life simultaneously highlights the division within WoDaaBe society in terms of division into different lineages. Globalization with all its changes, shows how people like the WoDaaBe continue – not only to resist – but to take advantage and manipulate new opportunities that arise within a changing world.

Ethnographer

When I took my undergraduate degree in social anthropology at the University of Iceland, anthropology demonstrated that things I found dissatisfying could fruitfully be seen as problematic. I feel that some of the most important characteristics of anthropology are its incitement to look at an environment in a critical way yet also with compassion and its attempts to "understand" the reasons for other people's behavior and thoughts. I think that my interest in anthropology also has to do with my hope that the world was a certain way and that there were better worlds somewhere, which explains my interest in indigenous communities, which I had cherished before. My imagining of communities existing in isolation, with perfect harmony among people, soon started to break down, the final point being an article that I read by Terence Turner while still in Iceland. Turner emphasizes in this article the importance of emphasizing agency and inequality within indigenous societies, not only seeing indigenous people as victims of the world (1979:2). I had placed an order for this article on interlibrary loan, because I knew that it was a criticism of the "romantic" representation of indigenous communities. I remember holding it in my hands when I finally received it five weeks later, knowing that by reading it some of my innocence would fade away. It did, but it was replaced by an interest in my own need for this image, as well as in understanding the actual situations of indigenous people today. The motivations for my research were influenced by the positioning of my goals in relation to a metanarrative that has been "popularized" about the WoDaaBe. These narratives have served for Westerners to imagine a world, somehow untouched by modernity, which they can visit either through colorful books or expensive travel packages. My orientation was also shaped by the present-day political and historical circumstances of the WoDaaBe – their lack of animals, weak rights to land, lack of sustainable pasture – and how these factors that are simplified or ignored in the popular imagination have affected the lives of the WoDaaBe, and furthermore, how WoDaaBe resist and create better living conditions for themselves.

Doing Fieldwork

A year prior to my fieldwork, I conducted a six week exploratory study in Niger and established contact with several migrant workers, formulating my research goals. Walking through the hot streets of Niamey, I met a few WoDaaBe selling handicrafts at a little store in the district where many of the development project staff are based. Two persons, young men who had worked for many years as migrant workers, took special interest in my project and were more easily able to communicate with me due to their ability to speak English. When they suggested that they should show me the "real" life of WoDaaBe in the bush, I reluctantly accepted their offer somewhat concerned for my safety and took on a difficult five-day trip to the bush. Afterwards, I saw that I had unknowingly and unwillingly started to shape the circumstances even before I started the research. After this initial visit to Niger, all kinds of processes started taking place; expectations being made in relation to gains which could possibly be made from my friendship, friendships being damaged due to the same reasons, and new alliances being constructed. As I understood later, Westerners are seen by many WoDaaBe migrant workers as a road to prosperity, and thus friendship with me was seen as a possible way of improving one's situation. I think that this, perhaps more than anything else, showed me how research takes place in a historical and political environment, which shapes the research itself.

My ethnographic fieldwork consisted of formal and informal interviews, questionnaires, research in government archives, participation in various private and public events, and systematic observation of daily life. Observing, interacting and participating with people in their daily life where conditions are often not under the control of the anthropologists, helps in creating an understanding of how subjectivities and identities are formed in the field of social practices. I did fieldwork mostly in two locations: the bush west of Tchin-Tabaraden and in Niamey, the capital of Niger. I traveled back and forth between these localities just as many of the migrant workers do, though I traveled more often. In the pastoral area, I was a part of households, most of the time staying within the same lineage group. I participated in their daily lives to the greatest extent possible, traveling in their fashion, eating the same food and drinking the same water as other household members. I also visited various other households to enrich my ethnographic data. In Niamey I interacted with migrant workers and collected institutionalized material relevant to my research. Even though I interviewed migrant laborers from lineage groups from different areas in the country, I emphasized interviewing the WoDaaBe migrant workers belonging to the same lineage group with whom I interacted in the bush. Such an approach better demonstrates the difference between lives in the bush and in the city, and of course enabled me to make use of the personal relationships developed in the bush. In Niamey, I collected archival material and tried to get overviews of recent studies of the WoDaaBe, and I interviewed individuals working with international aid institutions and civil servants in various state institutions working in relation to natural resource policies. In addition, I transcribed some of my interviews with the assistance of a WoDaaBe in order to improve my Fulfulde and to gain greater accuracy in interpreting the texts. As much as I wanted to live with a WoDaaBe family in Niamey, it was not possible. Those WoDaaBe families that were the subject of my study lived on the street and they considered it unsafe for me to sleep outdoors. Circumstances in Niger were unstable, crime in the city high, and "white" people generally seen as being much more valuable victims than local Nigeriens. So for a large part of my stay in Niamey, I rented a small flat where I resided with a few WoDaaBe migrant laborers. People stayed at my flat and there were a few instances when I slept in front of houses that were where my WoDaaBe friends worked as guards. As my writing shows, I have tried to bring this intimate experience into the text, focusing on real individuals and their stories.

Also, in order to make the text more readable, I present the ethnographic data regarding the bush and my stay in the pastoral area in one part and data relating to migrant work and my stay in Niamey in another. In fact, these data were collected during overlapping periods, as I undertook several trips between Niamey and the bush. Those chapters referring to personal events and narratives are still presented in the correct chronological order.

Theoretical Influences

My research is based on previous works on the WoDaaBe society (see Appendix III) but attempts to demonstrate further the relationships of the WoDaaBe to global practices and changes. Even though Bonfiglioli's research focuses on WoDaaBe in a historical context, he barely mentions migrant labor, which increased considerably during the 1980s. Other writers discuss migrant labor (White 1990, 1997; Bovin 1990; Wilson 1992) but focus mainly on the reasons for migration and outline the different occupations. There has, furthermore, been a general tendency to ignore pastoral people in urban migration studies (Mohamed Salih 1995:183). My research tries to grasp the experiences of the migrant workers, their views of their work and lives, in addition to tying these conceptualizations in with WoDaaBe identity in general. WoDaaBe ethnic identity has not received much attention, even though there exists an extensive body of material on the identity of other Fulani (such as Azarya et al. 1993; VerEecke 1989, 1993; Stenning 1959; Riesman 1977; Virtanen 1998; Zubko 1993). Both Stenning and Dupire provide discussion on the main components of WoDaaBe identity but in my discussion I try to connect identity to the recent historical changes involving the WoDaaBe, in addition to locating them in relation to Fulani identity in general. Previous research conducted among WoDaaBe has not focused much on the WoDaaBe in a larger context of power and representation of the West, i.e., in relation to the environment of the researchers themselves. My focus on representation and power tries to turn attention to the social environment of the WoDaaBe today, an environment of tourism, development workers and researchers.

Lila Abu-Lughod's (1991) important phrase "writing against culture" criticized how anthropological discourses tended to focus on timelessness, underlining coherence and boundaries of culture, freezing differences. Generalizations about societies created a sense of homogeneity, coherence and timelessness, thus supporting essentialized notions of cultures as different from "ours", of people different from "us." Abu-Lughod suggested that in order to move away from this construction of the Other, anthropologists should attempt to "write against culture", by focusing on connections and interconnections, contemporary and historical, as well as to write ethnographies of the particular, focusing on individuals and their relationships (1991:154). My focus on identity is inspired by this moving away from culture as a fixed unit toward emphasis on how identity is negotiated by different actors.[3] Identity, as a way of experiencing one's self in relation to the

---

[3] Similar strands of theoretical development have taken place in relation to ethnicity, which like "culture" has often been substituted for "race" (Visweswaran 1998:75). This has involved a move from seeing ethnicity as fixed and coherent definitions of social groups towards a more historically constituted understanding of ethnicity as both fluid and negotiated in society (for example Little 1998 on the Maasai).

world, is a crucial part of understanding power and domination. Identities are not about things but about relations (Comaroff 1996:165; Barth 1969), people constructing the sense of who they are in relation to other people, identity thus never being a finished product but an ongoing process (Hall 1990). Identity has to be seen as fluid and contextual, and as created in relation to the present historical developments. Following emphasis by various feminist scholars I, furthermore, emphasize class, gender, age, ethnicity and sexual orientations being dimensions of identity, which are crucial for the negotiation of power and status in society (Alonso 1994:391), these different dimensions interacting in complex and unpredictable ways.

Focusing on WoDaaBe identity, I try to be sensitive to the various aspects of social formations such as ethnicity, age and gendered dimensions. Theoretical perspectives developed in the context of gender and women's marginal position in general are, in my view, useful for understanding the position of marginal groups in general. Thus, I find the writings of many so-called post-modernist writers significant in pointing out that women are not a homogenous group, but are situated in power relations among themselves, characterized by difference rather than similarity (Parpart and Marchand 1995). Udayagiri makes an important comment in this context that even though some theorists have rejected universalistic categories of women, the world itself continues to treat them on this basis (Udayagiri 1995). These theorists remind us that members of marginal groups are not homogenous, neither within the group, nor across groups, and that inequalities and differences of power exist on those levels as well. The world, as Chandra T. Mohanty among others has reminded us, has to be understood in relational terms (Mohanty et al. 1991:2).

I find it important to both focus on WoDaaBe ethnic identity as relational and dynamic, and to identify the placement of the WoDaaBe in the larger imagery of indigenous people in the Western world. My approach seeks thus to place the WoDaaBe's contemporary status in a broad political and ideological framework. Important criticism on representation of indigenous communities is found in Johannes Fabian's (1990a, 1990b, 1983) ideas regarding coevalness, and Jan Vansina's (1990) and Hobsbawm's (1983) critical views of tradition. I pursue Johanna de Groot's suggestion that it is necessary to move beyond a functionalistic view of ideas of gender and "race" as simply tools for establishing and maintaining Western male power over women and non-Western peoples. Instead, we need to look at these ideas as a reflection of conflicts and desires that have been parts of lived relationships among these different groups (de Groot 1989:100). I suggest that these ideas are ideologies, which as such make otherwise incomprehensible social situations meaningful in order to make it possible to act purposefully within them, involving a general process of the production of meaning and ideas (see Geertz 1973:220; Williams 1977:54). The concept "hegemony" is important for ideology, involving a process where domination is maintained, compromised and negotiated in society (Eagleton 1991; Gramsci 1971; Hall 1981; Williams 1977). As Smadar Lavie has pointed out (1990:35), culture works on making invisible the affiliation existing between the world of politics and ideas. My analytical approach emphasizes that human beings are creative agents capable of resisting, formulating their own conditions, and affecting the structures of power that dominate them (see Bourdieu 1990; Gramsci 1971; Miller 1989; Roseberry 1994).

Globalization has become a growing interdisciplinary field of study, scholars increasingly focusing on mobility of people, images and commodities through time and space (Appadurai 2001,; 1996). The intensification of local identities should be seen in connection with global processes (Friedman 1990). Even though the concept of globalization has to some extent been glorified and globalization somewhat incorrectly been emphasized as something new, it has still been useful to grasp some aspects of current conditions. As I have claimed elsewhere (2004a), I find anthropological studies of globalization and resistance important in counteracting simplistic notions of globalization as merely "westernization", even though to some extent failing by under-theorizing the great inequalities that are involved in globalization.

International development can be seen as one of the great globalization projects of this century (Loftsdóttir 2004a). As Anna Tsing (2000) has stressed, the charm of the notion of globalization brings to mind much of the charm of modernization, which development was seen as a part of, especially as imagined in the post-war period. My understanding of the concept "development" follows the criticism of post-structuralists (see Escobar 1995;, Ferguson 1994, 1999), who emphasize the importance of placing development within a historical context, analyzing how development discourses create both their objects and subjects. Many development projects have reproduced their own cultural biases, emphasizing women's work as non-productive and less significant than the work of males, as well as ignoring the importance of local strategies and different ways of being (see AID Policy Paper 1982; Boserup 1970; Mazumdar and Sharma 1990:185; von Braun and Webb 1989; Ferguson 1994; Henderson 1995). At the same time, many of those working in development desire to change the world, hoping to accomplish that, as I saw often in during my fieldwork in Niger. Powerful institutions like the World Bank can thus maintain and perpetuate a certain institutionalized framework which does not necessarily reflect the desires of its personnel or the activities of other smaller institutions. Development has thus been constituted by various contradicting discourses, where important criticism on development has, for example, been derived from anthropologists working within development, criticizing its ideological basis at the same time as stressing the possibility of development to improve people's lives (Little and Painter 1995). The world is, of course, characterized by gross inequalities and poverty and as James Ferguson (2002) reminds us, many people feel excluded from the modern world, desiring what is usually labeled as "development." Ferguson's comment on exclusion importantly draws attention to the fact that development is not only about technical solutions for certain problems but is a field of social practices, being part of people's social environment, hopes and desires. Also, as pointed out by Carmen Martínez Novo (2007) we have to emphasize that development has included the participation of non-Western elites and states who have benefited, participated and shaped localized development practices (p. 121).

In the text, I discuss the way in which groups such as the WoDaaBe have been made into subjects in Western discourse of the Others and how issues of power and globality are played out in interactions between WoDaaBe and whites. My own subject position as a white woman must be particularly relevant. Rabinow argues that there is a need to anthropologize the West (1986:241), referring to the need of deconstructing ideas of self and others, in order to demonstrate how the West's claims to truth are historically linked with certain social practices. By simply discussing the Other, anthropology is reproducing the hegemonic view of the West as universal and unproblematic. My attempt to juxtapose the WoDaaBe with the Western imagination of them is an attaempt to capture the webs of power and global connection in which the WoDaaBe are entangled. Thus, including the ethnographer as an object of study can give glimpses of global connections and relations of the

West to "the rest." Theorists such as Edward Said have often been criticized for over-emphasizing the hegemony of the West (for example Porter 1994:152; Ahmad 1994:165), thus reducing people outside the space of the West (and also within it) into passive masses. Henrietta L. Moore (1994:132) has similarly pointed out that "Western" and the "West" are problematic terms, assuming much homogeneity. I believe that in some contexts it is useful to identify hegemonic ideas in a certain socially defined environment, historically certain ideas have gained very widespread acceptance as "common sense" or "truths." Hegemonic ideas are of course contested and struggled against on the various levels of society. I thus use the concept West and Western as relational terms, constructed in opposition to non-Western Others. As Frankenberg (1993:265) has pointed out, these terms can be seen as relational concepts, denoting those belonging to the centre of the world economy as opposed to those on the margins, furthermore expressing certain relationships to power and colonial expansion. Foucault's concept of "regime of truth" implies that there is a dominant hegemonic idea in society, without excluding that there also exist counter-canon or subaltern ideas. Various forms of agencies exist and hegemony is neither static nor complete.

I hope that the focus on the ethnographer and the West's imagination of the WoDaaBe will contribute toward the deconstruction of "whiteness" as a neutral, invisible social category outside the realm of social science (for example Hartigan 1997). Even though most whites may not experience themselves as racial subjects in the encounters between predominantly white Westerners and WoDaaBe, the WoDaaBe most certainly do so. These encounters also take place in a world that is constructed in racial terms. As argued by Frankenberg, "whiteness is a location of structural advantage" (1993:1). Even though my research does not focus on race as such, I attempt to acknowledge this dimension of power and identity. To make the text more readable, I avoid placing the value-laden words that are frequently used in the text, within quotation marks. I do not use these words to refer to real phenomena, but rather to describe social ideas about particular issues. By asserting these concepts as social constructs, I do not minimize their social and political influences. Thus, to give examples, I use the term "primitive" not to imply that there actually were some homogenous groups of people more primitive than others, but rather to refer to the Western idea of some groups being more primitive than others. Also, I do not consider "white" people to be actually white, no more than some are "black", but these are much used social categories, which tell us something about how people classify their world. I find it especially important to emphasize, as many other anthropologists have done, that the word "race" is a social construct, not a biological reality (for example discussions in Anthropology Newsletter 1998:3; Mukhopadhyay and Moses 1997).

Organization of the Book

The book starts with two chapters introducing some important contexts in the WoDaaBe social, historical and political environment. The first chapter discusses development as a global modernization project and the conditions of the national and pastoral economy in Niger. International development has been important in shaping pastoral projects in Niger as elsewhere, furthermore, the Niger State itself is very dependent on international development institutions. For the WoDaaBe development in itself is also a site of desires and hopes. Development institutions have global hegemony for conducting development in the Third World, often involving Western specialists engaged in various projects in poorer parts of the world. I show how the WoDaaBe's present day situation of marginality has to be seen in the context of broad policies of natural resources and development as conducted by the state and international development organizations. In chapter two, I show another global context of the WoDaaBe, the popular media, and its contextualization of the WoDaaBe within the global imagery of indigenous people. These romantic visions of the WoDaaBe have stimulated interest in their cultural artifacts, whose production and selling has provided income opportunities for WoDaaBe migrant workers.

The discussion turns toward a more micro perspective, focusing on WoDaaBe practices and lives and my ethnography among WoDaaBe in bush and the city. Chapters three to eight stress the basic values and social structure of WoDaaBe lives in the pastoral area of Tchin-Tabaraden. I attempt to give insight into the meaningfulness of pastoral life as embedded in the relationship with cattle and the environment, and further how ethnic identity is understood and interwoven with gendered realities of WoDaaBe society. These chapters reflect the difficulties and pleasures associated with pastoralism as a way of living. In chapter nine, the focus moves to the more global context introduced in the first two chapters. Chapters nine and ten focus on WoDaaBe migrant work in cities, demonstrating the different survival strategies and the political-historical reasons for the relatively recent migration in a city context. In chapters twelve and thirteen, women's strategies are in closer focus, stressing the individual women's stories. Chapters eleven, fourteen to sixteen focus more intimately on identity within a city context and the WoDaaBe's ambiguous relationship with Westerners and development. The text looks at the lived relationship between *anasara*[4] and the WoDaaBe, and how many WoDaaBe actively manipulate these encounters. In this section, relationships embedded in development and the images of WoDaaBe in the West, are explored in relation to WoDaaBe lives, dreams and identity.

---

[4] The term anasara, probably originating from Arabic, is used by various ethnic groups in Niger. Tylor's dictionary defines the term (spelling it as Nasaradjo) as referring to a "Christian", (Tylor 1995 [1932]:147) but other Fulfulde dictionaries reflect, however, the general present day use of the term as referring to a "white person" (there written as annasaara) (see: Osborn et al. 1993:522; CRDTO 1971:22).

THE EVER CHANGING WORLD

When in Niamey for the first time, I was struck by the visible poverty expressed in almost everything around me: beggars following my every footstep, the broken cement and dust roads beneath my feet. What was still even more striking, perhaps especially because of the visible poverty, were all the different signs, large and small, some new, others old, pointing out the direction to different aid institutions, advertising their work at the same time. I found myself asking: "How can a country with all this development be so poor?"

After staying for a long period of time in Niger, it became even more evident that development was in fact very much a part of the social and historical landscape of the nation state Niger. While Niger appears at first for someone coming from a country far away in the North, as "left out" somehow, on the margin of the interconnected world, the signs reveal, as the top of an iceberg looming in the blue sea underneath, Niger's long relationship with the world at large. In this chapter, I will explore this relationship, situating the nation state Niger within the context of international development which has been important for the country since colonial times. In doing so, it should be stressed that this is of course not where the history of the people of Niger starts. We do not have to go far back to remember areas of Niger as the sites of prosperous and powerful states such as the Songhai in the eastern part of Niger, the Hausa states in the southern part, and Tuareg confederations in the south. The Fulbe to whom the WoDaaBe are ethnically related, waged *jihad* in early 19th century, creating the Sokoto empire. History tells us that these were not isolated states West-African scholars being connected to Islamic scholars elsewhere as well (Hunwick 1997).

In the present, Niger has repeatedly been listed in the Human Development Index as the poorest or one of the few poorest countries in the world. Compared to many other countries, it is seen as poor in its natural resources, the main revenues coming from cultivation and herding until uranium production began. Niger's economy depends on its natural resources and uranium export so that rainfall patterns and the uranium price affect the overall

Dro with his youngest son.

state of the economy. The high price of uranium in the late 1970s led to heavy debt in external loans to finance various expansions and projects (World Bank 1992).[5] When the price of uranium fell in the early 1980s, Niger was faced with a major economic crisis which has continued until today (World Bank 1991:2). During 1989 and 1990 a major effort was made to reduce Niger's foreign debt burden, and it has undergone several structural adjustment programs in the context of its difficult economic situation (World Bank 1992:2), as well as the CFA being devalued (the currency of francophone Africa), leading to various negative effects such as educational strikes and high unemployment rates (Alidou 2005:13). In 1999, a year after I completed my research, debt service as a percentage of government revenues was nearly 44 percent (US Department of State 2007). To make things more difficult, rainfall has been below average since 1968, which affects the yields of both cultivated land and natural vegetation (World Bank 1991:9),[6] coupled with Niger more than doubling its surface under cultivation during the period of 1960 to 1985 (World Bank 1991:9). This has increased the stress on natural resources. Total agricultural production has been growing, but at the same time yields per hectare have been decreasing. Population growth is identified by the World Bank as the main factor leading to the degradation of croplands (World Bank 1991:10).

The visibility of development in the streets of Niamey is no coincidence. Close to 95 percent of Niger's investment budget is provided by aid donors (Matt 1994:2), making Niger's economy greatly dependent on foreign aid. 96.5 percent of agriculture, livestock and natural resource management is dependent on foreign aid (World Bank 1991:18). Niger's dependency on international development is also expressed in the high numbers of development institutions operating in Niger and the vast number of projects being carried out. The number of projects is so high that it has proved to be difficult to evaluate their total number in the country. A report from 1994 shows that ongoing projects carried out in Niger concerned with natural resources numbered one hundred and twenty six during that year (SDSAP 1994). Other projects

---

[5] During the years 1975–1989, uranium export accounted for 80 percent of Niger's export revenues (World Bank 1991).

[6] In the past 10–15 years, the 300 mm isohyet has moved south about 70–100 km (World Bank 1991:2,9). Taking Tahoua as an example, the average rainfall during the period 1948–1967 was 456.6 mm, between the years 1953–1982 rainfall was 406.5 and then only 328.9 mm between the years 1968–1987 (MHE: Republique du Niger 1993:4).

than those classified under natural resources were not included in the report. This information indicates the importance of international agencies as a part of Niger's society and economic life, with various effects on people's lives and expectations. The scope and focus of all these projects differ greatly, and the different developmental institutions in Niger have different policies and funding mechanisms. Lisa M. Matt states in a consultant's report prepared for USAID and the Niger Ministry of Livestock and Agriculture in 1994 that programming of investment budget activities is not based on other projects or experiences gathered in relation to them, because the communication from diverse field activities to the central ministries is weak. In addition, the success or failure of a project has usually been estimated on the basis of whether the prescribed quantity of goods has been delivered, rather than if the situation of the project's beneficiaries has actually improved (Matt 1994:2; World Bank 1991:18). The lack of communication between government services and donors, in addition to changes since 1982 in the names and organizational structures of different ministries, further increases confusion. The World Bank has characterized the general situation as "scattered interventions by different ministries and different donors in different directions" (World Bank 1991:18; see also discussion in World Bank 2003).

Creating the Developing World

During the interwar period, new structures of relations between the colonies and metropolis were created with the establishment of "development" based on the powerful – as James Ferguson (1999:13) phrases it –"myth" of modernization. As Ferguson remarks "[i]n the mid-1960s, everyone knew, Africa was 'emerging'" (Ferguson 1999:1). The United States took the lead in the ideology of development, formulating the basic ideas behind its development programs based on older ideas of 19th century social scientists that human societies developed from simple to complex social organization. The political redefinition of the world into three distinct sets the "free" capitalist world, the communist world and the Third World re-conceptualized the world in a new way, which was quite apt for the new idea of development. The United States' development programs were to some extent policy responses to prevent the spread of communism in former colonies and the countries affected by the war (Hoben 1982:351), and in general it believed that if the poor of

Third World were not rescued from their poverty, the Communists could gain power in these countries. Of the numerous wars fought in the Third World during this time, many entailed direct or indirect participation of outside forces (Escobar 1995:34). Predating the usage of the term globalization, development can be identified as a global phenomenon both due to its extensive effects in various parts of the world and to its entanglement with global political issues.

US President Harry Truman's announcement of the concept of a "fair deal" to the world in 1949, which among other things aimed toward solving the problems of the "underdeveloped" areas of the world, was, according to Arturo Escobar, a powerful statement in shaping ideas of what development should be about. The solution was the replication of the characteristic features of the West, its high level of industrialization, urbanization, and technology, in addition to embracing the West's cultural and economic values. In Truman's vision, these goals would be accomplished with the use of Western capital, science and technology (Escobar 1995:4). The strong hegemonic and political position of the United States was probably important in gaining wider acceptance for its policies and formulations of development. As described by Escobar, Truman's idea was not only conceived in the United States, but was also the result of conditions after the Second World War and within a few years was universally accepted by those in power in the West[7] (Escobar 1995:4). The term "underdeveloped" replaced other older terms used for "outsiders", such as the terms "barbarian", "pagan", and "wild man" which now belonged more to the colonial period (Minh-ha 1984:54).

Many different perspectives are gathered under the label modernization which share the assumption that development is based on a division of the world into "modern" countries, serving as models of modernity, and "backward" countries into which modernization has to be transplanted in order to replace the "traditional" elements responsible for their backwardness (Worsley 1984:183). The assumption that development is the transfer of the "modern" has led to a tendency to focus on technological solutions rather than social ones, these technological solutions seen as belonging to the sphere of

---

[7] The objective of development as prevention of the spread of communism was thus seen as consistent with the expansion of trade, strengthening of democratic institutions, and various humanitarian goals. All these goals seem to have been considered attainable by simply replicating the above mentioned features of the West (Escobar 1995:227).

modernity (Horowitz 1986; Hoben 1982; Marcus and Fischer 1986:16). In addition, development experts' discourse concerning problems is sometimes divorced from its political and cultural realms and placed in neutral scientific rhetoric (Escobar 1995:45). The polarization of the modern and the traditional has of course a long history within Western scientific tradition. Nineteenth-century social scientists such as Ferdinand Tönnies, Emile Durkheim and Max Weber, tried to explain and understand the transformation of the former into the latter. These theorists generally characterized this transformation as problematic but the translation of these ideas into modernization theory framed the transition as unquestionable and highly desirable (Wolf 1982:12). Walt Rostow's book *The Stages of Economic Growth: A Non-Communist Manifesto* published in 1960, was highly influential, which could to some extent be due to the fact that Rostow played a major role in the foreign policy of the US government, anthropologist Clifford Geertz being, for example impressed by his theory (Edelman and Haugerud 2005:15).

During 1973 and 1975, new amendments to the Foreign Assistant Act were legislated by Congress which became the "New Directions" (or the "McNamara Doctrine" in the World Bank), focusing on improving the conditions for the rural poor (Hoben 1982:357; Horowitz 1986:251; Horowitz and Painter 1986:2; Bourque and Warren 1990:85). This change in emphasis beyond rather narrow economic indicators created new employment opportunities for anthropologists (Edelman and Haugerud 2005:14) but according to Michael M. Horowitz and Thomas M. Painter, anthropologists were employed by development institutions to try to change these traditional ways, even though most anthropologists themselves rejected tradition as an explanatory tool (Horowitz and Painter 1986:3). Furthermore, the claimed essential core of the New Directions (targeting the poor) seldom became the actual focus of the projects (Horowitz and Painter 1986:8). The criticism of development in the 1970s came from various directions, including the Dependency and World System theories (Wallerstein 1974; Amin 1976) claiming that the relationship with the West had in fact created *under*development, which was the root of poverty in these parts of the world. Development institutions were criticized as well for ignoring women, leading to the establishment of *Women in Development* (WID) emphasis (Boserup 1970; Cloud 1986:41; Moore 1988:56; Tinker 1990:39). Since the 1980s and the 1990s, the World Bank and the International Monetary Fund have promoted structural adjustment reforms, which have been greatly criticized even by Joseph Stiglitz (2002) a former vice president and chief economist of the World Bank. In addition development institutions have in the last two decades tried to respond to criticism by stimulating Non-Governmental Organizations (NGOs), thus attempting to mobilize the civil society more in the development process (Fisher 1997; Murphy 2000), as well as responding to continuous criticism on gender in relation to development issues (Cornwall et al. 2007), even though with mixed and disputed results (Fisher 1997; Murphy 2000; Cornwall et al. 2007). As claimed by Marc Edelman and Angelique Haugerud, the ongoing debates over globalization clearly confirm that "development is still hotly contested" (2005:51).

Pastoral People and Development

How have these abstract theories and ideas played out then in relation to development among pastoral people in Africa and in particular West Africa? Modernization theory seems to have been a dominant paradigm in major development institutions working in Africa (Hoben 1982). During the colonial period, an important infrastructure was created which facilitated the control and design of projects later on (Gefu 1992:23), as will be seen better later in relation to projects among pastoral people in Niger. A major trend in pastoral development in the post-colonial African states were attempts to commercialize production through replicating Western systems of livestock production (Gefu 1992:23, 27). Pastoralism was supposed to develop from subsistence production into more commercial modes of production and in the spirit of modernization, this was supposed to be done by transferring "foreign" technology to change the pastoral economy from what was considered to be simple and traditional into something more modern and scientific (Gefu 1992:36; Galaty 1981:7; Scott and Gormley 1980:93). Projects directed at pastoral peoples in the 1960s and the 1970s were concerned with developing commercial beef production, mainly intended for the world markets (Bennett 1988:551; Scott and Gormley 1980:93; Riesman 1984:171) and this was supposed to take place through strategies such as crossbreeding, ranching schemes, grazing reserves, and feedlot operations (Gefu 1992:38; also de Bruijn and van Dijk 1999:117). As a result, some of the best grazing land was taken over by commercial ranches (Galaty and Bonte 1991:270). According to an article by David W. Brokensha, Michael M. Horowitz and Thayer Scudder in the late 1970s almost none of the projects directed at indigenous communities in the Sudano-Sahelian zone were "well informed on the relevance of local cultural practice on project implementation, nor on the likely impact of the project on local ways of life" (Brokensha et al. 1977:2). It is perhaps not surprising that the planners felt these "traditional" elements were irrelevant to their understanding, considering the basic ideology behind modernization theory, assuming that "traditional" elements must be replaced by "modern" elements. Michael Horowitz, when analyzing development projects during the 1970s and early 1980s, argues that the failure of many projects directed at pastoral economies during that time can be explained by the planners' idea of pastoral people. According to Horowitz, they frequently based their strategy of development on unexamined ideas about the "typical" herder, ignoring the diversity existing in herd management in the Sahel (Horowitz 1986), the major obstacle for development in the pastoral sector being seen as this "irrationality" (Turton 1988:137). Anthropology did probably reinforce this stereotype of the traditional society (Hoben 1982:354), among other things with its concept of culture as having natural unproblematic boundaries[8] (see Abu-Lughod 1991). The resistance of the pastoralists to changing their production system and to embracing technology has been seen as the reason for the massive failure of development projects (Gefu 1992:14), thus blaming their attachment to tradition for failure of the Western model. Melville Herskovits' ideas emphasizing certain social values attributed to the herders, popularized the conceptualization of the "cattle complex" as he called it, and came to be seen as reflecting the irrationality of pastoral people and production systems.[9] The idea that herders place so much symbolic value on animals, that they fail to use them economically has been surprisingly resistant to change (see criticism on the idea in Grayzel 1990:35-36; Park 1993:311; Prior 1994:33; VerEecke 1991:185–186).

---

[8] It should be pointed out that such views have also been expressed in relation to farming practices in Africa. An article by Pepe Roberts, for example, discusses the French colonialists' views regarding farming technologies of the Hausa in Niger (Roberts 1981).
[9] David Turton has pointed out that Herskovits never intended the concept "cattle complex" to be used in the "Freudian sense" as the concept became used by others, referring then to "sentimental and obsessive attachment to cattle". Rather, Herskovits was using the term as referring to various collective cultural traits (Turton 1988:138).

Bennett has, furthermore, claimed that many pastoral projects have failed due to their focus on the development of cattle, ignoring that pastoral production is a part of a social and political system (1988:54). A similar point is emphasized by M. A. Mohamed Salih writing in the early 1990s, when claiming that development discourse blurs what he calls "pastoral development" and "livestock development" (Mohamed Salih 1991, 1990) The former, in his view, should be a social development concern with pastoral people while the latter focuses on livestock production and productivity. His distinction points out that it is important to identify whether projects conducted among pastoral people are aimed toward the people themselves or toward other goals such as involving livestock rather than herders. A similar criticism is voiced in M.E. de Bruijn and H.J.W.M van Dijk's discussion, stressing that a different approach is needed in development policy toward pastoral people, that involves appreciation of "instability, variability and diversity" (1999:135–136), instead of attempts to control the environment and pastoralists.[10] Scholars have in fact pointed out that the concept of drought is frequently used in a way that assumes that reduction in normal rainfall automatically explains both desertification and famine. Variation in rainfall is the normal feature in the Sahel, rather than an unusual state, the environment being in fact so variable that it is difficult to distinguish between change and fluctuation. Thus, it is more useful to define drought there as an "abnormal reduction in water supplies for a particular land use" (Agnew and Anderson 1992:110–111). In the light of these theories, scholars have stressed in more recent times, that pastoralism seeks in various ways to adapt itself to this insecurity, which is to a certain extent inherent in its conditions (de Bruijn and van Dijk 1999:133–134). Ranches, either privately or government owned, have, however, continued to replace pastoral households during recent decades (Fratkin 1997:248).[11] Eliot Fratkin bluntly asserts in his overview of pastoralism in relation to development and governance issues that "the future of pastoralist populations is far from certain" (1997:254). That is not to say that

---

[10] A similar view can be seen expressed in David Rain's (1999) discussion of mobility of both pastoralists and peasants as constituting a meaningful way of responding to unpredictable situations, constituting an economic strategy in itself.
[11] Ranches differ in many aspects from the family based production of the herders. Ranches obviously require substantial infrastructures and large enclosed fields, making ownership of land well defined. There are other aspects, important as well, which suggest the ranch is a different mode of production from herding, bringing about different relations of production, and a different kind of space usage.

it needs to be so, but policies in regard to pastoral people have to be clear on what they are attempting to do and whose interest they are benefiting.

Niger and Development

The colonial administration of Niger emphasized peanut cultivation and export, leaving herding somewhat marginal in the economy (Bonfiglioli 1988:114). Yet, herding had been a source of state revenue for a long time, both the Hausa rulers and Fulani having imposed taxes on the pastoralists. The French administration taxed herders heavily in addition to envisioning herding as able to provide the metropolis with leather and meat and with products for export to English colonies (CIDES: Mazou 1991:12).[12] It seems that World War I increased interest in the colonies as suppliers of meat for the "home" countries (Dunbar 1970:112). In order to accomplish the goals of increased production, the *Service vétérinaire* was established in 1918 in Niger and the *Service de l'Elevage* in 1927. The main policies regarding herding were directed at health issues, focusing on vaccination (Breman et al. 1986:28). This is not surprising considering the risk of rinderpest that had killed many livestock in northern Nigeria at the turn of the century, and continued to break out in Niger, especially with increased numbers of people. The success of vaccination, in combination with a growing interest in investing in herding (such as former slaves becoming herders) led to an increase in the animal population in Niger (Bonfiglioli 1988:121). The colonial government also sponsored attempts to develop fresh-meat shipping facilities to facilitate export of meat abroad (Franke and Chasin 1980:101). Meat was, for example, transported by air from Niamey to Lagos (Dupire 1962b:353). The colonial authorities considered it necessary to change the mentality of the herders regarding production, in order to increase the productivity of herding (CIDES: Mazou 1991:12).

The push of agriculture in Niger toward the north led to the colonial administration's decision in 1954 to place northern limits of cultivation, thus reserving areas for herders. This divided Niger into two main zones, the pas-

---

[12] A capitalized abbreviation in front of a reference indicates that the documents are found in one of Niger's archives. The capitalization refers to the name of the archive. All archival sources are listed separately in the list of references. These institutions are IRSH, IST, MHE, DANIDA, CIDES, MAL, TA, and NAN.

toral and the agricultural area. This order was revised by the government in 1961 and made law (Eddy 1979:137; MAL: Habou et al. 1990: Sutter 1982), and during the same year, the pastoral zone was redefined and labeled "the zone of modernization of the pastoral economy", thus opening the way for initiating projects in there (MAL: Habou et al. 1990:27). A document written during the same period emphasises the need for researching different breeds of animals, in addition to identifying factors that "limited" the development of pastoralism (MAL: Republique du Niger 1960).

The French colonial government emphasized building wells and vaccination to counteract lack of water and problems of animal health seen as the important constraints to the development of herding. This emphasis was carried into the post-colonial state, when Niger gained independence from France on August 3, 1960. In 1961, laws were put in place regarding *"des stations de pompage"*, and then in 1963, the OFEDES (*Office des Eaux du Sou-Sol*) was created, which was connected to *Ministère de l'Hydraulique* and responsible for the construction and maintenance of pumps and watering stations in the pastoral zone (Breman et al. 1986:28). The new independent government of Niger, led by Hamani Diori, emphasized the evolution of export-oriented livestock management that had been advocated by the French. The creation of ranches and a refrigerated meat abattoir in Niamey was supposed to facilitate this enterprise. Meat was to be exported to neighboring countries in the south and French consumers were to be provided with low priced beef (Franke and Chasin 1980:101).

More recent development programs have emphasized growth to increase national revenues. In 1984, livestock products constituted 42.7 percent of export revenues (apart from the revenues from uranium) (MAL: UNCDF 1984:9). Production increase in the pastoral sector is, however, considered to be somewhat restricted by a "limited resource base" (World Bank 1991:11). The period of the late 1960s and early 1970s was characterized by a massive loss of livestock, followed by famine and human suffering. Even though many people lost all their animals in the drought, tax collection was rigorously continued.[13] Policies after the drought period generally emphasized rebuilding the animal stock of the country, in addition to finding ways of reconstruct-

---

[13] Discontent with this in combination with other factors, led Lt. Col. Sayni Kountche to initiate his *Coup d'état* in 1974 against Hamani Diori (Lund 1993a:9–10).

ing the pastoral economy (MAL: SEDES 1974:75). This orientation was reflected in Nigerien policies after 1973, when a previous focus on animal health was criticized and a more "progressive" orientation advocated, namely strengthening the herding infrastructure so that herds could be rebuilt and their products increased and improved (Breman et al. 1986:28). A document from 1974 identifies the major focus of herding policies as responding to growing demand for meat and, to a lesser extent, milk[14] (MAL: SEDES 1974:75). The general emphases of policies after the drought period were to rebuild the stock of animals and find ways of reconstructing the pastoral economy (MAL: SEDES 1974:75; CIDES: Sidikou 1994:37).

The government plan *"Programme triennal 1976–1978"*, formulated in the aftermath of the drought, emphasized the "liberation of the economy from natural forces" (CIDES: Sidikou 1994:37), which presumably was supposed to be done by reconstructing the economy. The goal of improving and increasing production was, among other things, to be accomplished by stratifying the steps of production into three phases, each carried out in a different area of the country. However, most monetary resources were still spent on health and water as before (Breman et al. 1986:28; see also MAL: Republique du Niger 1983:15). Similar emphasis on pastoral production was reflected in the goals of the government plan *Plan quinquennal*, for the years 1979–83 (MAL: Republique du Niger 1983:14–17). This period also carried some important institutional changes in terms of organization of development, and Kountche launched the ambitious *Société de Développement*[15] (Lund 1993a:9–10). In addition, some legal changes were made in the organizational structure of the pastoralists, providing the basis for organizing co-operatives and interest groups (*les groupements mutualistes*) (CIDES: Sidikou 1994:37–39). In 1980, it is estimated that livestock levels reached pre-drought levels (White 1986:243), but the ownership pattern of these animals had changed considerably. During the dry season of 1970–1971, it was estimated that herd ownership distribution was that 39 percent of animals were in the hands of the pastoralists (*elevage pastoral*), 53 percent belonged to semi-sedentary populations, and 9 percent were controlled by sedentary people. 40 percent of livestock was in the pastoral zone in 1970 (MAL: SEDES 1974:10).

---

[14] Milk is written within brackets and I assume it has less importance than meat.
[15] The *Société de Développement* aimed towards increased participation of the population in developmental activities, and establishing different bodies on various levels of organizations in Niger's society.

In 1968, there were 4.45 million cows in Niger, but in 1973 only 2.2 million (MAL: Republique du Niger 1978–1979:88). Losses of livestock were much greater in the pastoral area, loss of cows being 63 percent as compared to 50 percent for Niger as a whole. For all animals, the loss was 52 percent in the pastoral zone compared to 32 percent for the country overall. The livestock lost was primarily young and adult cows, thus affecting the reproduction possibilities after the drought. In addition to losing their animals, the herders also had to sell their remaining starved animals in massive numbers, in order not to lose them through death as well (Breman et al. 1986:38; Bonfiglioli 1985:30). These animals were sold at a low price and thus provided a very good investment for those holding capital, because prices increase after droughts. When a drought is prolonged, animal prices start to rise due to scarcity of animals. This dynamic makes it very difficult for the herders to buy back animals later on (White 1990:244). In 1980, only 20 percent of the total livestock of the country was in the hands of pastoralists while 60 percent was owned by agro-pastoralists and 20 percent by sedentary people (Breman et al. 1986:38; MAL:SEDES 1974:9). Thus, the general situation was that livestock ownership had in fact moved from the hands of herders to absentee-owners that were often rich agriculturalists, businessmen and *"fonctionnaires."* The herds were merely managed by hired pastoralists (Breman et al. 1986:37). Thus, it does not make much sense to advocate, as development projects tend to do, that pastoralists such as WoDaaBe should destock more animals. As pointed out by White, the herders were in fact "obliged to sell more animals than they should" (1990:248).

Another drought, during 1983–1984, further increased awareness of the problems of the pastoral economy in Niger. The seminar *Débat National sur l'Elevage* held in Tahoua was initiated by Niger's president Kountche and organized by the Ministry of Development, to address the difficulties of the pastoral economy. The conference's major objective was to address three key issues: a) the need for environmental protection; b) the basic safety of the herders; c) the contribution of herding to the self-sufficiency (*autosuffisance alimentaire*) of the national economy. The last concern can be translated into an emphasis on production of meat and milk for the national economy (Breman et al. 1986:26). In the World Bank policy framework paper for 1996–1998, it is stated that "agriculture and livestock breeding have some potential in Niger", and that there are "plans to take greater advantage of the size and quality of the livestock herd, as well as the traditional expertise of cattlemen, to encourage the development of beef, hide, and leather industries" (World Bank 1995:4). This document also points out opportunities in the intensification of traditional exports, placing in that group livestock on hoof, hides and skins (World Bank 1995:13). Since the mid-1980s, Niger has undergone IMF's structural adjustment programs, as well as the devaluation of the CFA, leading to various negative effects such as educational strikes and high unemployment rates (Alidou 2005:13). According to David Rain (1999) the relationship between the Niger government and development organizations has been fraught with difficulties, Niger being known to the developing community as having "one of the most demanding and rigid governmental frameworks to be adhered to in West Africa", with many bureaucratic obstacles (p. 102).

The Importance of Land

It would be simplification to see the livestock losses of WoDaaBe and other pastoralists as due to environmental factors alone. Natural and social factors leading to drought and famine cannot be fully separated. The Sahel drought has to be seen in the context of increased population in the pastoral area, and the reduction of land space available due to agricultural expansion. Drought can become a good impersonal scapegoat, pointing away from the political and historical factors which have created its conditions (Scott 1984:3). WoDaaBe have both been pushed further north and pastoral people have more limited areas of land to graze their animals on.

Various factors have led to reduced areas of land for pastoral people. One major factor was the French colonial government's heavy emphasis on peanut production. Various campaigns were conducted to encourage and increase the production, such as the French giving a guaranteed price for peanuts. Also, some new varieties of peanuts were developed in Senegal that facilitated expansion into new areas where cultivation had not previously been possible. In addition, it led to decreased fertility of the soil as fallow periods work to restore the necessary nutrients (Franke and Chasin 1980:83). Decreased yields have meant that the farmers have to cultivate larger land areas. Since 1976–1977, the fallow periods have been declining by 10 percent annually, and the rural population growing at 2.3 percent. Yields for groundnuts, millet and sorghum in Niger were about half the average of yields in

WoDaaBe mobility makes use of the variability of the Sahel environment.

other West African countries for 1980–1985. It is not surprising in this context that Niger doubled its surface under cultivation from 1.862 million ha in 1960 to 3.86 million in 1985 (World Bank 1991:4, 9).

Development projects have continued this trend of encouraging an expansion of cultivated land. Self-sufficiency in stable food grains has become a national goal of Niger's government after 1974. This effort, backed up by large amounts of developmental assistance, was supposed to be initiated through promoting more intensive rainfed agriculture. Projects, starting in 1972 and seeking to introduce new agricultural techniques to increase rainfed agricultural productivity in yields per hectare, were intended to accomplish these goals. In 1984, the Ministry of Planning concluded that the increased aggregate production of rainfed crops was not the result of greater yields per hectare but the result of larger and larger areas being cultivated (Painter 1987). Also, alarmingly, large development institutions such as the World

Bank have ignored these political and historical conditions of pastoralism as recently as 1991 referring to Hardin's theory of the commons to explain problems of deterioration of land:

> Pressure on land mounts through the fact that livestock herds are privately owned whereas the rangelands are common property. Grazing rights are thus "free for all" implying economic and ecological inefficiencies, commonly referred to as the "tragedy of the commons", after Harding (World Bank 1991:12).

At present Niger faces serious problems of land degradation, which are often blamed on the nomadic populations. Desertification is often seen as resulting from nomadic activities while drought is seen as a force of nature. As we have seen, it is believed that Niger's pastoral economy needs to change in order to respond to these problems, to "free" itself from the forces of nature. The World Bank ranks desertification as one of the top major global environmental problems (Thomas and Middleton 1994:3,48). Desertification has been described as a rash that is centralized around settlement (Thomas and Middleton 1994:3). Thus, the "desert is not invading from without: the land is deteriorating from within" (Goudie 1981:58).

Since 1986, Niger's government has been preparing reforms in terms of land tenure, referred to as the Rural Code, which aims towards clarifying rights to land in Niger (Lund 1993b). The Rural Code has the objective to "establish a legal framework for the appropriation, tenure and management of the natural resources vital to agriculture and livestock production" (Lund 1993a:2), establishing a coherent land policy for all land use in Niger. It is also believed that the Rural Code will encourage private investment in land and interest farmers in investing in and developing their land (Ngaido 1993:1). The principle orientations of the Rural Code were made law in 1993 (DANIDA: Guindon-Zador 1995:5). The Rural Code is likely to have fundamental affects on the herding populations of Niger, but land tenure legislations have generally been ambiguous in the Sahel concerning the status of pastoral people's right to their lands (Thébaud 1995:21). As discussed by Edward D. Eddy in 1980, existing laws in Niger at that time did not recognize individual rights to land of pastoralists. Agricultural populations were given rights over land and could collect compensation from pastoralists as a result of damage inflicted by herders on grain plots and by their clearing and planting of a plot they gained private rights to it (Eddy 1980:27; see also Swift et al. 1984:816). One of the most important rights assigned to the herders in the Rural Code is its acknowledgement the existence of "areas of attachment" for nomadic groups (*terroir d'attache*). According to Lund, this means that pasture becomes protected common property with priority access to pastoral groups who have claim to it as their area of attachment (Lund 1997:98). Area of attachment can be defined as "a geographical area which regularly, for the majority of the year, is essential for a group of people and to which they are attached and to which they move back and forth due to transhumance, migration, or exodus done by a part or the whole group" (MAL: Habou et al. 1990:35).

This appropriation of land is not assigned on an individual basis, but rather on a collective basis (MAL: Habou et al. 1990:52–52). As Lund points out, this creates problems in determining what groups should be recognized as having legitimate claims to the area (Lund 1997:98). Investments in an area, such as building wells and the length of a particular group's stay are factors that strengthen resource claims (MAL: Habou et al. 1990:35). The Rural Code laws take "*mise en valeur*" (to give value to) as being important in claims to land by both pastoralists and agriculturalists. This emphasis on and lack of clear definition of the meaning of "*mise en valeur*" gives a priority to agriculturalists' use of land, and can lead to difficulties for pastoralists in maintaining or recovering pasture (Terraciano 1993:48–49).

In Conclusion

Policies and ideologies of development have to some extent created the social and political environment in which the WoDaaBe live. The cultural ideas embedded in development have to some extent shaped conditions in which the pastoral economy operates, through direct interventions but much more importantly through reforms that are not necessarily targeted at them or the pastoral economy. Policies of land allocation in Niger during colonial and post-colonial times, projects among agricultural people have affected pastoral people in Niger greatly, reducing the overall land they have to graze their animals and pushed them further north where risks are higher.

In contemporary discussion, "development" is often labeled as either good or bad, as either doing good or harm. For the first, the phrase development aid encompasses a wide variety of approaches and different types of development institutions, ranking from the IMF to small individual projects. What has mainly been the focal point of criticism here are the overall policies and ideologies of the large development institutions that continue to shape the living conditions for people all over the world. Secondly, within these institutions individuals have conflicting interests and views. Anthropologists and others working within development institutions have often provided valuable criticism of the ideology and implementation of different projects. Development is still a global issue involving policies or projects implanted at local level designed and arranged in another place far away. Current WoDaaBe economic marginalization within the nation state Niger can only be understood in such a context.

WoDaaBe migrant workers at a dance gathering in Niamey. Tourists and other Westerners pay to take photographs at this event.

A GLOBAL WORLD OF IMAGES

I had just finished my M.A. thesis, and started on the PhD. program at the University of Arizona. I knew of course what topics interested me, but not how to connect them, where to do research or what I should focus on. I enter a store and there is a book about people in Africa, called WoDaaBe. The pages, full of life, portraying sand and dust in combination with exotic images of different people, are similar to the ones I had both desired and criticized before. They were presented as one of the world's indigenous peoples, living as they had for centuries. More as a joke, the friend accompanying me said that I could do my research among this people. The day after browsing at the University Library for a different project, I explored what references I could find in relation to the WoDaaBe people. To my own surprise, almost immediately a project started formulating in my head where I could tie together my diverse interests.

When I told people that I was going to do my doctoral research with the

WoDaaBe, many knew right away what I was talking about. They were familiar with the images of men with painted faces, the beautiful and exotic WoDaaBe who I had originally seen in the book store. It was thus not surprising that those I met in Niger working for development institutions knew these popular representations of WoDaaBe. Images in the contemporary world have wide distribution, which involves a constant recycling and repeating of particular themes. In the real world, the "hard" issues of development cannot be separated from "softer" issues of representations and images. Development practices, as other social and historical praxis, are based on specific ideas of their subject matter, meaning that representations and discourse translate easily into praxis.

Categorizing the World

The division of the world into the "free" capitalist world and the communist world after the second world war reflects changed relationships between different parts of the world (see discussion Worsley 1984; Pletsch 1981). Even though originally coined to refer to newly independent states and their independence, the term "Third World"[16] soon gained meaning as containing "left-outs", characterized by tradition and less developed. The Fourth World, added later to this division is, however, often seen as synonym for indigenous people[17] and as applying to those seen as a more traditional than those usually characterized as belonging to the Third World. Mary Douglas' structuralistic perspective on categories and boundaries can be useful here. She argues that ideas of purification and separation are important in imposing a system on an untidy world, and that it is only by "exaggerating the differences between within and without, above and below, male and female, with and against, that a semblance of order is created" (Douglas 1966:15). The process of establishing this order involves ambiguous aspects being treated as if they "harmonize with the rest of the pattern." Aspects that do not "fit in" are thus ignored or distorted, in order for them not to disturb the established assumptions (Douglas 1966:14). Categories thus have to be "clean" and contrast with each other to become structurally meaningful. Utilizing Douglas'

---

[16] According to Philip W. Porter and Eric S. Sheppard the term was coined in 1955 at the Bandung Conference where representatives of 29 nations met in Indonesia (1998:3).
[17] It is also occasionally used about the poorest people of the world (Burger 1987:6).

theoretical perspective, it can be suggested that the binary opposition of the modern and the traditional is recreated in the opposition of the First and the Fourth World, due to the Third World no longer being seen as purely "traditional" having become more like the West. As Renato Rosaldo argues, culture is perceived as more "pure", when assumed to be more different from Western culture (1989:198–202). Changes and influences from other cultures are seen as corrupting this purity, and through an individual's movements from one culture to another, the individuals become "stripped" of their culture. This view of the Third World characterized by a decay of the traditional and pollution of the modern is expressed in an article by Robert D. Kaplan which became instantly popular among US foreign policy officials and analysts, being faxed from the Department of Global Affairs to every US embassy in the world (Englund 1996:180). Kaplan presents an alarming vision of chaos in West Africa, with an indication that this is what America will be like in the 21st century:

> Disease, overpopulation, unprovoked crime, scarcity of resources, refugee migration, the increasing erosion of nation-states and international borders, and the empowerment of private armies, security firms and international drug cartels are now most tellingly demonstrated through a West African prism. West Africa provides an appropriate introduction to the issues, often extremely unpleasant to discuss, that will soon confront our civilization (Kaplan 1994:46).[18]

The concept "primitive" became unfashionable after World War II (Bétaille 1998:188) and the term "indigenous" has gained increased popularity. Contemporary popular representations of WoDaaBe locate them generally as indigenous people and it is within such categorization that they are often known to most people in Europe and North America. I find it necessary to contextualize the discussion within definitions of the concept indigenous, because some of the problematique with how the concept has been appropriated and used reflects very clearly in the representations of WoDaaBe in the "popular" media.

---

[18] Kaplan followed this article with a book, *The Ends of the Earth: A Journey into the Dawn of the 21st Century* (1997), about the same issues as were discussed in the article (see Englund 1996).

The first international conference of indigenous people[19] was held in Georgetown, Guyana, in 1974. Following that conference, a definition of indigenous people[19] was created:

> The term indigenous people refers to people living in countries which have a population composed of differing ethnic or racial groups who are descendants of the earliest populations living in the area and who do not as a group control the national government of the countries within which they live (Sanders 1977).

As pointed out by Sidsel Saugestad (2001) most definitions have since stressed indigenous people as 1) first comers, 2) people in position of non-dominance, 3) culturally different from the majority and as 4) perceiving themselves as different from the majority (p. 43). Paradoxically, the idea of indigenous people has become more and more important when scholars are reconstructing and historicizing their concept of culture, ethnicity, nationalism and tradition, seeing these not only as politically and historically constituted but as fluid and dynamic (Anderson 1983; Abu-Lughod 1991; Barth 1969; Hannerz 1992:11; Hobsbawm 1983). Featuring highly in debates about the concept is how it essentializes culture as a "fixed and corporeal thing" (Brown 1998:197) and how the designation of the term "indigenous" seems to presuppose that others in the same area are "settlers" or "aliens" (Bétaille 1998:189; Bowen 2000). The idea of the "indigenous" thus applies well in places like Australia, because of the clear distinction between the small aboriginal population and the "white" settler population which dominates the state but much less so in other parts of the world such as West Africa (Bétaille 1998:188). Jeffrey Sissons' book *First People: Indigenous Culture and Their Futures* (2005) addresses this problem by importantly stressing that we have to recognize that the distinct cultural struggles of ethnically distinct minority groups within the new and the old world (or in settler societies as he calls them) and within the Third World are quite distinct in many ways. In some sense, Sissons discussion reserves the use of the term indigenous for communities within settler societies,[20] even though simultaneously stressing the

---

[19] Indigenous people have also been simply called "first people" because "their ancestors were the original inhabitants of their lands, since colonized by foreigners" (Burger 1990:16).
[20] He defines the term indigenous as "cultures that have been transformed through the struggles of colonized people to resist and redirect projects of settlers' nationhood" (p. 15).

importance of analyzing how tribal or subsistence cultures within the Third World have been marginalized or threatened by global capitalism and their own governments. Sissons' comment that we need to see how the project of nationalism, tied to globally funded development, has affected small communities (p.21), is particularly applicable when placed in the context of the development of pastoral and agricultural communities in Niger, and the effects of those on the WoDaaBe. Even though Sissons is probably correct in that we have to distinguish settler communities as distinctly different, abandonning the concept indigenous in relation to the Third World could have negative effects for marginalized communities there. Especially since the Declaration for indigenous people was adopted in 2007 by the United Nations and even by powerful development institutions such as the World Bank in 2005, the definition of oneself as indigenous becomes strategically significant within the contemporary political context. The labeling of a particular group as indigenous has been and will continue to be a fluid political process where different actors can utilize the term for various ends (Novo 2007; Nyamnjoh 2007).

Representations of Indigenous People

Sissons interestingly shows that the prioritizing of indigenous people's self-definition by the International Labour Organization's definition and the UN special Rapporteur in 1986, contributed toward a growing confusion around the term, in addition to paving the way for what he calls "eco-indigenism." Eco-indigenism associates indigenous communities with a relationship with Mother Earth and subsistence economies resulting, for example, in that that urban indigenous people tend to be excluded from the category (2005:17–18). Sissons' identification of eco-indigenism is extremely important because it points toward the political and global appropriation of the term indigenous for various ideological and even commercial goals by indigenous people themselves and others. As Sissons himself states indigenity is a "project", (p.13) and one could add that it is a project appropriated for various ends, having compelling global significance to a variety of people.

In order to understand the potency of the concept, it has to be contextualized within the changed relationship with nature within the West. Donald Worster identifies a new paradigm of environmentalism in the Western world as emerging on 16 July 1945, when the first nuclear bomb went off in the New Mexico desert (1977:339). This was, according to Worster, a factor creating a sense of nature "as a defenseless victim", vulnerable and sensitive, demonstrating that humans had finally gained power to completely destroy nature. A few years later, Paul Ehrlich argued that the population explosion was threatening all life on earth, and his statement was followed by an identification of other threats such as solid waste, oil spills, and toxic metals, to mention a few (Worster 1977:340–341). The general interest and concern with environmental issues in the Western world today is manifested in the fact that magazines like Vanity Fair include articles about environmental problems, addressing issues such as the state of the Brazilian rain forest, overpopulation, and pollution (Nugent 1990:173). In Western popular narratives, indigenous people tend to be contrasted with the "modern" world, and are seen as free from destructive materialism, living peacefully in a closer relationship to nature and each other, something from which "we" in the West should try to learn (Conklin and Graham 1995:698). The association of indigenous people with the environment, has led to environmental issues often being diffused with interest in the rights of the indigenous people, images of them frequently being used to advocate the significance of environmental issues. Environmentalism's public image had become so strong in the 1980s that many "human rights" groups started to recreate their image as environmental groups. A Rainforest Foundation spokesperson stated that without identifying indigenous people with the rainforest "indigenous people wouldn't have a chance in hell" (quoted in Conklin and Graham 1995:698). A spokesperson for Cultural Survival, an organization working for the rights of indigenous people, also reports that the diffusion of human rights with ecology "works better" than simply focusing on human rights issues. For the environmentalists the identification of their cause with indigenous people can also strengthen their moral position, legitimizing First World environmentalists' involvement in the internal affairs of other nations (Conklin and Graham 1995:698). The association of the native with nature has, therefore, in no sense disappeared, even though in accordance with a more positive assessment of nature, the native is also addressed in more positive ways. Following Conklin and Graham, it can be argued that images of the native are integrated into the "global ecological imaginary" and the ideas of the native as the Other is utilized to create a sense of solidarity among people from different backgrounds (see Conklin and Graham 1995:697).

Kaaplan's image of the Third World discussed previously can be contrasted with the representation of the Fourth World in an interview with a Kayapó leader in *Parade* magazine. On the cover there is a picture with the heading "A Man Who Would Save the World", and a smaller text underneath stating: "I am Paiakan, a chief of the Kayapó Indians of Brazil. What is known as the Amazon rain forest is the land upon which my people live. Help me to save lives – ours and yours" (from Conklin and Graham 1995:696). The visual imagining of the Third World is generally characterized by masses of nameless people, while the indigenous people are seen as small and few in number. In such narratives, there are bad and good others, the former bringing chaos to the world, while the indigenous, good others carry a hope of saving it. The good savages represent Eden before the Fall, as phrased by Taussig, the bad ones are signs of the "permanent wound inflicted by history" (1993:143).

Ideas of the native and nature stating that the natives have been in their natural place for a very long time, present the image of a certain stability in a world that is changing fast. Thus, the idea of the native as rooted in a particular timeless space, can be understood as a nostalgic desire for a world of stability and safety. While the older concept "primitive's" association with nature and timelessness implies negative values (lacking civilization, culture, morals, and intelligence) the newer concepts native and indigenous carry positive implications from their same social identification (such as balance with nature, egalitarian and peaceful society). It could be suggested that the "new" relationship of the West with the environment has led to new way of conceptualizing those perceived as closer to nature.

Imagining the Fulani

The appeal of the WoDaaBe in the popular media is not new because Westerners have had a fascination with Fulani people (that the WoDaaBe are a part of) for a long time[21] (see discussion in Amselle 1998:43–49). The main characterization of the Fulani took place by contrasting "the" Fulani to a "black" person, establishing him as different from his "black" neighbors, and/or locating him somehow in a more "civilized" context. An example of

---

[21] No ethnic distinction was made between WoDaaBe and Fulani at that time. I have discussed the ethnic boundaries of WoDaaBe and Fulani more extensivly elsewhere, stressing the historical fluidy and contextualization of the way in which they are placed (Kristín Loftsdóttir 2007).

this kind of construction is found in C. K. Meek's "The Northern Tribes of Nigeria", published in 1925. Meek divides the population into three races, the negro, the hamite/caucasian, and the semite/semito-negro. His phrase that "the basic Negro characteristics are almost too well known to need description", indicates how well established the classification of types was during the time of his writing. The description of the hamite/caucasian is most interesting here, because Fulani are seen as belonging to this category. He writes:

> In marked contrast to the Negro is the Hamitic element, whose purest representative are the nomad Fulani. Their color varies from a light to a reddish brown; their physique is slender and sinewy, and sometimes even effeminate; the face oval, the lip thin... the eyes are almond shaped and overhung by long black silken lashes (Meek 1925:26).

Other examples can be taken from other texts, such as that: "the Cow Fulani [...] are a very different people from their negroid neighbors is evident enough from their physical appearance" (Wilson-Haffenden 1930:96–97). A similar view is echoed when the races of Niger are seen as two, black and white, the Fulani belonging to the latter race (Abadie 1927:185; see also Morel 1911:119). Such imaginations of separate races, and that some people inhabit the category of "blackness" are in no way items of the past, being reproduced through some more recent texts addressing the WoDaaBe. One text draws the distinction between WoDaaBe and their neighbors by stating: "They differ completely from their neighbors, the Kiri, who express their virility in wild competitive games and violent rituals" (Chesi 1977:66). Another text states: "they are distinguished from tribes among whom they live by their stiltwalker elegance, their delicate features, their light copper skins" (Englebert 1971:179). The ideas on the origin of the WoDaaBe are usually directed at showing that they are actually not "black" like the rest of the Africans. This is done by either establishing them as having a pristine origin in other places from those of the "black" masses of Africa, or by ignoring history all together and discussing them as original primitives without history. Fulani have been said to be of the same ancestry, to take a few examples, as the Gauls, the Romans, the Jews, the Hindus, the Egyptians, and the Ethiopians (criticized in Ki-Zerbo 1978:60; discussed in Kirk-Greene 1958:22;

Burns 1929:52). Thus, instead of focusing on the rich history of the Fulani, Westerners were preoccupied with myths of their pristine origin outside Africa. One theory was that the Fulani were a mixture of Jews and Arabs with a Sudanese tribe of Cushitic origin, who came to Africa in the early days of Islam (see discussion in Meek 1925:95). Lieutenant Boyd Alexander argued that the Fulani are "interesting people of Eastern origin, who are believed to have settled in Egypt from farther East, and to have been driven out of their adopted country during the Theban Dynasty, 2,500 years ago" (Alexander 1908:190). One well known theory regarding the origin of the Fulani was M. Delfosse's thesis that they were a group of Armaic-speaking Judaeo-Syrians who entered "Negro" Africa from Cyrenaica about 200 A.D. (see discussion in Greenberg 1949:190) and then became the white rulers of Ghana from the fourth to the eighth or ninth century (Meek 1925:95). To maintain this conception of the caucasoid origin of the Fulani, it was often argued that the language of the Fulani was Hamitic, an idea which was met with wide acceptance[22] (Greenberg 1949:190).

Contemporary representations of WoDaaBe in the popular press[23] have in common placing a great deal of emphasis on visual images, containing many photos and in most cases only minimal amounts of text. Interestingly, even though the purpose and the length of these discussions differ, the general emphasis in relation to the WoDaaBe remains the same. The best known discussion in the US of the WoDaaBe is, probably, the book *Nomads of Niger* by Carol Beckwith and Marion van Offelen (1983), which has been translated into French and can be bought in Niger among other places. The mass publication journal, *National Geographic*, has also published an article on the WoDaaBe written by Beckwith and included a discussion about the WoDaaBe in its publication *Nomads of the Worlds* (Englebert 1971). The texts I discuss constitute only a faction of the material that makes reference to the WoDaaBe in one way or another.[24] The recent picture of painted WoDaaBe

---

[22] Peter Rigby has pointed out that the existence of the "hamitic type" came about as a result of the need to explain how Africa could have a rich and exciting history, i.e., history or civilizations could not have been due to a "negro race". His discussion also shows that other groups also seen favorably by Westerners such as the Nuer and Maasai were also conceptualized as being hamitic (Rigby 1996:65–66).
[23] When using the concept "popular press", I refer to texts that are widely distributed and intended for mass consumption.
[24] It should be noted that the goal and length of this material differs. The Body Shop (1995) and Camphausen (1997), for example, only mention the WoDaaBe in a few places of their overall discussion, while the Beckwith and van Offelen narrative is an extensive work on the WoDaaBe.

men engaging in dance ceremonies in a recent World Bank brochure (which has no reference to the WoDaaBe but discusses World Bank general policies) and in the Niger web page for the US Department of State, Bureau of African Affairs (2007), shows how dominant these images have become in presenting the WoDaaBe. In addition the US embassy web page for Niger which features condensed and short texts, gives an elaborate discussion of the WoDaaBe obsession with beauty and dance,[25] and does not address their present economic and environmental conditions.

The WoDaaBe placement as indigenous people is indicated by their inclusion in work that concentrates on "tribal people" written by Maybury-Lewis, the head of Cultural Survival (1992:xiii), and their description as people in "danger of becoming extinct" (Nkrumah 1978:7). Their association with the indigenous is also seen by their inclusion in work that focuses on diverse peoples such as the Bambuti pygmies and the Bajau (described as the "gentle" boat dwellers of the Philippines) (Englebert 1971). I have previously discussed the interest that Westerners have shown in the physical characteristics of the WoDaaBe, using ideas of "blackness" to characterize the WoDaaBe as different from their neighbors. The contrast to their neighbors is not only expressed in their beauty, but also in their isolation from the rest of the world. They "live as they have for centuries" (the cover of Nomads of Niger). Chesi states that "they are among the last Africans who live completely unaffected by the progress of civilization" (Chesi 1977:66). In another coverage it is stated that the WoDaaBe are an "amazing nomadic tribe which has survived in the desert for more than two thousand years despite living constantly on the brink of starvation" (Roddick 1991).[26]

---

[25] The text romantically states that "the young Bororo must first seduce his fiancée and then arrange to kidnap her from her family. The couple then embarks on a journey which takes them all over the region and sometimes beyond the country's borders. They will decide to settle once the "wife" has become a mother and when she feels that she has traveled enough and is tired of this bohemian existence. Every year the Bororos organize a traditional and colorful festival known as the *Guérewol*, which is the occasion for celebrations, engagements, kidnappings of wives, and baptisms". This information was posted on http://www.nigerembassyusa.org/profile.html, accessed 30 December 2007.

[26] The view of the WoDaaBe as isolated and traditional is established even further in one of these books, where it is stated that this book "is the first to be published about a unique (sic) and colorful people" (Beckwith and van Offelen 1983). Aside from evoking images of Western "penetration" and colonialization, supplemented by the value of being first, the statement is simply incorrect. When the book itself is examined carefully, this becomes obvious to the reader. On the last page a little note can be found, which acknowledges the existing studies and ethnographies of the WoDaaBe as providing "useful background material" (Beckwith and van Offelen 1983:224).

WoDaaBe are used in the world of images through the commercialization of products. Anita Roddick, the founder of the multinational cosmetic company the Body Shop, has associated images of the WoDaaBe with her beauty products (see Zinn 1991). Probably, the Body Shop's association with the WoDaaBe is intended to underline the company's association with nature, which the company's identity is based on. In a research trip for the television series *Millennium*, Roddick spent two weeks with the WoDaaBe (Roddick 1991:182). She recounts that: "I have also learned the pure joy that is to be obtained from mixing with simple people whose lives are untainted by what we have laughably described as 'progress'" (Roddick 1991:181).

The more recent discourse on the ethnic origin of the WoDaaBe shows in some respects striking similarity to the older ones discussed earlier. Wenek states, when referring to the origin of the WoDaaBe: "All this makes you think of the American Indians, or Gypsies, or the Egyptians. Those who are interested in the mystery of their origin, claim that they are Indians who migrated through Syria or Ethiopians"[27] (IST: Wenek n.d.(1):8). The WoDaaBe have been referred to in more recent publications as primitive fossils having survived through the twentieth century. One text describes them as "unique people, believed to have been among the first inhabitants of Africa, the descendants of the mysterious people of an ancient area who sculptured fantastic drawings into the rocks" (Chesi 1977:65). Another relatively recent text states that nomadic Fulani have a striking similarity to rock paintings in the Tassili caves in Algeria dating from 4000-2000 B.C. (Beckwith and van Offelen 1983:30). The text claims to be able to separate "negroid figures" in these ancient paintings (Beckwith and van Offelen 1983:30), thus again separating the nomadic Fulani from "blackness."

Ki-Zerbo claims that the imaginary exercises regarding the origin of the Fulani would have been more useful if, instead of placing a "pure" Fulani against something called "pure negro", the Fulani had simply been placed in the context of other people of the Sahelian zone[28] (Ki-Zerbo 1978:60). It

---

[27] My translation: "Il suffit de regarder leur trait pour constater qu'aucun ne témoigne d'une origine negroide, leur yeux orienteaux, leurs nez aquilins, parfois retroussés, leurs lèvres minces: leurs longs cheveux tressés qui ne sont pas crépus et surtout leur couleur, ni noir, ni blanche, tout ceci fait penser aux Indiens d'Amérique aux gitans, ou aux Egyptiens. Ceux qui se sont intéressés à l'énigme de leur origine pretendent que ce sont des Indiens émigrés par le Syria ou des Ethiopiens."
[28] Greenberg has shown that Fulfulde is closely related to Serer-Sin, a language of the Senegal area, and has some remote connection with the Wolof language of the same area. All these languages thus belong to the sub-group West-Atlantic section of his West Sudanic family (Greenberg 1949:192). It is today generally accepted that the Fulani originated from the Futa Toro in the Senegal area (Hunwick 1965:121; Ki-Zerbo 1978:60)

A typical picture of the Gerewol ceremony in the bush, similar to those featuring in the popular media.

seems as though the Fulani and the WoDaaBe in particular were bent and molded in an attempt to distinguish them from other Africans. The WoDaaBe served as exotic fossils of lost civilizations, placed in contrast to the blacks and thus moved closer to whiteness.

Taken together the images in popular literature have a coherent theme. They focus on the WoDaaBe as beautiful, peaceful, isolated and connected to their natural environment. This description is intensified with another dominant theme in the description of the WoDaaBe in the popular press: every representation themes to a great extent on the same social event, the *geerewol* ceremony. *Geerewol* is the name of a dance, but this ceremony refers to a seven day annual celebration, which unites the two major lineages of the WoDaaBe. The most handsome males of each lineage dance in competition, wearing specific types of clothing with their faces painted in a special way (see for example discussion in Beckwith and van Offelen 1983:180). The popular narratives connect the ceremony predominantly with tradition and beauty (Chesi 1977: Beckwith and van Offelen 1983: Englebert 1971). The performance is described as "the freedom to follow their tradition" (Beckwith and van Offelen 1983:279), "they dance with delicate and graceful movements, passionately but without aggression" (Chesi 1977:83) and they "dance erect and noble" (Englebert 1971:194).

The strong focus on the annual *geerewol* is underlined by the fact that usually between half and one third of the photographs following the narratives are devoted to it. It is interesting to note in this context that Lutz and Collins in their analysis of representations in the National Geographic Magazine observe a similar pattern generally in that magazine's representations of non-Western people: nearly one fifth of the pictures of non-Western people focused on rituals. The authors point out that the accompanying narratives tend to downplay the rituals' temporality and the historical changes that have taken place, presenting them rather as features of custom or tradition (Lutz and Collins 1993:91; see also Spitulnik 1993). The representations of the *geerewol* gathering in the popular press do not discuss the dance in relation to historical changes or to social interactions among those participating. Also few of the narratives emphasized the relationship established between individual men and women during the ceremony concerning affection, sexual relations, a jealous husband, and a marriage between two lovers etc. (Englebert 1971:189; Maybury-Lewis 1992; Beckwith and van Offelen 1983). One text (which gives a very short summary of WoDaaBe culture) states "it's clearly the men who are the most given to the cult of beauty and who are in modern terms, the objects of sexual attention" (Camphausen 1997:44). Another text states casually, " (...) Mokao may disappear into the bush with another woman after a long evening dance" (Englebert 1971:187), yet another states "the idea is to seduce the prettiest girls with erotic looks and grimaces"[29] (Villiers and Hirtle 1997:285). This emphasis on sexuality evokes a preoccupation of the West with the untamed sexuality of so-called primitive peoples.

The wide distribution of these images is perhaps reflected in that contemporary handbooks for travelers in Africa, which usually offer very few pages on Niger, often include brief descriptions of the dance, all of which seem to emphasize the WoDaaBe as highly sexual creatures (Finlay et al. 1998; Newton 1992; Trillo and Hudges 1995 [1990]). Sexuality in the dance is empha-

---

[29] The book is a historical overview of Africa, written in a comprehensive and somewhat poetic narrative. It has five pages on the "Fulani", and very briefly addresses the WoDaaBe, then in connection with the *geerewol* dance.

sized with statements such as "a man who isn't happy with his new partner has some difficulty getting out of the social obligation to spend a night with her" (Trillo and Hudges 1995 [1990]:985), and even more bluntly reports that the men "adorn and beautify themselves so that only the most obstinate female will refuse their advantages" (Finlay et al. 1998:668). The same text further emphasizes casual sexual encounters by stating: "With luck, they find a wife – a woman brave enough to move forward and demand his services, at least for the night" (Finlay et al. 1998:668).[30]

In Conclusion

The representation of the WoDaaBe in the popular press frames them in the context of traditional people, as separated somehow from the "dark nameless masses" surrounding them, being more beautiful, more traditional and having exotic rituals on which to pride themselves. In Western thought, those conceptualized as primitives were seen as existing closer to nature, bound in tradition and performing exotic rituals, in addition to having a strong sexual appetite. The popular representations of the WoDaaBe construct them as a people that have lived the same way for centuries, participating in exotic rituals where sex plays a large part. Their present historical conditions and dynamic remain a matter of little interest and the same can be said about the internal dynamics of their society. No political context is given to the dance exhibitions, meaning that descriptions of the dances have no specific time to them, but could generally be applied to something occurring hundreds of years ago. One may suggest that the focus on the dance ceremony as such is desirable because it can easily be divorced from political issues, and thus becomes more easily consumable, simply a part of tradition and aesthetics, rather than connected to a complex political reality.

In key with Benedict Anderson's (1983) analysis of the nation state, it can be argued that through images and texts, people have imagined themselves in relation to others whom they have never seen and never will see, as Western people have done in relation to the WoDaaBe. Arjun Appadurai (1996)

---

[30] The way in which these images influence the perception of those in Niger, can be seen in the following experience. Occasionally, when I introduced my research subject to Western men working in Niger, they offensively indicated that someone doing research among the WoDaaBe must also have some sexual goals in mind.

has pointed out that images in the global world are constantly removed from their original context and reproduced. Benefiting from Geertz (1973) it can be claimed that representations are symbolic systems that provide models *of* and *for* reality, making the world meaningful and affecting and shaping the relations that they are part of. At the same time that representations give some reflections of reality, they embody cultural values affecting the way in which reality is conceptualized. A regime of truth – in Michael Foucault's sense – is created through a constant interplay of signs, enacted through representations (Pollock 1994:14; Foucault 1980 [1972]:131). Representations as models *for* reality thus reflect that representations have to do with how people conceptualize their relationship with others, as well as shaping the way in which the world is acted on.

The table (*saga*) in everyday use. Next to it is the bed (*leso*). Both these items are major components in the making of the WoDaaBe home in the bush.

AT HOME IN THE BUSH

In a letter to my parents, I describe my first arrival to a WoDaaBe home in the bush in following terms:

> The day after, we continued for an hour and then stopped. It took me a while to figure out that we were actually there. From my perspective, we were just sitting out in the middle of nowhere. Suddenly people just appeared and sat down with us. Akali told me proudly that this was his house, but there was nothing visible indicating this to me. I just saw a few women far away, children and a donkey, but nothing like a tent or a shelter.

The Sahel area is usually defined as a "zone approximately 200–400 km wide, centered on the latitude 15°N in sub-Saharan Africa" (Advisory Committee on the Sahel 1984:3). The Sahel climate consists of fluctuating rain and dry heat. Rainfall is unpredictable because of its interannual variability, its unequal distribution in space and its unequal distribution in time. Crops and vegetation depend on the rain, which differs from year to year. The variability of rain increases in the more arid areas (Nicholson 1984:73). In the northern part of the Sahel in Niger, rainfall is between 100–350 mm, while in the southern part rainfall varies from 350–550 mm, making rain-fed agriculture possible (Beaumont 1989:202). In the district of Tchin-Tabaraden, the climate is characterized by a long dry season usually from September to May), and a short rainy season from June until August (Franke and Chasin 1980:27). The harmattan wind comes from the northeast, blowing dry air and carrying with it large amounts of dust. There are days when the layers of dust in the air severely limit visibility. The harmattan wind can also be a source of erosion, blowing away topsoil deprived of plant cover (Franke and Chasin 1980:24).

The department of Tahoua is 73,340 square km at the approximate altitude of 450 m (from Loutan 1982:2). The town of Tchin-Tabaraden is populated by around 2,000 inhabitants and situated in the center of the Tchin-Tabaraden district. It has a Sunday market, a police station, health care facilities, and a college. The markets at Kaou and Abalak are also popular among nomads. The district population was estimated at over 100,000 in 1977, the majority engaged in pastoral production (Loutan 1982:4–5). According to information from the government offices in Tchin-Tabaraden, the WoDaaBe in the Tchin-Tabaraden district are 13,398, the Tuaregs 60,364 and Arabs 8,500. No information was available regarding the numbers of Hausa, Fulani or other ethnic groups. It was pointed out to me that this information was more than ten years old. Its general value should also be taken with caution because it was read out to me from an unidentified census. In 1990, around 400 Tuaregs were killed and tortured by the military in Tchin-Tabaraden, leading to great political unrest in the area and continuous conflicts between the government and various Tuaregs groups (Lund 1997:32).

The bush in Tchin-Tabaraden consists of hilly platforms with low bushes and shrubs; in the depressions between the platforms are clusters of small trees. The trees stand in clayish ground, and the area becomes a shallow lake during the rainy season. The vegetation of the platforms is moderate. During the cold and hot seasons its color is yellow, with large patches of nothing other than light reddish brown sand. Or perhaps it is sometimes more appropriate to say, in certain places, at certain times, there are patches of dry grass within the large area of sand. The soil in the Tchin-Tabaraden area is classified as sub-arid, and is not very fertile, in addition to being prone to erosion (Michel 1980:18). However, ecological studies have shown that even though the annual grasses in such areas have a low biomass, they have a relatively high protein content which makes them quality forage (Netting [1977] 1986:45). The most important vegetation in the area of Tchin-Tabaraden is various *Panicum* and *Aristida* grasses, and *Acacia* and *balanite* thorn trees (DANIDA: PNUD 1991:8). The shrub *Calotropis procera*, *Asclepiadacea*, which thrives well in inferior soil, is widely found in the area, even where there are no other trees. This strange and almost clumsy looking shrub with leaves which look too big, is almost as if it came from an old fashioned adventure story.

The Ecology of the Bush

His name is Kala'i and he is the head of the household (*jom wuro*). He is an ultimate authority, feared by my assistant, his son, and gradually by myself, as is appropriate. During the year when I had not realized that I had already become part of their lives – the year before I arrived to do the fieldwork – Akali has asked his father if I can stay with them. He has presented me in this way for his father and to the lineage group as a whole. In addition, he has received permission from the *laami*Do, the highest political authority of the WoDaaBe, for my stay among them in Tchin-Tabaraden. The two men, a father and son, are responsible for me and my actions to their broader society, and as they see it, they are responsible to my own society for my well-being.

When we have moved to a new place, I often sit down with Kala'i, because the two of us are usually the ones who are supposed to relax. These are somewhat strange moments, involving the head of the house and a young female anthropologist trying to communicate. Kala'i has never been to a large city, and has not interacted as much with *anasara* as most other WoDaaBe. He loves his cows; they are his life, and the only life he finds worth living. Almost two years later, when I am about to leave Niger, he confesses to me that only one of his sons has inherited his passion for cows. His eyes are sad when he tells me this, but he is a man who has seen and experienced many painful things, and learned to accept life as it is.

We left in the morning; my camel was lost, so I had to walk. But it is not far to go this time and it is refreshing to walk for a change. Usually I go with Akali to find my camel but I am tired and I know that he is faster going by himself. It is noon, the hottest time of the day. The communication between Kala'i and me is difficult due to my limited language capabilities, but Kala'i is patient. As usual, he observes me quietly, and I wonder how it feels for him to have this woman as a part of his household. He gets no rewards, no compensation. He has no specific interest in 'whites.' Contrary to the other WoDaaBe, he does not ask me about the lives of 'white' people in particular. Also different from most other people who always saw me as belonging to a big homogeneous group of *anasara*, he identifies me as *"surbaajo Island"*, (young Icelandic girl) and has an interest in my family and my Icelandic-ness, rather than my "white"-ness. He learns the names of everyone in my closest family, their ages, likes especially to hear about my historical past when Icelanders kept animals in the bush, just as the WoDaaBe do today. He gives me long speeches that I am later supposed to recite to my family. He always speaks gently to me, slowly, always in the same sweet tone as if to one of his grand-children, not in the strict way he would address his own children. It is this day that he teaches me the names and characteristics of the seasons. As usual he tells me to unpack my notebook and write it down, which I gladly do. Each season which Kala'i defines for me is, of course, a reflection of the different ecological times of the Sahel area, and thus the different tasks and difficulties associated with them. As remarked by Bonfiglioli (1981) the seasonal cycle state lies at the basis of the life of the WoDaaBe. People's lives follow these different seasons, greatly affected by the environmental conditions at each given time. Kala'i lies on his side on the mat; I am sitting by his side, using one of the poles of my bed as a support for my back. He starts with the *yaawol* season, which is the season of prosperity and pleasure, and presents the seasons one by one in the order of their arrival, telling me their names and major characteristics: *dabbunde*, the time of cold, wind and sandstorms; *ceeDo*, the hot season; *kokke*, when the first rain starts to fall; *korsol* when the rain has started for real; *ndunngu*, when there is plenty of grass. And then the cycle starts again... endlessly.

WoDaaBe Homes

The WoDaaBe home (*wuro* pl. *gure*) in the bush is composed of several smaller units called *cuuDi* (sing. *suudu*). In English, both the terms *suudu* and *wuro* can easily be translated as "house", even though they do not refer to the same structure.[31] In the Fulfulde language, the concept *wuro* has several meanings, sometimes used to describe a single hut, compound, village or town (see Sa'ad 1991:207). It can be seen as describing a sociographic unit, headed by a man, which is usually tied together by kinship (Riesman 1977:31). A half circle of dead branches (*lise*) marks the area of each house-unit, its opening always facing west. The WoDaaBe are patrilocal and patrilinear, and thus a father and his sons or several brothers usually make their home together. The house-units are lined up from south to north, in a specific hierarchical order depending on the relationship between the people of the *wuro*.[32] Riesman points out that a *wuro* "does not exist where there is no woman" (Riesman 1977:31). A WoDaaBe[33] man told me laughingly that a man who is left by his only wife is basically left with nothing except his cow, because she owns all the objects and will take them with her. The husband is still the head of the *wuro*, deciding aspects such as with whom to compose a wuro, and where to move. The *suudu* is, however, almost exclusively a wife's space (see also Sa'ad 1991:212). The composition of homes (*wuro*) is quite flexible according to the seasons, life spans, and personal circumstances. Members of "different" families stay temporarily, wives frequently stay at their parents' house (always when they give birth to the first and second child), and children are often in other households during long periods. Migrant laborers in most cases stay at their homes during the rainy season for 2–3 months a year. However, some of the migrant laborers regularly send money to their *suudu*, thus contributing to the household in a direct way even though they are away a great part of the year.

---

[31] For the sake of clarity, I often refer to wuro as "house" in the text, and suudu as "house-unit".
[32] The hierarchy in the relationships of men is represented from south to north, but for women from north to south. Thus, if two brothers make a wuro together, the suudu of the older brother would be to the south of the younger brother, and the father has a suudu to the south of his sons. The first wife, however, has her house to the north of a second wife.
[33] The singular of WoDaaBe is BoDaaDo, but to make the text more readable in English I use the plural form as both singular and plural.

The calf-rope (*dangol*), used to tie the calves during milking of the cows, is in front of each *suudu* and can be conceptualized as a part of the house, making the house of a WoDaaBe home an integrated space of human and animal settlement. Frequently in the night, the cows sleep behind the calf rope and roam freely within the space that is the home. The calf rope is also a sign of prosperity. In order to symbolize how difficult a certain year was people say "that year we did not have any calf for our calf rope." A man who has more than one wife cuts his calf rope, placing parts of it in front of each wife's *suudu*. The integrated community of humans and animals in WoDaaBe society is also demonstrated when a child is born; its navel cord and afterbirth are buried next to the sticks (*kopeeje*) which the calf rope is tied to. I ask my friend Amina why, and she tells me that such is the tradition of the WoDaaBe; the calf rope is the place of the calves and thus the newborn.

During the rainy season the *duDal* fire is constructed in front of the house. The *duDal* is an area of fire for the herd to give it relief from mosquitoes and other insects that are more numerous during this season. During the night the herd stays around the fire, not bothered by the smoke, and is free of insects. The *duDal* also contributes to the general cleanness of the house, because the animals will not enter the human sleeping place, and thus that area is free of their droppings. When the rainy season (*ndunngu*) is over, the fire is not made. The area of *duDal* carries various taboos; a clay bowl can never been carried into the *duDal* because it can break; someone from another house does not have the right to take fire from the *duDal*, married women with unbraided hair should not enter the *duDal*. The disrespect of these taboos causes misfortune, perhaps the death of a calf or a cow, illness or that an animal gets lost. Sometimes people sit down within the *duDal* but that is not common, and people do not sleep there. The *duDal* is simply seen as belonging to the herd.

Some WoDaaBe origin myths state that the cows of the WoDaaBe originated from water and were lured to join people by the *duDal*. *LaamiDo* Bayre bi Tuka'e tells me: "Two children came out of the water and they made a grass house (*cuurel*), and sat down at that place. Later, some cows came out of the water, and they stayed during the evening with the children. They wanted to come because the children had made a fire for them. The cows came and stayed for the evening until they became used to the children. And then the children did a *gurgiisi* (a short migration movement). The cows followed the children to every place they went, because they had made them a fire" (7 September 1997; see also Dupire 1962a). This origin myth sees the cows, people and fire all as elements of coexistence, fire being the tie that unites animals and people.

WoDaaBe homes are thus an assembly of highly regulated spaces, having various rules and taboos associated with them. The *wuro* can be seen as an integrated settlement of human and animals, which is not surprising when we consider how much the house is adapted to human-animal coexistence. The material culture of the WoDaaBe shows an adaptation to the mobility that has such an importance for the health and well-being of their animals.

Living in a *Wuro*

I have of course read Dupire's description of the house, but it is different reading about something and actually being within it. Somehow everything is confusing so I am not able to fit the description to what I have read. There are too many elements to be identified and they blur together, creating chaos. During my first time in the bush, I go to the *Cure Sallée* festival where I am introduced to many faces and people who add more chaos to my mind rather than solving it. Only marginally do I see the wives and sisters, and at night I sleep in the bush with two male friends sleeping close to me. This organization is confusing and rather disrupting. I am not able to identify who belongs to my family because there are so many families crowded together in a small area. The reality is that the everyday structure is dissolved to some extent during this festival, the families are not staying together as much, people do not even eat with their households most of the time. But because I have just arrived, I am not aware of this. In the day, I eat with men, I am observed and inspected in greatest detail by older men, who unlike the young men, do not hesitate to touch me, especially my toes and fingers. I have never seen a guide on how to react in such a situation, and I just sit quietly and shy while being observed. I had thought about myself as an anthropologist, as someone who is there for a purpose, an adult; yet I find myself being perceived by the older women and men as a child. I desire to be with the women, interact with them, talk and laugh with them. I am new and because it is the time of the festival, the women stay in large groups; being left "alone" with them (a WoDaaBe man would generally not join a large group of women) means being talked about, not being talked to, laughed at, and in general being a source of entertainment for the group.

My next placement is also unusual. When the rainy season is over, people break camp and start to move to the dry season pasture. All of sudden I find myself within an actual household. The first night, my bed is placed next to my friend and his wife, so I won't be afraid, as he explains. I find his concern ridiculous. However, when I have been in the field for a while time my bed is all of sudden placed further away from everyone, more in accordance with the norm in WoDaaBe society. To my own surprise, I miss this rather unusual but very safe arrangement. My house-unit, *suudu*, is small and not really a true house, because there is no table nor water and I am only an unmarried *surbaajo* (girl, young woman). My *suudu* is placed within the *wuro*, and after drawing the house a few times in a few different places, and trying to remember Dupire's description, I finally realize that I have been placed between my friend's wife and the father's wife. It is a strange placement, which I even today do not see as making much sense from the point if view if the organizational structure of the WoDaaBe. At the time, I vaguely recalled that there was a place called *daDDol* where guests were to be placed; I wonder for a long time if I could remember it so wrongly, and whether the *daDDol* could actually be within the *wuro*. I finally got the courage to ask my friend, able to make myself comprehensible to him (which back then was often difficult), and he told me that this is not the *daDDol* at all, the *daDDol* is over there, far from the house, it is the place where guests and travelers come. "Is there a problem?" he asks, and there was none.

I am happy with my house; a bed, two bags with my belongings and my blanket. The women and a young girl who became my friend right away carry branches for my house forming a small fence (*lise*). When the dry season wind starts blowing, my house is usually constructed in the shelter of a bush or a low tree, also with a small fence. When it starts to get cold, a fire is lit in the evening and morning. It does not keep me warm at night, but makes the cold manageable in the early morning. Kala'i, the father, comes into my house-unit in the morning and makes his tea next to my bed, along with other males in the household. The women come as well when only the closest family is there. During the day it is too hot to stay in the *suudu* and the woven straw and wood mattresses used for the bed are foldedwith my belongings placed inside to prevent children and animals from playing with them. At night, people gather again around the fire by my bed, usually only the men in the household and the mother. If only the younger brothers are home, the women come as well and sit by my fire. I have no privacy, except when I pull my green blanket over my face. During the evening people like to sit on my bed, relax on it, even take a nap. Even though my house is still some distance from the other house-units (as is the rule with a *suudu*), there is always someone there who sleeps on a mat next to my bed. Usually several people, young children, my friend Sollare, the younger brothers, or the sisters are still at home. There is always someone, again according to instructions from Akali and his father, in order to prevent me from becoming afraid. I sleep alone in my bed, which becomes important for me due to the lack of privacy. There are a few exceptions, but they are unusual and out of the ordinary.

During the frequent seasonal movements, the women and girls of the camp pack the house for me and my bed is carried on one of Akali's donkeys. My camel cannot carry this, only my two sacks, the man conducting my camel, and myself. I want to ride it myself, but am not allowed to do so. My friend or one of the brothers sits in the saddle, but I am in the rear. I try to explain that I know how to ride a horse, but my friend tells me that I can still fall off. Instead of sitting on the hard back of the camel, as the young WoDaaBe girls do, he makes a small saddle for me by tying a half empty millet sack to his saddle, softening it with a blanket. I should not take hold of the man in the saddle, he tells me, but should only put my hand on the saddle itself.

A year later, at the end of the rainy season, my placement within the structure changes again. As in the previous year, the social interactions are intense, and the houses made not far from each other. Now my *suudu* is placed between the two wives of one of my friends, not with the usual distance, but in the space which otherwise would provide a barrier between these two *cuudi*. I announce that I liked where I was before, but am told that this place is now better for me. The father does not enter my house anymore because it is too close to those of the two wives of his son, and he would show them disrespect by entering into their space. Male friends and relatives come, but a mat has to be dragged a little into the open for them to feel comfortable when sitting down. They place themselves within a liminal space of my house, not really within it, yet not outside it. My lack of privacy increases but my placement also makes me more isolated from the world of men, hence more approachable from the world of women. I learn that you cannot be placed in two locations at the same time, as the quality and nature of my information changes, my own relationship with the family changes and develops. Anthropologists can perhaps move between places, or social spaces, but they cannot be in two locations at the same time. The build up of confidence and friendship, so necessary for ethnography, within two different and at times almost hostile groups, takes time and more time. Making friends in every culture is like walking along a long path where it is not possible to rush. No matter how fast you try to go, the number of steps remains the same.

James Clifford writes, in relation to location: "Nowadays, when we see these pictures of tents in villages, we may find ourselves asking different questions: Who, exactly, is being observed? What are the political locations involved? What are the relations of power? What reverse appropriations may be going on?" (1997:20). My location within the structure had a dialectical dimension, both reflecting *how* people related to me, as well as *affecting* the way in which they related to me. It reflected my placement in their lives as lived through social interaction, as well as affecting my position in their lives. One's location also limits and affects the kinds of information gained because data is gathered through interaction with real people, who are confined to certain domains and so are you, the researcher. The myth of neutral research objectivity reformulates itself in the idea of the anthropologist as a neutral being, existing in neutral spaces. Being where I was limited my research activity along with giving it new and exciting dimensions.

WoDaaBe live very close to their animals, the herd is standing in front of the bed and the table.

ANIMALS IN WODAABE ECONOMIC AND SOCIAL LIFE

"Allah gave WoDaaBe the life of the herder " (Akali)

Melville Herskovits was one of the first anthropologists to draw direct attention to pastoral people in Africa. He saw the herding economies characterized by what he labeled a "cattle complex", which among other things refers to the social values which cattle have in pastoral societies. Herskovits' writing tried to explore the economic systems of pastoral people who at that time were not seen as keeping cattle for economic reasons, but out of emotional closeness (Herskovits 1926). As Robert Netting has pointed out, later anthropologists have looked at the herders in an ecological context, seeing the herders' attitudes in relation to their environmental context, thus placing them in a more pragmatic frame (Netting [1977] 1986:43). However, the idea of pastoral economies as irrational and emotional seems resistant to change in some discourses, especially outside anthropology (see criticism in Grayzel 1990:35–36; VerEecke 1991:185–186). The binary opposition of the herders keeping their cows either because it is either economically rational or because they are attached to them, is furthermore simplistic and unfruitful. Cattle especially have multiple roles in WoDaaBe society that cannot be reduced to a single meaning, as they have interconnected symbolic, social and economical significance in people's lives.

The most common species of animals kept by the WoDaaBe are cows, goats, sheep, donkeys and camels, but the WoDaaBe conceptualize themselves as being primarily cattle herders. Cattle, especially the *Bororo Zebu* breed, have a special meaning and their value and role cannot be compared to other kinds of animals. Animals are part of WoDaaBe most intimate environments. Late in the afternoon, the herd returns to camp and the cows gather in front of the home area, close, just a few steps away. From my bed, I frequently watch young children play with an older calf. It is sitting on the ground, and the children play on its back. They hold on to its horns, rest on its head, move on it like it is a natural extension of their own bodies. The young children know that they have to watch out for some of the older cows, but they are familiar with this calf and know that it is harmless. A little boy less than a year old walks around every day with a stick in his hand. His face is determined; he follows the little goats and lambs, beating them with the stick. In another place, a mother is packing her house items because the camp will move soon. She is putting the baggage on the donkey which, as usual, refuses to stand still. Her two year old girl is too small to help her but at the same time as her mother struggles to control the donkey, she tries to keep the donkey's foal in line. She experiments with getting it to move to different places and then tries to make it stand still. These interactions are scattered pictures, taking place at different times and places, and concern different people. But they have in common the socialization of humans and animals; everyday interactions where human children and animal offspring get to know each other, explore each other, test their own boundaries and limitations, establishing and defining relationships which will become an integrated part of themselves and their lives later on. The animals are a part of a child's social environment, moving freely around and inside the space defined as house.[34]

---

[34] For more detailed discussion of the WoDaaBe conceptualization of their natural environment see Kristín Loftsdóttir 2001a and 2001b.

Different family members often sit down for a while around a small fire in the morning to have tea.

When I asked children to make pictures of their homes for me, they always included the calf rope, and sometimes the *duDal*, the fire lit in the rainy season to keep mosquitoes away from the cattle. As I fall asleep at night, seeing white horns around me, the cows themselves are only shadows in the dark. Sometimes I wake up during the night hearing the whispering steps of their feet when they move for pasture.

Djelgul, the Symbol of Ownership

I am told to repeat, "*E mi jiidi mi jela na'i am*" and everyone around me laughs because I do not have any cows. The *djelgul* is a mark of ownership, made by cutting into the ears of the animal, done during a specific time of the year (the month of *Jeletenduudu*). The WoDaaBe only mark cows, sheep, goats and donkeys. Discussing the reason for this with Akali, I suggested that this could reflect a difference between animals which have traditionally been owned by the WoDaaBe (the animals marked), and those which are recently integrated into their economy. Akali did not find this explanation convincing and suggested instead that this would rather be affected by the marked animals being owned in greater numbers than those without a mark.

Akali and other WoDaaBe males told me that the mark is made to show WoDaaBe ownership of the animal, distinguishing it from the other ethnic groups' ownership. This definition of the mark heavily emphasizes the practical aspects of marking and assumes interestingly enough that the WoDaaBe themselves would not dispute the ownership of animals. Dupire, however, emphasizes the *djelgul* as an important manifestation of WoDaaBe identity. According to her, the mark signifying an animal's ownership becomes a symbol of a common ancestry, justified with circular logic: "the same ancestry hence the same sign, the same sign hence the same ancestry" (Dupire 1962a:286; my translation). At the time of her research, there were only four types of marking in all the WoDaaBe lineages. She reports that only one mark exists for all the different lineages within the Degiredji but within the Alidjam lineage[35] three types of marks are found. When discussing Dupire's argument with Akali, he wanted to de-emphasize the importance which Dupire places on the *djelgul* as a unification symbol for the WoDaaBe, pointing out that the concept *djelgul* can simply be translated as a "symbol" or "mark" in English. The concept itself thus simply refers to the marking of one's property and can be used in other contexts as well, not having anything to do with the WoDaaBe or livestock. He also pointed out that humans have *djelgul*, just as animals, the *djelgul* of the WoDaaBe being a stick, the braiding of hair, etc., and the *djelgul* of the Hausa being different from the Tuaregs' *djelgul*. This is an interesting observation in my view, stating that both people and animals are marked to classify and distinguish them from their neighbors. The *djelgul* could simply show to whom a certain person belongs, and to whom a certain animal belongs. This observation is not all that different from Dupire's observation, but instead of seeing the *djelgul* as a source of unification, it suggests that it is a sign of boundaries, of borders rather than identification. The concept implies some kind of similar metaphorical separation of WoDaaBe animals and WoDaaBe people from 'others' seen as belonging to other groups.

Perceiving the *djelgul* as a sign of boundaries between groups, it is interesting to observe that the marks on animals which appear to be the same are not

---

[35] The WoDaaBe are divided into two major lineages: the Alidjam and the Degire'ul (see discussion in Kristín Loftsdóttir 2002).

so when closely observed. I received detailed information regarding the marks of the Bii-koro'en, Japto'en and Gojanko'en lineage groups, but all my informants confirmed that the mark is actually not the same if closely observed. The Bii-koro'en cut deeper into the ear than the Gojanko'en, and the Japto'en take the top part of the ear (*djebite*). Fulani groups in Tchin-Tabaraden, according to WoDaaBe informants, cut the ears of their animals in a similar way, but unlike the WoDaaBe, who cut both ears, the Fulani only cut one ear of the animal. The Tuaregs, however, use a very different method in marking their animals, branding instead of cutting them. According to Nicolaisen (1963:138), all northern Tuaregs cut the ears of the sheep and goats, but brand camels and donkeys.

The Affection for and Economics of Cows

I was told that the WoDaaBe say that they never stop *muusini* (in this context, breast-feeding) because when they stop drinking the milk of their mother (*o koDaaDo*), they continue drinking the milk of their cows. People did not seem to view their relationship with cows as one of dominance and use, but somehow in terms of equality, emphasizing the symbiotic aspect of the relationship. Akali argues: "My people are like *maccuBe* (slaves) for the cows, all you do is for your cows. If it is the dry season, you want to go and get water for your cows. Your cows only wait, observing you working. You have to do all the work, you have to think about how to get the water" (3 October 1998). The products of the cows are seen differently from the products of other animals. The feces (*belade*) from the cow are used for healing purposes. Women sometimes cook the *belade* and rub it into their hair to make it look darker. Cow urine is considered to have healing capabilities as well, and people who have been ill for a long time wash with the urine. The skin of a dead cow is used, but its horns are placed quite high up in a tree, sometimes along with the tail (*BookorDe*). The hair from the tail is sometimes used as a body decoration for the dances of males. The concept "*BookorDe*" has also entered the language of gift exchange. When someone reciprocates a gift, he or she is said to be giving the *BookorDe*.

The various taboos associated with objects having to do with cattle show the importance of the cow, both in terms of subsistence and symbolic terms. A few can be mentioned here; the calf rope (*dangol*), has several taboos, one of its most important being that it should not be stepped on or walked over. The milking bowl (*birdude*) also has various taboos associated with it and should not be used for any other activity than milking. A woman with unbraided hair cannot enter the *duDal* (the fire for the cows during the rainy season), and no one can take charcoal from this fire. The breaking of these taboos will usually cause something bad to happen to the livestock, such as a calf dying or a cow getting lost or ill. Dupire points out that the concepts *yiite* (fire), *nagge* (cow) and *naange* (sun) all belong to the same class (*nge*) in the Fulfulde language, being the only concepts constituting that class. She suggests that this can mean that these three elements can belong to an ancient primitive cult of which no traces are left today (Dupire 1962a:93; Dupire 1971 [1960]:49).

Social Life and Livestock

As pointed out by Dupire (1962a:53), the animals do not only satisfy physical needs of the humans taking care of them, but are also important in their social needs. All important events in a person's life cycle, usually marking a transition of their defined roles in society, such as birth, marriage or death, involve the killing of an animal (see also Stenning 1964:199). Livestock is thus the basis for all social relations. Through *haBBanaaji* loans of livestock, an extensive network of social relations is formed and reinforced. *Kobgal* marriage takes place through the slaughtering of a bull, uniting two families of the same lineage group. The *kobgal* marriage is arranged by the parents for two young children, and consists of a series of steps which take many years, but always involve either the boy's family killing an animal or them giving gifts to the girl's family.[36] In performing a *teegal* marriage ceremony (which is marriage between mutual consenting adults), a sheep is usually slaughtered. In some few instances, a bull is slaughtered; this is usually done if the man is trying to demonstrate a great affection for the woman, and imitates

---

[36] The first step, the *puDDol*, usually takes place when the girl is very young. It is not important how old the boy is when this is done, but the girl has to be under 15 years of age. The *puDDol* involves the killing of a young bull or a sheep, depending on the wealth of the household. The *puDDol* is not necessarily done at the annual lineage festival. The next ceremony is simply called *kobgal*, which involves the killing of a bull (2 or 3 years old) or a big cow, depending on the situation of the household. Usually the girl is around 11 to 14 years old. The next ceremony is called *bosDi kobgal* and involves the killing of a sheep, whose meat is eaten by both families. Finally, there is a series of several gifts.

WoDaaBe usually only slaughter animals for some specific social events.

kobgal marriage. *Suka'en* is an institution where the father gives his son his first calf. In some cases, if the man has a great many cows or few sons, the daughters receive a *suka'en* cow from the father. The calf stays with the father's herd where it grows and will become what later constitutes the son's herd. It is important to note that the herd of a household does not only belong to the male head of the household but also includes animals belonging to sons who still make their home (*wuro*) with their father. These animals will form the basis of what the sons can have later in independent households. Animals thus play a central role in social institutions, constituting a medium where relationships are established in WoDaaBe society.

Cattle-loans (*haBBanaaji*) are another important way in which animals are part of WoDaaBe social life and relationships. Briefly stated, *haBBanaaji* is the borrowing of a female animal for a certain period of time, usually until the animal has given birth to two calves (see Scott and Gormley 1980; White 1990). After that time the original animal is returned to its owner. Cattle-loans take place with cows, sheep, goats and donkeys. Women have very few cows, which can explain why fewer of them have *haBBanaaji* cows. Of eighteen women asked, only two participated in cattle-loans, and in both cases the women had only one animal. In contrast of the twenty-one men surveyed, only one did not participate in cattle-loans, but most had more than one *haBBanaaji* cow. Cattle-loans are an important institution in WoDaaBe society, both in terms of redistributing resources, of sustaining relationships and in giving meaning to what it is to be a WoDaaBe. Cattle-loans involve generosity which, as I will discuss later, is at the heart of a definition of being WoDaaBe. Ibonou, a young herder, told me that if someone did not want to give cattle-loans, that same person was not a WoDaaBe. Cattle-loans are a way of making friends and allies, but also a way of earning respect and prestige among people. One man confessed to me that his dream was to get a big herd, and be able to give a lot of *haBBanaaji*. Sometimes, when people describe someone as having power they say, "He is a big man, he has given a lot of people *haBBanaaji* ." But primarily, a *haBBanaaji* animal is the animal of friendship, involving an act usually not forgotten. When people talked to me about other people, they usually told me if the person had given them a cattle-loan, thus showing the nature of their relationship. Cattle-loans increase the safety of the group as a whole, by distributing resources to more people. Credit can thus be seen as collected in a more secure form, by transferring livestock into a debt of reciprocity. Someone who has given a lot of *haBBanaaji* and loses all his cows will be much more able to depend on the generosity of the people around him than someone who has been reluctant to give such loans. As Stenning points out, in terms of the obligation of reciprocity to kinfolk, a man is "wealthy because of his kin and not in spite of them" (Stenning 1964:195). Although the WoDaaBe see cattle-loans as a part of their ethnic identity, similar institutions also exist among other ethnic groups in Niger, and probably most herding communities have a similar system to ensure the safety of the community as a whole (Wilson and Legesse 1990:7; N.n 1983:53; Scott and Gormley 1980:103).[37]

---

[37] Development projects, attempting to base themselves on indigenous methods of survival, have used the cattle-loans to reconstruct WoDaaBe herds. Such was the case with the project Oxfam Abala, which helped the WoDaaBe to reconstruct herds after the 1968–1974 drought (see Scott and Gormley 1980), and with the Range and Livestock Project in 1982 (see Swift and Maliki n.d.).

THE COLD AND THE HOT SEASON

> I think it is surprising to Akali, and to people in general, how useless this *anasara* is. She gets tired very fast, she is always falling down, and she is always getting stuck in the thorns of the bushes (a letter to my parents 16 October 1996).

Akali is trying to find my camel and I sit down on a blanket while his wives pack the house items. "Can I help?" I ask, but as usual, I am told that I help most by just sitting and waiting. Akali comes back and the camel struggles before it lies down stiffly. Akali puts a quilted cloth on to its back and places the saddle (*kirkje*) on top. My two bags, his own radio and small bag are tied to the saddle.

Unlike the young WoDaaBe women, I am made something to sit on. From a half empty sack of millet and my blanket, Akali makes a "saddle" that is tied to his saddle, forming something like a swing. It will prevent me from slowly sliding down the camel's back. I take my shoes off, lift up one leg carefully over the camel's back and sit down. Camels have a tendency to jump up as soon as the rider places himself in the saddle, and thus it is important that this one does not get the impression that I am the actual rider. I hold tight to the back of the saddle, not afraid but determined not to fall. Akali has gently explained to me that I should not take a hold of him, because it is improper and would never be done by a WoDaaBe. Instead, I should take hold, preferably with one hand, of the back of his saddle. His younger brother Gidado rides by our side and the two men talk.

My bottom is sore from the previous ride; still, there is something magical about riding into the endless landscape, to merge with the hilly platform. The camel has soothing movements, its steps are quiet. The items of the house have been packed, but we have not waited for those to be placed on to the donkeys. I look back and see the women and children start to move on their donkeys not far behind us. Akali's father has left earlier with the herd.

It is late rainy season (*yaawol*), and thus water is still taken from the ponds.

Yet, it is difficult to find ponds where there is water, in most of them only a watery mud remains. My own water is almost finished and Akali worries about me becoming dehydrated. He knows about a pond not far away, and we ride to it. Gidado, a younger brother, gets off his camel, pulls his trousers up his legs as far as they will go and walks into the middle of the pond in an attempt to get the best water. It is dark brown. "This water is not very good", Akali tells me after having tasted it, "We should try to find another pond." Gidado still fills the container with water, and we ride a little further, where there is another larger pond with purer water. Gidado pours the dirty water out and fills up on fresh water. We catch up with Akali's father after a little while, where he is riding his son's camel. Ibrahim, another of his sons, is walking with the herder's stick (saaru) on his shoulder. He limps because a few weeks earlier a snake bit him and he has not recovered yet. He has probably not walked for a long time. Kala'i calls something to Akali and I only understand that he is asking about me. Akali tells me that his father wants to stop now because he can see that I am really tired. I try to tell him that I am doing fine, but a decision has been taken. Akali tells me quietly that he does not want to argue with his father.

We are making a long migration movement, and every time we move somewhat further south. It is the time of the migration movement *jolol*, when the herders move from the rainy season pasture in the north to the dry season pasture in the south. The *Cure Sallée* and the small festivals were all held in the rainy season pasture to the north-west of Tchin-Tabaraden. The areas in the south, where the lineage group will make use of the waterhole area, form what the WoDaaBe call their country (*lehidi am, gari am*). There are several waterhole areas that the lineage tries to return to each year, but rainfall and the region's situation will affect what waterhole area will actually be used. Prior to the *jolol*, the migration is discussed in the men's council (*kinnal*). Even though everyone has, in theory, a right to speak out in the council, the elders' authority is highly respected. The person, however, having the most authority is the lineage chief (*arDo*). People are not obligated to follow his direction, but should communicate to him if they leave for another area. The name *jolol* is for the movement in general, the term thus simply referring to the displacement from rainy season pasture to the area of attachment (*gari*). Short migration movements, even those done within the context of *jolol* are simply referred to as *gonsul*.

The sun is shining and we are moving again to a different place. It will not be far today and so I am walking. My camel is led by Akali, while Gidado and Ibrahim lead the other two camels. I have been told to walk in front and not come too close, as the camels are mean spirited and could try to kick me. The high grass is yellow and dry. The *saabeere* grass, characteristic by the late rainy season, is everywhere with its thorny seeds sticking to my clothing. The seeds not only stick to one's clothing but also painfully pierce the skin like little needles. "No, no", I hear Akali call again. "Don't go over there! Where are you going! You just went right into the *saabeere* again! Can't you see the road?" He is frustrated. "No, I am sorry, I just don't see any road", I say almost as equally frustrated, having gone through the same conversation with him several times. "This is because you don't look where you are going", he tells me harshly, "This is not a street in a town, you have to look where you are going." Only a few minutes earlier he had been angry at me for only looking down. As he said, I was like a cow, only watching my own feet. He told me then that I should look far ahead. I do not remind him of that, feeling that I should say something but instead remind myself that I am an ethnographer, not a child. I just try to follow the path that to my eye is invisible, trying to look down and see far ahead at the same time. Before too long I am again stuck in *saabeere* land.

WoDaaBe generally do not show their affection for someone in words. "Words are nothing", Akali will tell me over and over again during the following months. To experience that people are fond of you, you have to look for little things, sometimes things almost invisible. There is a little girl called Sollare whom I have a strong affection for. She usually sits down silently on the blanket and observes me, and then moves closer and closer full of curiosity and questions. Perhaps it is because she is around eleven years old, just like my sister's oldest daughter. Her patience in trying to communicate with me is endless, and every spare moment she has, she wants to spend with me. Like other WoDaaBe women, she fears men and only approaches me when I am alone or surrounded by other women. If I am with any of the men, she comes to me, but sits next to me silently, perhaps only holding my hand or leaning her head against my shoulder. Sometimes she finds for me dry, crunchy leftovers from the pot where the millet porridge is cooked. She gives them to me and I eat them along with the other children. This is children's food, but I like it. Sometimes she tries to find lice in my hair, looking under my braids and fondling my scalp. That is her way, I think, to show that she likes me. As with others, I cannot show her in the way that I know that I like her and love her. But what I desire most is a word of encouragement, some token showing that I am doing fine, someone to say something about my own value as an anthropologist, as a researcher, as a person. But the world around me is silent. I do not know it then, but a direct compliment is not much practiced in the society that I live in. To compliment something invites the risk that it will suffer bad luck somehow. A Tuareg goldsmith was a jewelry maker. His jewelry making was well known and people complimented him a great deal regarding it. Then this man became blind and unable to carry out his craft. People know what happened, it was people's *hunnduko* (literally mouth, but in this context talk) that had caused his misfortune.

During my stay at this household, I usually eat with Akali or with him and his brothers. I get a large share of milk, which I have to drink as appropriate before it is mixed in with the porridge. Akali then pours it into the porridge bowl and mixes together the two items to make *suuDam* (*suta* is to mix). Because of me, he mixes it carefully as is usually done for the younger children. No big pieces. Milled porridge is the food for most occasions; it is cooked in the late afternoon, eaten after the cows have been milked and what remains of it is eaten the morning after. Usually people only have these two meals during the day. As a result of my presence in the house, there is always a little something cooked at noon, usually rice or a mixture of rice and pasta, because as Akali claims, this is the food I am used to. He also asks every couple of weeks, for people going to the market to buy me a little piece of meat. He eats one piece of my meat because I tell him that I do not want to eat alone, and then carefully separates with his hands the rest of the meat into small pieces for me. I tell him I prefer to eat millet porridge like everyone else, but he tells me that I am not used to eating only millet porridge and I have to get a little meat occasionally. The rules of eating are complicated and I always seem to be making mistakes. He corrects my mistakes; after all, did I not come here to learn the life of the WoDaaBe? I make so many mistakes in terms of eating in a proper way that I write down the rules in my notebook, collecting them in the hope of learning them. He is right, they do say something about being a WoDaaBe, as in probably all other cultures eating is part of social interaction, and its rules of conduct thus become crucial for being functional in a social context.

The first rule is in the morning before eating, I have to wash my mouth and nose. I also learn that when taking hold of a calabash to drink from it, I should put my index fingers inside the calabash but leave all the other fingers outside it. I used to grab the calabash firmly, causing people to laugh. When I am drinking from it, I am not supposed to place my hands very close to my mouth (i.e., when I am holding it). The oldest of the group should start to eat first, meaning that if it is only Akali and I, he takes the first spoonful. When eating, I have to finish everything in the spoon and preferably in one mouthful. This list of rules in relation to this simple act seems endless.

The times when the family has visitors are the most stressful because this is when my table manners are tested along with my language skills. A man comes for a visit who is the friend of Kala'i. His camp is not far from ours, and he has not seen Kala'i for a long time. It is during the evening, and I am writing in my notebook, trying to make use of the diminishing light. We had been moving in the day and I am tired but relaxed. Other members of the house are sitting with me. The man is curious about this *anasara* (white) woman, and I hear him asking Akali and Kala'i questions about me. He is an old man and has been Kala'i's friend for a long time. Finally, the man turns to me and asks me my name. I manage to answer well. Then he asks "*To wi'ete lehidi ma?*" I had earlier learned the word *lehidi*, then in the context of meaning earth or sand, but its meaning is in fact much broader, extending to a place, country or area. I cannot understand what the man is saying, and he repeats it. Again, I do not understand. I do not know what to say, and there is this silence where people wait for my response. Finally, Akali tells the man that it is "Iceland." Akali then turns towards me and explodes with disappointment, "This is not difficult, you know this, *lehidi* means country, he is only asking what is the name of your country! You should be able to answer this, you know what this means!" I am silent, feeling incompetent and confused. We eat soon afterwards. Akali and I have our meal together, because the guest dines with Kala'i. It is a quiet meal, his sudden anger has disappeared, his face is sad and blank. After we have finished eating, I go to my bed instead of talking to him and or to other people and just pretend to be playing cards. I am hurt and do not understand why he was so angry with me. I feel anger myself, but also frustration. I hear him coming and I see that he is embarrassed somehow, as he does not know what to say.

"Oh, you are playing with your cards" he says. "That is very good." I nod

Camels are useful for travelling fast in certain area, but young men also like to have a camel to more easily visit other WoDaaBe households in the surrounding area.

and there is a silence. When I do not say anything, he starts making excuses; that he has not had time to help me as much as he has wanted to because there were always so many things he has to attend to. He would like to take better care of me but it is hard because he has so many other responsibilities. I look at him, and realize that he is somehow trying to make me happy, somehow trying to reach out to me but not knowing how, and all of sudden instead of feeling sorry for myself, I feel sorry for him. I feel sorry for him to have an alien woman whom he feels for some reason responsible for, and puts so much emotional pride in, that he becomes hurt when she "fails." I think about the assistant, informant, consultant or whatever-we-want-to-call-it and I ask myself if his work is not much more demanding than the work of the anthropologist. He is the true borderliner, trying to make the meaning and behavior of the anthropologists understandable to himself and to his society, as well as making his society meaningful to the anthropologist. He is caught in between. He must in a sense feel that he has to present the anthropologist in a favorable light to his society, and his society in a favorable light to the anthropologist. When I try to go to sleep that night, I am awake for a while. I lay on my back and think about all this. The sky is dark blue and the moon is almost full. I feel happiness because the moon looks at me through the holes in the branches. I look back at it and feel good to be part of something, even though it means causing disappointment sometimes.

We migrate to a new place the day after. We do not go far, probably a little less than an hour and I am walking along with some of the younger men. The house is created again at the new place. Sollare is, as usual, responsible for my bed. The next day, everything is packed to move again, but contrary to most times we start packing late in the day. The *wuro* moves together, the donkeys, camels, cows, sheep, goats and people moving slowly in the yellow landscape.

When the sun sets, Kala'i decides that we should find a place to sleep during the night and continue early in the morning. Instead of reconstructing the houses, the baggage is taken off the donkeys and mats are placed on the ground for people to sleep on. Akali and I play cards in the night. It is my only form of entertainment. Akali, who plays most often with me and did not know how to play cards before my arrival, is becoming so good at playing that I suspect him of voluntarily losing in order not to beat me too many times. When I lay down on my mat, I feel very tired, even though I miss sleeping on my bed.

Gidado sleeps very close to my side on another mat. I fall asleep right away.

Suddenly, I wake up. There is a strange sound and I am not sure what it means, I only know that something is wrong. Half asleep, I hear people calling out but cannot make out what they are saying. All of a sudden I realize what is happening, something has scared the cows and they are running like mad towards the camp. I jump up. They are so close, they are running past me on both sides, some so close that I fear they will run me over, one steps on my straw mat, but moves away at the last moment. Their speed is so high that they are not able to stop even though something is in the way. Gidado is right by me but the chaos is so great that I cannot reach out to him. Suddenly, as fast as it started, it is over, only dust is left everywhere. The cows have been stopped, which is important so they do not get lost. I hear people laughing, happy that the crisis has been solved. My own body shakes like a branch, and Gidado takes my hand. "Is everything fine Mariyama?" he asks and I nod. The sun is rising and I am happy that I do not have to go back to sleep.

The *yaawol* has ended and the *dabbunde* season arrives. It is marked by wind blowing all day and a brown-grayish sky. It is the sun, but it is pale in the sky. The night and morning are cold. I have a wool blanket with me, originating from my native country. We are proud of our blankets in Iceland, so when Akali told me that I would be cold with only this one, I laughed and announced that being from a cold country I would never be cold here in Niger. The blanket was fine during the rainy season, but as soon as yaawol is over and the cold *dabbunde* starts, I feel very cold in the night. I only have my bed and then this blanket to cover myself with. I sleep alone unlike most others, who have a spouse or a child, or siblings to sleep with and keep warm with. I am freezing even though I sleep in most of my clothes, as the others do. The first night after the *dabbunde* starts, I shake in the night because it is so cold. Akali never goes to sleep in his *suudu* before making sure that I am safely under my blanket. I am shaking from the cold but try not to show it, hoping that it will be better later in the night. It is not better. I try to sleep but my body is too cold for me to rest. Akali observes in the morning that I have not slept well. "You don't look very well" and he asks me, "Is there a problem?" Before I answer, he has guessed the reason. He laughs, "You are cold." I laugh as well, even though I feel miserable, not knowing that he will make fun of this for the rest of my stay. The next night he brings me one of the two blankets that he and his wife use. I feel guilty in accepting it, but try to convince myself that he would not accept my refusal. For the next few days other people in the household comment on this, feeling sorry for me, asking me "*A nani peewol Mariyama?* Are you cold Mariyama?" Stories travel fast. This one traveled before me to Niamey and was known to most people of the lineage staying there.

The small ponds where we used to get our water have dried up and the time has arrived to make and use small hand dug wells at the waterhole areas. A lot of work is ahead which includes digging the wells and later maintaining them, occasionally making new ones if the old ones become dry. Our migrations are short, and aim at using the area around the waterhole area, not migrating to a different area. Migration can only take place on certain days, as in WoDaaBe society certain tasks are often reserved for specific days. Some days of the month have a taboo on migration movements, having to do with the moon's location in the sky. Some weekdays are worse suited for *gonsul* than others, those days that should be avoided being Monday, Wednesday, and Saturday (Maliki 1981:70). If for some reason, however, it is seen as absolutely necessary to move the camp, then these taboos can be circumscribed. The animals are often moved to a new pasture during the day and the house follows only at night, justified by the reasoning that a new day has actually started.

Migration is important for the WoDaaBe in various ways. It is a way of utilizing a resource where grass cover is not equally distributed over a given space and also a way to prevent over-grazing in a specific area. Thus, migration is an adaptation to the ecology of the Sahel and has to be seen in the context of its ecology. However, migration movements also have a more direct importance for the well being of people and animals, because they translate into milk production. After staying a few days at the same place, the area around the house is conceptualized as dirty. It has animal dung all over, which has not become assimilated by the ground. "People in towns have flies because they always stay at the same place", various WoDaaBe tell me, "and flies carry illnesses. We are more healthy because we move." The cows are also sensitive to the cleanliness of the place. If it has dung all over, they do not feel good and will not lay on the ground, thus not resting enough which diminishes milk production. It can also be pointed out that with moving to a new area, the pasture for the animals is closer and the task of collecting firewood is much easier. WoDaaBe women collect dead branches as firewood and because their house moves so frequently, firewood collection is usually not very time consuming. Migration movements are also important for the definition of being WoDaaBe. I think the psychological effects of the migration lifestyle as part of one's life experience from birth cannot be completely ignored. Kala'i tells me:

> *Gonsul* [migration movement] is the inheritance of WoDaaBe. When God created WoDaaBe, he gave them *gonsul* as their tradition. So when WoDaaBe came into existence they had *gonsul*; that is to be WoDaaBe. We are WoDaaBe because of *gonsul*. All of us do *gonsul*. WoDaaBe leave a place, we find grass, call our cows, and take them there. WoDaaBe do *gonsul*, take their house, milk their cows, drink milk and are full. If we would not do *gonsul*, we would not get a lot of milk from our cows" (2 February 1997).[38]

After returning from my research, I was asked by someone who had also worked in Niger and knew the WoDaaBe whether I really liked the seasonal movements and felt if this was a good way of life, going through the hassle of unpacking everything once again, just to have to pack it again two or three days later? I thought about the question for a while, inspecting my own feelings. I have to say that I liked it and understand why WoDaaBe value it. I think *gonsul* involves a certain embodied experience. There is an excitement in the air almost every time when the house is packed, a sense of liberation, freedom which one perhaps has to learn to value by being a part of. A new place is refreshing, like a welcome change from the rather dull routine of the day. As Kala'i said, *gonsul* is a gift from God, intended both for the well being of animals and people.

I am never alone. During the day people gather on my bed, usually women during the day, and men in the evening. Who it is depends on what tasks have to be done and who is close to our camp. Sometimes Sollare or one of the other women moves my bed from the open area of the day, to better shelter from the sun. Sitting on the bed instead of on the ground, in the shadow of a few trees feels good. "How wonderful your bed is, Mariyama", Jumare tells

---

[38] The majority of interviews are translated by me from Fulfulde with the assistance of a WoDaaBe consultant. A few interviews are, however, "translated" from broken English into standard English in accordance with the request of the person interviewed.

me when she and four other women are resting on my bed, taking a short break before they start pounding the millet. She, as the other women, is of course not resting without any work, but attending to her embroidery, a handicraft that WoDaaBe women frequently do if they have any available time. She makes beautiful, imaginative patterns and small carefully crafted stitches.

"*Gollal yari'en WoDaaBe*. The work of WoDaaBe wives", she tells me proudly. The embroidered clothing usually consists of three types of clothes, the small shirt for young girls (*surbaajo*), the long shirt for a young man (*kajejo*), and the skirt cloth (*wudere*) for women (*surbaajo* and *ja'eriijo*). The thread and the cloth are expensive and I admire their ability to keep their work clean in the middle of their daily chores. In order to protect what has already been done, plastic is sewed on to the patterns, and then the cloth rolled up, leaving only the part exposed where work still remains. My nomadic lifestyle and lack of transportation other than my camel leads to me only having one big notebook to write down all my observations. I also draw pictures in it, creating much pleasure for the people around me. During my first months in the bush these pictures are a medium to communicate. When the men are away, the women come to see the old pictures and if there are any new ones. All the drawings of people must have names in my notebook and often people ask me to make pictures of them. In the evening the men and the women who went to the waterhole area to get water or to some other household come back to the house. Sollare comes back from the waterhole area but she has to go there almost every day to get water. Long before I see her, I hear her singing from a distance, coming back from her day's work. "My work is difficult", she tells me once when there are only the two of us. "I wake up early in the morning to go to the well, only to come back in the evening. I am tired of going every day."

Akali's young brother Gidado is for some reason not particularly shy towards me. I eat with him and Akali and sometimes Ibrahim. Unlike most of the other young men, he is not shy to hold my hand, and his handshake is light and friendly like a brother's hand in mine. He has a girlfriend who lives in a camp nearby and thus he is usually not at his *wuro* in the evening. I see him leave with his long iron spear and his blanket on his shoulder, disappearing into the night. His girlfriend comes to the house for a few days and stays with us. She is beautiful and graceful, looks down when the men get close, but keeps her head high otherwise. She has no interest in engaging in conversation, just getting me to repeat things that she laughs at with the other women, or asking me something which I do not know the answer to. It is Jumare who most often saves me from such situations. Jumare and I calculate our age, discovering that we were probably born exactly in the same year, both being twenty-eight years old, born in the year called *gol Makruu*. We find it fascinating, perhaps because we both realize how different our lives have been. Ironically, we also become friends because she is often ill and thus has to stay more at home than the other women, recovering from her illnesses. When her stomach is hurting, I help her to place the cow dung on it. She is thin and fragile, and I am shocked to discover the scars on her stomach. "What happened to you?" I ask her astonished. She laughs in a friendly way at my ignorance, telling me that I am seeing the consequences of childbearing. Our different experiences are sometimes a gulf between us and my inability to master the language contributes to this gulf and hence my sense of isolation. It is strange not really to know anything, to be ignorant like the smallest child in the camp. I discover that it is not difficult to ask people standardized questions, but to "talk", to really talk, discuss, and explore is more challenging because our lives are so different and thus so few things can easily be chatted about. These valuable moments with Jumare described above are not an everyday occurrence, but valuable breaks from the mundane, where our experiences touch and we manage to move temporarily beyond cultural barriers.

An aspect of WoDaaBe reserved behavior is that it is generally considered somewhat inappropriate to ask many questions. Questioning is often seen as a way of demonstrating dissatisfaction with something. For an ethnographer, whose work consists basically of asking questions, this can be difficult. Some questions are of course well taken and seen as appropriate, especially if they are not too many and asked at the right moment, but others are understood as criticism or an indication of a "problem." I frequently have to explain to Akali that my questions are not because of any problem, but instead I just ask because I want to learn things. He says that he understands, but at the same time it is hard for him to comprehend why everything has to be questioned, and often he forgets that I am not criticising when asking about something. I ask, for example, why a particular girl has the hair style of a man, rather than of a woman. He takes the question as dissatisfaction on my part and becomes upset. I explain again to him our cultural differences, and he tells me that his people just do not ask questions like this. Our discussions on posing questions and behaving appropriately help me to ask other people questions without distancing them. Sometimes, especially when Akali is not around to direct me, a long awkward silence meets my inquiries, which means I have said something that is not meaningful and probably not polite. I fear this silence, this looking away, people not knowing how to react, how to behave.

Questions can also be tiresome. Once, after moving to a new place, I notice that all the *bambammbe* trees are dead. They are without leaves, just the white dead trunks standing naked in the open. A few meters away there are three *tanni* trees in much better condition. I am curious to know why, and ask Akali why all the *bambammbe* are dead. He looks at me, silent for few moments, then says, "You want to know why all the *bambammbe* have died? I will tell you. This is because *bambammbe* were at war with the *tanni*. The *tanni* killed all the *bambammbe*, so now they are all dead." He looks at my face. It is probably rather surprised because he adds, "Of course I don't know how these *bambammbe* died, how could I know that? I don't know everything, Kristín. Only God knows this."

A Letter to a Place Far Away

I tell my friend Sollare that I know a girl in Iceland, the same age as her, my sister's child who I care for deeply. Sollare has observed me many times writing something in my notebook. She has learned to write a few numbers and she makes beautiful drawings to give to me. One day she decides that she wants to write a letter to the girl in my family, who is as old as she is, just like I am writing letters to my parents. We sit down for a short time almost everyday for three weeks working on the letter. She talks and I write down her narrative, parts of which I present here.

I greet you my friend Garun. Sollare greets Garun. You gave me a sweater. I have two brothers, Njunju and Gabidi. My age is eleven. Gabidi is three years old. Njunju is five. How old are you? My friend Mogamany is eleven. Yesterday, I went to the well, I got lost, I came back only now this morning. The sun went down, and I was still working at the well. The well is really far away. The cows have to be given water, the well has to be cleaned. The well has almost no water, and we are far from it. It is in front of

CHAPTER 5 — THE COLD AND THE HOT SEASON

Djiibiiri. [...]. My grandmother's name is Fatima, my other grandparent is Kala'i. My sister's brothers are Gidado, Akali and Ibrahim. […]. Their mother is Fatima, their father is Kala'i. I have finished writing, I feel tired. Greet your home, greet all people of your home.

(February 5)
We decided not to migrate. I did not go to the well, which is really far. Yesterday it was cleaned and tomorrow I will go. Garun gave me a sweater. She is eleven years old.

(February 6)
Today, I went to the well. The well has water now. That is because it was cleaned, the earth taken away so the water would come. I went to the well and was there early this morning. Budju deepened and cleaned the well.

(February 7)
Today I went to the well. Tomorrow, I want to stay at the house. Then the day after tomorrow, I will go to the well.
[…].
(February 14)
Today we will migrate but I have to go to the well anyway. Yesterday, I went to the well, I came back very tired. The day before yesterday I went to the well. It is like this but I got porridge, and I had millet porridge to eat with a sauce. I was still tired.

(February 16)
I went to the well today. Now for two days I have gone to the well. I am very tired, I have a headache, and I can't find the donkeys. Four donkeys are lost. I have two water sacks (sakjijii) and I have to go to the well. Today, we are far from the well. Tell my friend that my work is to carry water to my house. The well is really far away.

(February 17)
Today, I am not going to the well. I will rest; the well is very far. The well is so far away that only when the sun has gone down, do people return to the house. Tomorrow, I have to get water at the Abalak well. Abalak is very far away. Tell my friend that my work is to get water for the house, I never rest during the whole month, my work is really difficult. Today, I pound millet. I pound, I cook, I carry wood to the house and tomorrow I go back to the well. Fatima, Gidado, Dida and Karetuu came back from the market

today. *Tomorrow I have to go to the Abalak well which is really far away. Abalak is far away! We are far away from that place. I want to greet my friend, Garun. My name is Madika, and my name is also Sollare. My grandfather calls me Sollare. Sollare is my different name. A'isa is my name, this people call me. Fatima calls me A'isa but I am also called Joo'gojl and Juumare and G'kassase. My younger sibling died, the child who was born after me. His name was Doteguul. I have Njunju and Gabidi. Gabidi is only three years old, but Njunju is five. Gabidi knows Mariyama well. […] Ibrahim's mother is called Fatima, and his father is Kala'i. […]. The youngest child [of Fatima] died at Tchin-Tabaraden. Its name was Amina.*

(February 17)
Today I did not go the well, I will go tomorrow and then the day after tomorrow. I was pounding millet. A cow kicked Ibrahim, [who was carrying a calabash with milk] and spilled milk.
[…]
(February 20)
Today, I go to the well, tomorrow I stay at the house. I pound millet, I cook and I make porridge, I give people different shares, I make sauce, I give people to eat. I don't have any shoes today, they are worn out. Mariyama told me that she would give me shoes.

(February 21)
I did not go to the well today. Only tomorrow I will go. Today I have work. Tomorrow, Mariyama will leave. I don't know if I go to the well, perhaps I will stay here at the house. Today, I pounded millet, I cooked, I gave people their share of the porridge, I made sauce, I ate with Mariyama when I finished cooking. Now, I pound millet, I take out sa'anjo *[the by-product which is given to the livestock] I add water, I make powder, I pound, I put water, I put water and pound. Dembe cooks, I put food into the calabashes. I take the sand from the millet. I separate the* sa'anjo, *I put the water in the pot to boil. Dembe puts millet into the pot, then she puts the millet powder and closes it. Today, I cook, I pound, I make powder. Today, I gave Mariyama millet to eat. I separated* sa'anjo, *I put different kinds of millet into plastic and told her to show her father and mother this millet. Tell my friend that I greet her, that she receives my best greetings. Tell her that I have reached eleven years. Tell her that I have a* kowaaDo *[the* kobgal *husband whom she will marry later]. His name is Saddo, he is older than I am, but until now we have not been married. Greet my friend. Tell my friend that if the man does not beat me, I want him. Tell her that I want to make a house and get children."*

WODAABE ETHNIC IDENTITY

It is late fall, the *dabbunde* season as the WoDaaBe call it, and the anthropologist has problems of her own. Her past, her "real" life, has knocked on the door, even though she is far away with the "exotic" WoDaaBe in the hot lands of the Sahel. She is lonely and there is no one who she can share her thoughts with, no one sharing her universe. In addition, the living conditions are extremely difficult. The sand is blowing, and has done so since the day before. Her mouth is full of sand, her hair cannot be combed, and her glasses dusty to the point of being useless. There is even sand between her teeth, her lips are dry and cracked with sand in every crack. What is even worse is that during the sandstorms I cannot write. I have tried, but only with the result that the layers of thin sand accumulating on the pages of my book have destroyed three of my pens. They will never write again. I have tried to pull the blanket over my head, but the sand blows mercilessly through it. I feel so frustrated and there is no one or nothing to take my frustration out on. I have no place of my own. My face has to remain expressionless, my voice free of stress. A strange picture comes into focus in front of my eyes; it is the picture of Malinowski on the cover of the book, *Observer Observed* (1883) edited by George W. Stocking. I see Malinowski sitting in a tent with a table, and I think angrily to myself, "Even Malinowski had a table to write on." I feel cheated somehow.

I go back under my blanket and Akali who can see my sadness and frustration, fearing that he is the one who has failed, when it is people faraway or perhaps just me, tells me to go to sleep. He has no other solution for this difficult woman whom he has decided to take care of. I pull the green blanket over my head, crawl into a fetal position, shelter my face with my hand from the sand and cry. Without a sound, because I cannot let anyone know that I cry. I cry inside my heart, my face wet with tears until I fall asleep.

I feel very tired the next day and I am hungry. The sand is blowing less. I need to bathe, but this is difficult because it is so cold at night and the sand-

The knife will protect this little boy from the evil spirits in the bush.

storms of the last few days have made it impossible. I am afraid to bathe in the day, afraid that someone will see me. When Akali comes back from giving water to his cow, he is also tired. He brings me *daniDam*, my favorite food, a milk which has been standing overnight, and has changed into white flakes and liquid both giving relief from hunger and thirst. *DaniDam* is usually only available during the rainy season, because most houses have so little milk at other times. I drink it, and Akali tells me that it is all for me.

"I want to tell you something, Mariyama", he tells me seriously, "If my speech is not pleasant for your heart, then you must forgive me for that. I only want to tell you this for your own good." His eyes are firm but his voice is gentle. "My people have something called *munyal*. *Munyal* is worth more than anything else. When you feel sad you want to do *munyal*. You want to pretend that you do not care, you want to laugh and not show that you are sad. Because whether you are sad or not, in the end it is all the same. If something is difficult you want to do munyal, because everything is in the power of God. Do you understand?" I nod my head, not knowing what to say. "I am sorry that I am sometimes a difficult person," I say hesitantly. He laughs gently, telling me that I am never difficult. He just wanted to tell me this for my own good, because perhaps no one had done so before.

I eat the *daniDam* eagerly, feeling better somehow, but the sadness has not completely left my heart. Akali observes me silently. "You were hungry" he says almost accusingly. I tell him no, the *daniDam* was just so good. He repeats the sentence more firmly and I ask myself almost in desperation if he is now angry again and disappointed at me. How is it that I can never do anything right? He looks at me and then asks: "Maybe now you want to go back to Niamey?"

He asks me this regularly. I usually just say "No" and we talk no more of it. Now I look up and think that perhaps he wants me to leave. I see a smile on his face, realize suddenly that he is teasing me.

"No", I say firmly, "the bush is very sweet." I realize almost at the same time the absurdity of this statement, because I am very dirty from not bathing due to the sandstorms the past few days. For the same reason I have not been able to comb my hair for two days. My eyes probably look as I have been crying and just before I was obviously hungry. He is probably noticing the same things, but he laughs, "You know now something you never knew before, you know hunger, you know thirst, you know hot, you know cold. You know how it is to not being able to bathe properly, how to sit down by yourself all alone. And you know how to stay with people. I think that now you know the bush." I do not try to protest, I just start to smile and we are suddenly both laughing for no obvious reason.

Mbodagansi

Mi hollataa e mi yiDi, mi wanaaka (I do not show what I love, I pretend that I do not care).

Mi yiiDi kamma mi yiDaa (What I love is the same to me as what I dislike).

I learn these sentences, not only because they are the heart of WoDaaBe conduct and thus of my research, but because they are guidelines for my own behavior and essential tools to comprehend others around me. Thus, they are crucial both for my personal development as someone living with people and for my professional development as trying to understand something about this people.

WoDaaBe strongly associate their ethnicity with herding life, as indicated earlier, and also base their identity as a group on certain moral rules that they perceive as unique to themselves. WoDaaBe conceptualization of *mbodagansi*, *semtuDum* and *munyal* are key concepts in this context. The idea of *mbodagansi* is particularly important because many WoDaaBe use it to differentiate themselves from other ethnic groups, including the Fulani. Fulani express the core of their ethnic identity in the idea of *pulaaku*[39] which refers (as the WoDaaBe's *mbodagansi*) to social-moral rules, seen as separating the Fulani from other ethnic groups. Scholarly works addressing Fulani identify *pulaaku* as a core concept in characterizing the Fulani identity (see for example Azarya et al. 1993:3; VerEecke 1989, VerEecke 1993; 4; Stenning 1959:55; Zubko 1993:202). Dupire uses in her study on WoDaaBe in Niger, the concept *mbodagansi* to refer to key components of WoDaaBe identity (1962a), while Stenning's research conducted among WoDaaBe groups in Nigeria at a similar time uses the term *pulaaku* (1959). According to Bonfiglioli's research, the WoDaaBe abandoned the term *pulaaku* in favor of the term *mbodagansi* in order to reaffirm their separation from the Fulani which, Bonfiglioli claims, the WoDaaBe felt had become too absorbed in values they associated with the Hausa (1988:63). The boundaries between these two groups are not always easily defined and these two concepts share in many respects a similar meaning. It should be emphasized that *pulaaku* and *mbodagansi* are not simply guides for appropriate behaviors and values but refer as well to other aspects of Fulani and WoDaaBe identity. Values associated with cattle are, according to VerEecke, an important component of a system that is embodied in the idea of *pulaaku*, cattle being extensively used in a metaphorical way to show values that are part of *pulaaku* (VerEecke 1991:189). The *pulaaku* guides the Fulani in their interpersonal relationships and their relationships with cattle (Ezeomah 1989:2). This same idea is reflected in John Aron Grayzel's assertion that cattle are the embodiment and reflection of values that are part of the *pulaaku* (Grayzel 1990:47).

---

39 In 1932, Reed defines the concept as employed to "denote the characteristics which distinguish the Fulani from surrounding races, but it is also used for the rules of conduct which should guide a Fulani in his intercourse with other people, and particularly with other Fulani" (Reed 1932:427). Stenning describes *pulaaku* as the "way of the Fulani", thus also in the inclusive ethnic characteristic of the term. He states that the term has several components, the most important being the *semteende (semtuDum), hakkiilo* (which can be translated as care, forethought), and *munyal* (Stenning 1959:55; see also Ezeomah 1989). VerEecke has noted that "in a broad sense, *pulaaku* is the path which guides one to be a just, moral virtuous and well-mannered person, which many Fulani believe to be peculiar to one's own kind" (VerEecke 1991:187).

The concept *mbodagansi* is, as argued in Reed's study, derived from the concept *mboDa*, meaning taboo or avoidance in English. The name "WoDaaBe" is derived from the same root (Reed 1932:424). The concept *pulaaku* is, however, derived from the same root as the concept Fulani (or FulBe (sing. Pullo) as they call themselves (Riesman 1977: 131). It is, in my opinion, very possible that the concept *mbodagansi* is simply derived from the name WoDaaBe (sing. Bodaado), (as *pulaaku* derives from Fulani), and is pointing more at "qualities appropriate to the WoDaaBe", than taboos per se, similar to *pulaaku* meaning "qualities appropriate to the Fulani" (Riesman 1977:131). Reed, for example, correctly points out that *mboDa* are not exclusively found in WoDaaBe society since many Fulani groups have *mboDa* as well (Reed 1932:431). I am here not disclaiming the importance of *mboDa* for WoDaaBe ethnicity, because following taboos is an important aspect of WoDaaBe everyday actions in all spheres of society, which integrated into being and behaving like WoDaaBe especially in relation to interaction with cattle and migration with the herd. When WoDaaBe are, however, asked to describe *mbodagansi*, most individuals mention formal acts, which they see as distinctive for WoDaaBe, including *mboDa*. These acts include respecting the different formalized *mboDa* in general; showing respect to parents-in-law; the inclusion of a mother after the pregnancy of her first child (*boofiiDo*), in addition to stressing the importance of obeying general rules of hospitality, and generosity towards one's kin. *Mbodagansi's* strong association with certain rules of hospitality can be demonstrated in the example of an elderly man's expression that someone with *mbodagansi* is generous in giving cattle-loans (*haBBanaaji*) (September 1997). Thus, *mbodagansi* seems to be associated with rather formal rules of conduct, some based on accepted taboos, others associated with general respect towards others, but in short it can be seen as referring to adhering to values of the WoDaaBe.

In addition to *mbodagansi*, WoDaaBe mention *semtuDum* and *munyal* (patience) as central to their ethnic identity. Translated roughly, the concept *semtuDum* can be seen as referring to shame; to have *semtuDum* is to know the correct moral behavior in certain situations, such as how to interact with one's parents-in-law and those who are older. There are several ways in which a person can behave shamefully, all involving the person in one way or another losing his or her self-control. Usually such situations involve the persons showing that they are not in control of their emotions or that they have some primordial needs, such as eating and defecating, and/or a need for other people. The need for self-control becomes more crucial when in certain culturally defined relationships, such as in interaction with one's parents and parents-in-law (see discussion in Riesman 1977). Children are, for example, said not to have *semtuDum*, because they act on their feelings and do and say what they like. Someone with *semtuDum* is thus generally reserved and respectful towards other people, not showing feelings or emotions (VerEecke: 1989). Catherine VerEecke further points out that the concept *dewal*, meaning "service", becomes part of women's *semtuDum*. Thus, the woman seeks to respect and serv her husband. This concept *dewal*, which can also be translated as "to follow", is the root forming the word for a "woman" (pl. *rewbe*, sing. *debbo*) in Fulfulde (VerEecke 1989:5). Again, we can benefit from Riesman's insights in terms of *pulaaku*, but he points out that people are said to lack *semtuDum* if they perform those actions that indicate lack of *pulaaku*. The concept *semtuDum* can thus, according to Riesman, be translated as the lack of *pulaaku* (Riesman 1977:131). Assuming that the meanings of *pulaaku* and *mbodagansi* are closely related (if not the same), it can thus be suggested that *semtuDum* in relation to WoDaaBe, refers to a lack of *mbodagansi*.

It should be noted that Fulfulde is often mentioned along with *mbodagansi* when talking about moral behavior. Fulfulde is of course the language of the WoDaaBe and Fulani, but in this context, the term refers more to a certain kind of conduct, to politeness and appropriate behavior, making it impossible to make a rigid distinction between the language and valued behavior. To have Fulfulde thus refers both to knowing the language and being able to act appropriately, but that knowledge is seen as embodied in the language itself.[40]

Munyal is also one of the principal positive characteristics of the WoDaaBe, embracing various interconnected ideas. *Munyal* can refer to showing patience to someone, not expressing dissatisfaction in order to avoid confrontation, of not showing one's feelings. The person who has *munyal* waits for something he or she wants, even though it may never come, not expressing his or her true feelings. *Munyal*, just like *mbodagansi*, is thus connected

---

[40] Bonfiglioli and Stenning also make this claim. Bonfiglioli writes: "Fulfulde is in this context not only a language, but a way of living" (Fulfulde dans le sens non pas d'un langage, mais d'une manière de vivre") (Bonfiglioli 1988:253). Stenning writes: "Fulfulde means not only the language spoken by Fulani but the whole range of rights and duties peculiar to a *pullo* [i.e., a Fulani]" (Stenning 1959:55).

with being in control of one's feelings. My personal metaphor for *munyal* is a car-trip that demonstrated for me both what *munyal* meant and its importance in an everyday context. I was sitting in the back of a pick-up with many people. The vehicle was supposed to take us the last short distance toward Tchin-Tabaraden. These vehicles usually have an iron frame built onto their rear, in order to load more people onto it. The women usually sit on the floor, on various commodities being transported while the men sit on the iron bars on the top. The car can become so packed that those in the center can hardly get enough air to breathe even though they are in fact outdoors. During this particular trip, I was sitting on the side with one hand holding onto the iron bar above me and the other hand holding onto a young WoDaaBe woman sitting to my left. Someone was sitting on the hand clinging to the iron bar, and I could find no other secure place to hold with my second hand. To my right was an blind old man, who was saved from the risk of falling because he was on the floor. Sitting on the side exposed me to the risk of falling off, and I constantly had to push myself further into the vehicle, making the blind man very uncomfortable. The other hand I used to support myself on the arm of the WoDaaBe girl who was further inside the vehicle than I was. I also had to bend my back forward to shift my balance into the right direction. The ride took over an hour and was extremely painful due to these circumstances. It was a rough ride, the car bumping up and down, which made it harder to concentrate on not falling and made the ride more painful for my back. I had earlier that same day been discussing the meaning of *munyal* and suddenly there I felt that I truly understood its meaning. Only by focusing on my pain as being irrelevant was I able to tolerate it. By imagining that it would never end, that it was a ride completely devoid of time, made me able to get through it. "What comes after *munyal*?" my friend Akali asked me when explaining the concept to me. "If you do not do *munyal* what can you do then?" Such a path is not easily followed. I am often guilty of not doing the right things in relation to others. My main problem in Niamey is a lack of working space and time. I need to do certain things to complete my research and my frustration increases because I have people napping and dining at my place in Niamey every day. The frustration increases when I have to postpone trips to important places in the city in order to play host at home.

"*Yaku munyal*" Akali tells me and explains that *munyal* is like meat that is difficult to chew, and thus has to be chewed slowly and carefully.

At a festival celebrating the name of new-born baby, a group of women sit in the shade drinking tea.

Scholars have for a long time now seen relations to others as intrinsic to the formation of ethnic self. As Fredrik Barth points out: "ethnic distinctions do not depend on an absence of social interaction and acceptance but are quite to the contrary often the very foundation on which embracing social systems are built" (Barth 1969:10). WoDaaBe explain their ethnic identity often by directly juxtaposing themselves more directly in relation to other ethnic groups, especially in relation to the sedentary Hausa. This is interesting when considering that the population in the Tchin-Tabarden area is composed of a majority of Tuaregs with a smaller population of individuals identified as Arabs, WoDaaBe and Fulani (Mabbutt and Floret 1980:126). This could be explained by the fact that, as Burnham and Last have discussed, Fulani ethnic identity was much articulated in the 19th century through a contrast with Hausa (Burnham and Last 1994). The binary opposition WoDaaBe generally draw between themselves and Hausa, marks a clear division of sedentary and pastoral life, constructing the world into coherent spheres of activities: WoDaaBe live in the bush, Hausa in towns or villages;

WoDaaBe are herders, Hausa cultivate; WoDaaBe migrate, Hausa stay in one place. To be Hausa and WoDaaBe means thus localization within different spaces that are appropriated by humans in different ways.

Horowitz has discussed the way in which division of labor correlates with ethnicity and the way in which people's understanding of belonging to a specific category can explain why they do not perform certain tasks (Horowitz 1972). As pointed out by Barth, ethnic groups are "categories of ascription and identification by the actors themselves", that work toward organizing interaction between peoples (Barth 1969:10). These "identifications by the actors themselves" take place through various mediums, both in speech interaction and in various kinds of public statements. Mette Bovin has discussed how ethnic terms are important for self-reference along with reference to others (IRSH: Bovin 1970).

Most classic scholarly works characterize the WoDaaBe as a part of the Fulani, speaking the same language and sharing many similar traditions (Dupire 1962a; Stenning 1959). Like the WoDaaBe, Fulani groups place strong emphasis on pastoralism as an aspect of their ethnic identity (see for example Azarya et al. 1993:38; Guichard 1990; VerEecke 1989). In spite of sharing the same language and many cultural traditions, the relationship of the Fulani and WoDaaBe is entangled in various ambiguities, contemporary WoDaaBe generally do not identifying themselves as belonging to the Fulani ethnic group. This relationship of the WoDaaBe to wider Fulani society is a good indication of the ambiguities and fluidity of WoDaaBe ethnicity. It can furthermore be pointed out that while Fulani draw also up typologies when characterizing their ethnicity (see Burnham 1999:271), studies have shown that Fulani ethnicity is in practice quite fluid, having changed in various ways. Some Fulani groups emphasis pastoralism as important to their ethnicity even in cases where they have become fully sedentary (Waldie 1990), while other Fulani groups have emphasized aspects not related to pastoralism in new conditions (Shimada 1993).

Today and the Past: The Council of Elders

Suura is the name for a council of older men. During festivals and social gatherings, the old men (*ndotti'en*) sit down at a specific place. Women and younger women do not, in general, enter the space within the boundaries of the council. The anthropologist, even though female, can cross these boundaries and take, at least briefly, a seat in the council.

I am with four elderly men on an ordinary day, Kala'i, Djuri, Ibrahim and Ganduu. They are all of a similar age, which I guess as being between at least 55 and 65. We are sitting not far from my bed, these men coming to visit the home that I belong to. We are talking about the past and the present, the changes of today. It is early in the morning, during the time of the rain, thus work is less extensive than later in the year. We are sitting on a straw mat under a tree. The women have started packing the camp because later that day we will move further south. I say: "I see that the young men have a lot of all kinds of things."

Djuri says, "In the past the young men had a *deDo* (leather shirt). I put on a belt, I had my *deDo*. I carried a sword by my side, but some people did not have swords. I had a turban, but it was different than the type people have today. Some men put *korol* (hair decoration) in their braids. I stroked my braids so they would fall down on my back, then put a hat on and rubbed cream on my face. I rub a special substance on my face."

"Yes, Dro [who is his age-mate] and I, we also did this. We went out to look at the girls, and they all liked me and not him!" Kala'i laughs when he says this because he is teasing.

I ask, "So what did the young men like to buy then?"

Djuri tells me, "The people in the past bought something very fine. People in the past bought fine cloth, and the older men swept it around their shoulders. They put the cloth around their shoulders, and then took a part of the cloth to make a turban. Then our shoes were made of cow skin, and the *deDo* made of sheep skin."

"Do you think that today the times are better or worse?"

Djuri: "The really old people say that in the past the times were better, but people today believe that today there are better times." They argue about this for a while, not in agreement if things are better today than in the past. Djuri says, "In the past it was better." Ibrahim adds very firmly, "In the past the times were better. At that time the children had a *deDo*. Today the children just do everything they want to, they have trousers. In the past, there were true WoDaaBe. The history in the past shows the true WoDaaBe. In the past when WoDaaBe got into problems, and someone wanted to beat them, they held their shoes in their hands and just ran."

"Do you not say anything to the young people today when they buy all kinds of things?"

Kala'i: "God has done like this. Today the children refuse the elders, their fathers, they don't obey."

Djuri: "They don't even want cows."

Kala'i: "Today the children go to the towns and stay there, there they get a radio, work and clothing. People in the past did not know towns in this way. It is different to stay here and herd your cows, than settle down in the town and do 'herding of clothing'."

Djuri: "Now today, there still exist some people who love cows more than anything. They don't have clothing, not even today. Those who are well dressed look at them and just laugh."

"What about the future?"

Djuri: "What I think about the future, the time that comes later, perhaps people's life will be different then, even now we don't know where all this is leading. Perhaps lives of people in the future will be very different from our lives today. This is what I think."

GENDER AND POWER

For an anthropologist who is a young, unmarried woman doing her first fieldwork, the issue of sexuality is difficult to approach. Her environment is foreign and sometimes disturbingly confusing. She has a research project in one hand, a notebook in the other. She is interested in women's lives and the relations between men and women. She has, however, experienced that this information is difficult to approach because people are hesitant to open up to a stranger. The anthropologist has read everything she could find about WoDaaBe women, finding it fascinating. The first thing she read about the WoDaaBe was, actually, an article entitled, *The Position of Women in Pastoral Society*, from 1960 describing the lifecycle of WoDaaBe women (Dupire 1971[1960]). She was interested in the issue of sexuality, even though she did not make it the topic of her research. She has read that WoDaaBe women have an unusual sexual freedom, demonstrated in that a woman can have many boyfriends and lovers before her *kobgal* marriage. The sexual freedom of women is especially emphasized in the popular press, which frequently discusses the sexual freedom of both women and men. The focal point of many of these writings, intended for a general audience in the West, is the so-called "*geerewol*", which in these narratives is seen as an important site for the expression of love and sexuality.[41]

When I arrive to the bush for the first time, a festival is taking place that is similar to those I have previously read about in the popular press. Dancing takes place during the night, young people going off together in pairs. I witness the dance of a small group of young men. I see the young women waiting not far away, and observe them sitting in a squatting position in a row. When the dance is finished, the men get on their camels and the women get up behind them. I see them disappear when they ride into the night. I ask, "Where are they going?" My assistant smiles, and tells me rather vaguely that

---

[41] *Geerewol* is a name for a specific festival but is often used by authors to describe all dancing activities.

they are going into the bush. I am impressed and excited by this freedom, perhaps because in my own society the sexual freedom of women is limited by the negative value placed on women as sexual beings.

Construction of Gender

Women and men pass through several life stages. As a newborn, the woman is called *Bikkon dewi kesi*, a few months later she is *Bikkon dewi jakul*; as a child *surba'el*; as a teenager *surbaajo*; after her first pregnancy and during the first years of motherhood, *boofiiDo*; as a married woman *yarijo*; and as an old woman *nayeejo*. Women are defined as *surbaajo* when they are old enough to be part of the nightly gathering of people, generally as a young, childless, unmarried woman.[42] A *surbaajo* is sexually available to men (excluding those with whom she would be seen as having an incest taboo). The *surbaajo* is well aware of her outer appearance, dresses well if she has the means (often her older sisters or parents give her this clothing or her boyfriend, *semaru*). A woman becomes *boofiiDo* when she is pregnant with her first child, but her whole period as a *boofiiDo* lasts for two or three years.[43] The *boofiiDo* is symbolically an "invisible" woman, dressed in black and without any decoration. She covers her body with a black cloth and head cover but has no shirt. After her child is born, she walks around with her breasts naked, a cloth wrapped around her hips. When becoming a *boofiiDo*, a woman leaves the homestead of her husband and returns to stay at her parents' home. During this period, she will not see her husband nor his family and she has in general no interaction with anyone except the members of her own household. Even during the annual gathering of the lineages, she stays secluded. If visitors arrive at her parents' homestead, she does not make her presence known. She has no relationship with males, neither her husband nor other men. The *boofiiDo* has a small bed at the house of her mother, which is situated to the left of the table. She is supposed to help at her parents' house, and is thus considered to be a valuable contribution to the work force. A woman is only a *boofiiDo* once

---

[42] *Surbaajo* can be a married woman (if her boyfriend does not make her pregnant), but most married women get pregnant soon and thus the role of the *surbaajo* is more identified with the unmarried women.
[43] If becoming pregnant by one of her boyfriends, a woman's actual marriage with her intended husband will be swiftly initiated, and her status is transformed into a *bofido*.

in her lifetime. When a woman's period as a *booftiDo* has ended, she becomes *yarijo*. She can dress again in a colorful way and interact with people. Her life has changed, she is a wife and a mother. A *yarijo* can obviously not have sexual relations with other men, she cannot be part of the night gatherings and she cannot go out late in the evening without her husband's permission.

A young man coming of age is, however, simply a *kajejo*, the term used about young unmarried men, married men, and men with a child or children. His role only changes when he is conceptualized as old, or *ndottiijo*. I ask men to define for me what a *kajejo* is, and they all emphasize that it is someone who goes out and does what he wants, someone who goes out to find dancing and find women. Briefly stated, according to these men, *kajejo* is someone who is enjoying life, and he becomes a *dotti'o* when he is old and ugly (i.e., no longer desired by women).

Gender Relations

WoDaaBe society is characterized by strict division of labor, which can be seen as a reflection of the gender segregation in the society as a whole. Women's sphere of activities is the home, the *suudu*, in addition to milking related activities, while men's preoccupation is with the herd. Men and women do not eat together, and a man would never sit down on a straw mat if women were gathered there, just as a woman would not join a group of men. The everyday relationship between men and women is characterized by reserve and avoidance (see discussion in Stenning 1959). Women are a source of pollution for men, particularly in connection with menstruation. The menstruation blood is considered to deprive traditional medicines of their powers, and thus women are not able to have many medicines for protection, which are an important part of the man's life and powers.

Women are generally treated with respect in an everyday setting but women's stories of themselves and their lives still directly express their fear of men. They fear especially physical violence from their husbands, who are considered to have the right to discipline them. A woman's parents are not able to interfere directly in the beating of their daughter, but the father or older brothers of the husband do interfere. When I ask men, "Do you beat your wife?" they usually respond without hesitating, "Yes, if she gives me problems." I ask women, "Why are you afraid of men?" and they laugh and

Guirgui with his small daughter.

tell me, "Why am I afraid! Because men beat women, I am afraid that they will beat me!" It is, of course, not all husbands who will beat their wives or find it to be appropriate action in the relations between men and women. Wife beating is, however, in general accepted conduct in WoDaaBe society. Disputes would probably not arise whether a man has the right to beat his wife, but more on the subject of whether a man was justified in beating his wife for a particular reason, or if he should have beaten her less. Wife beating can consist of everything between a slap on the face to brutal abuse.

Asking women how they felt about their role, the most usual response I got was laughter, and the statement that this was the way it is. They tell me that they do not want their husbands to have girlfriends or seek the companionship of other women, but add that there is not much they can do about it. "If I say something, he will beat me", is the response from most women. "What could I do about it?" In most cases the *semaru* does not enter the home of the husband, and thus it is more difficult for the wife to confront the husband about the relationship. Yet I have witnessed cases where the husband has a *semaru* staying with him in his house, something which I believe is more common in the city than in the bush. I asked one husband why his wife did not protest having his girlfriend living in the city with him and his wife. He told me, just as the women had previously expressed, that his wife was afraid of him. A co-wife, however, is more accepted, even though women admitted that they would like to be the only wife. Problems between wives occur in many cases, and in several cases a man divorces his *teegal* wife because she is considered as giving the first wife problems. The wife has the right to complain about problems which she experiences in relation to other wives, but such complaints could still be considered by the husbands as if she wanted to "give him problems."

A'isha is a young woman about my age. I do a formal interview with her, surrounded by a group of other women, and even though she does not know me very well, she knows the women accompanying me. When reflecting on marriage, she tells me, "What is good in marriage is if the man stays at home, gives you clothing, does not give you problems, takes care of you. But if he does not care about you, he will not help you, he will not give you clothing. Instead he will just give you problems, and beat you. This is not good." I ask her if she thinks it is correct to say that many husbands do not care much for their wives. "Yes, exactly!" she says, "Some men do not care for their wife, but others do not want to treat them badly, they give them clothing and take care of them. Others give nothing, do not take care of their wife, give her problems then take her and beat her." When I ask her what women feel about co-wives, she says: "They are tired of it. There is one man and two women, then perhaps three wives, and then four wives. WoDaaBe do it like this. The wives are tired of this. It destroys their heart, it eats the heart of the wife." She adds, "Only patience remains for the wife, to be patient and keep silent even though she does not want this." She continues on the same issue: "They [the men] are simply the ones in control. They force their wives to do something that they do not want to, the wives are patient, do not have a choice. But this is not what they want. All women do not want co-wives. Only they do not have any other choice."

When I ask A'isha why the women do not do anything when their husbands have a girlfriend, she gives me the same response as many women before her: "They see this but they do not have any choice, they see this, but they do not have a choice regarding what to do. They do not have any power. WoDaaBe men beat their women. We, women, do not want our men to have girlfriends, but we do not have a choice. If you complain to your husband because of a co-wife, he will beat you. He will let you feel pain. And as you know pain is not very pleasant." She starts laughing, and the other women and I laugh with her.

She tells me, when asked, that not all husbands beat their wives, but those who beat them are more numerous than those who do not. She adds, "They beat with the camel whip", laughing but not very cheerfully, "or with a stick. They beat and it is difficult. Our lives are difficult, marriage is difficult" (6 June 1998).

Teegal Marriage and the Lineage

A central focus of WoDaaBe life is the lineage which they are born into. Yet men and women have a different relationship to the lineage, a man never being able to leave his lineage and join another in the same way as women can do. A woman who becomes a *teegal* wife leaves her lineage or origin and stays with an other lineage group, quite likely in another area, which distances her from her own family and friends, her main social network. She can of course visit and stay with her family and the woman does not cease to belong to her

The millet porridge which is the staple diet of most families.

lineage of origin, her children, however, will belong to "different" people, even though they along with her brother will be her safety net later in life. A *kobgal* wife who decides to leave her husband to marry another man is thus not only leaving her husband but also her family and her life within the lineage. In many cases she would do so because she perceives herself to be maltreated by her husband. By divorcing her husband, she is leaving the security of the family network in the hope of finding a better life in a different marriage.

It is difficult for a woman who leaves her lineage in this way to return to her own lineage group. In some cases, the woman will leave and seek out the person whom she wishes to marry. If he for some reason is not able to marry her or not interested in such a relationship, she will try to find someone else to marry her within that lineage. This is due to a woman feeling degraded by going to a different lineage to marry and not being able to marry anyone.

For a man, however, the risk and conceptualization of *teegal* are different. One man told me, that because WoDaaBe do not have extensive possessions, the women serve as a measurement of one's quality. Men want women not necessarily because of desire for the women themselves but to acquire status, to gain respect among other young men. Men told me that sometimes they wanted to carry out a *teegal* marriage for the sake of the action itself, not because they were interested in the particular woman. I was told on one occasion: "Women do not know what takes place in the heart of a man. He tells her that he loves her, that he really loves her, but he knows that he wants to marry her and then will divorce her later. He knows he is only playing with her." Sometimes, during disputes (not necessarily having anything to do with marriage), a man would even be able to humiliate another by saying "What do you know, you never had a *teegal* marriage in your life!" One can also wonder how it feels for the woman to be the spouse of a man who is engaged in various *teegal* marriages. She must basically accept new wives brought into her home, trying to get along with them, yet not knowing if her husband is actually going to stay married to them or not. She will see them leave and other new ones coming in their stead. One woman told me: "Women have to have *munyal* [be patient], one day her husband will be ugly and old and no woman wants him. Then he will only have his wife."

The *BoofiiDo*

Victor Turner talks about the importance of "rites de passage" in transforming individuals into different kinds of individuals or different roles in society. Transition rites can according to Turner (1967) be seen as marked by the following stages: a) separation: involving a symbolic behavior signifying a separation of the individual or a group from a fixed point in the social structure, b) liminal phase: the status of the ritual subject is ambiguous, c) aggregation: when the ritual subject is in a stable state once more and thus has clearly defined rights and obligations.

Turner argues that as a result of the basic model of society being a structure of positions, the period of liminality can be seen as an inter-structural situation (Turner 1967:93–94). This inter-structural situation in the liminal period is manifested in various ways, expressing the ambiguous situation of the ritual subject. In some cases the subject is structurally invisible, meaning that the person is no longer or not yet classified within the structure, or it can be seen as both living and dead, and often without a particular sexuality. Another characteristic of transitional beings is that they have no status, property, rank, kinship position, etc. Finally, Turner argues, the relationship between the transitional being and elders during the liminal period is characterized by the authority of the elders being absolute (Turner 1967:100).

I find it useful to look at the *boofiiDo* from Turner's ideas of liminality. In that light, the role of the *boofiiDo* is essential to understand the status and conceptualization of women in general in WoDaaBe society. It can be suggested that the *boofiiDo* is a period aiming at transforming the sexually available woman into a wife. The behavior of the *boofiiDo* is in many ways out of the ordinary for WoDaaBe. She is socially isolated and as a part of that social isolation she should not greet people or respect other general rules of politeness. Such rules of general conduct are some of the key expressions of being a WoDaaBe, and thus the *boofiiDo*'s lack of conducting these underlines her existence in a structureless realm. Her black clothing when keeping in mind how much value people place on colorful clothing and jewelry can be seen as depriving her in some sense of her individuality. The *boofiiDo* is invisible in the social structure because she is supposed to stay invisible, not only to "outsiders" but also to people in her own lineage, her relatives, husband and parents-in-law. She is supposed to have no sexual relationship, and thus she is in a sense a "sexless" person, even though she has at the same time the role as a mother. By looking at *boofiiDo* as a liminal period between *surbaajo* and *yarijo*, the *boofiiDo* is a transitional state between the different types of women, transforming the "free" sexually available *surbaajo* into a *yarijo*, who belongs to the home.

Asking *bofi'en* (pl. of *boofiiDo*) to reflect on their experiences, I found it interesting how they described their roles in an objective way, almost like describing a role in a performance, completely excluding themselves as persons. One woman told me, when I asked if she did not find it difficult to be a *boofiiDo*: "To be a *boofiiDo* is difficult, because the *boofiiDo* is afraid of people, she does not greet people." In her response she does not state that she as a person is afraid of people, but that the *boofiiDo* is. Another woman, who had finished her role of *boofiiDo* several years earlier, also always used the pronoun *be* (they), when describing why women become *boofiiDo*: "They say this has to be done." The *bofi'en* that I knew best told me about how difficult the experience was. They talked about the hard work they do, their lack of rest, and the difficulties of being excluded from social interaction. A young girl, who had just became a *boofiiDo*, told me about how much she missed her boyfriend and her life previous to her new role.

Women's breasts can be seen as one of the strongest symbols representing their different roles. A *surbaajo* has firm breasts, a *yarijo* sagging ones.[44] One of my friends told me that the *surbaajo* is not afraid of men. "Why?" I ask, and she laughs and tells me: "*sabooda endu maBBe dara*" (because their breasts stand up).[45] I felt that this was an interesting remark, and believe that it can be understood in connection with the importance of women's breast as symbols for their different roles, as well as indicating men's power over women. When a *surbaajo* becomes a *boofiiDo*, her breasts are tied down in order to make them sagging. This is a painful process, lasting for several months, creating sores and blisters on her skin. The transformation of the breast is thus intentional, and seen as desirable from a certain perspective. A young *surbaajo* will not uncover her breasts in public. A young *yarijo*, however, will do so if feeding her child. Her sagging breasts are no longer objects of desire, and are sometimes left hanging outside the opening of her shirt. She is not in any hurry to put them back in after breast-feeding. The old women are, however, the only ones who would go around without wearing a shirt.

I ask the women themselves why the breasts are tied down and some tell me that otherwise the child could not suckle its mother's milk.[46] This action must, however, in my view, be placed in a context of the *boofiiDo* period being aimed towards transforming the sexually available woman into a wife. I heard the men several times discuss how beautiful the *surbaajo* were because their breasts were "standing up."

The sagging breasts can in this context perhaps been seen as a multivocal symbol. They are part of transforming a woman into a different role, marking her body as the body of *yarijo*, as opposed to *surbaajo*, transforming her into a sexually unattractive woman as opposed to a sexually attractive and available woman. The sagging breasts can be seen as a symbol of women being subjugated by men. Women who have "standing" breasts do not fear men, because they have not been controlled, neither they nor their breasts have been "tied" down.[47]

---

[44] The association of *surbaajo* and breasts is reflected in Taylor's dictionary which defines "*surbajo*" as a "woman whose breasts are still firm" (pp. 185). However, Osborn et al. (1993) define "*Surbaajo*" as a girl "who has attained the age of puberty and is not yet married" (pp. 451).
[45] Later, another woman made the same statement to me.
[46] This statement is obviously incorrect, because WoDaaBe themselves see women from other ethnic groups, who have not gone through this process, breastfeed.
[47] A male informant, interestingly enough, also felt that *bofido* served as a transitional state between a girl and married woman, even though he did not mark this transformation as negatively as I do. But as I have argued here, he argued that the transformation of the breasts was important in that respect, explaining it as an attempt to maintain "pure" categories. He explained this to me, after I had formulated my own theory on this (but not expressed it to him), and I find it impressive how he analyzed his society in this very anthropological way.

Resistance and Agency

Paul Riesman writes that men and women live in different societies, and I find his statement correct when seen from a certain perspective. They perform different tasks, stay in different places, and interact with different people in different ways. I entered the society of men, but the society of women seemed far away and it is hard to gain their trust. I certainly do research in both societies. I observe women's work, just like men's work, I do interviews with women just like men. The women are proud and distant, as if they do not really have any interest in being represented. They seem to need nothing from an outsider. But later in my fieldwork during the night, when I am "alone", when my male friends have left me because "I should not go out in the night" (i.e., I am not a sexually available woman), when I am going crazy of loneliness, when I want to cry because of frustration, the women come to me and tell me things; these are the times when they are willing to share their disappointments and desires on a more intimate level. I think that it was only during these times that they saw me as someone like themselves. As someone who has to be advised and informed, who for her own good has to learn to accept the way life is. I write in my diary after being in the field for almost a year: "Why did I not notice this forced inequality before? Perhaps I was stuck in the perception that it was just different, perhaps I just did not want to see it. Perhaps it is not visibly seen from the "outside", especially if you are surrounded by men, and the women always carry their heads so high, as if they do not care. Perhaps I would never have noticed, had I not been left behind 'alone' with them. Perhaps I noticed only because I was treated as one of them, feeling powerless as they."

WoDaaBe women have the reputation of being fearless and without particular attachment to others. Dupire documents an old woman stating that "Bororo women are not like other women, they want to move around, they go off and leave their husband" (Dupire 1971[1960]:48). Men fear women for this reason; women do not show their feelings and are ready to leave their husband and their children without any particular reason. One man told me, "What is different in relation to men and women is that a man has a knife and sword, stick, gun and bow, but the wife is not afraid of any of this. Everything she likes to do, she does.... If you want to beat her, she does not care" (February 1997). Another man states during the same interview, "The heart of the woman is such that if she is sad, she will leave everything, even her own children. She will leave and never come back" (February 1997). These interviews point to two aspects that I found very dominating when men discussed their relations with women: women do not have an attachment to anything and that they are even able to leave their own children behind, which is used to support the first claim. The women are thus dangerous to men because of their lack of feelings. Many men have experienced their mothers leaving them, either because they had divorced their husbands or because they left the home temporarily. Jumare leaves her little boys, Gabidi and Njunju behind for seven months, which the men point out to me as a symbol of the way women are. "Women love in a different way" the men tell me on various occasions. "They are not really interested in men."

A woman who leaves packs her things together without anyone observing. She leaves in the night, without telling anyone. She will use an opportunity when her husband is not close by. In the morning the next day, he will find her gone. The men fear this behavior, and seem to conceptualize it as unpredictable. They stated that a man had to avoid making his wife upset because no one can know what she will do then. It can be pointed out that this behavior of the woman as not showing her feelings and attachment to others is very much in accordance with the moral code of the WoDaaBe, *mbodagansi*. Reserved behavior both shows an existence of *semtuDum* (shame, respect) and *munyal* (patience). The men told me in relation to discussing the moral code that some women did not even cry when their child died, or at least not so anyone could observe it. The emotionally distant woman thus both awakens fear in her husband's heart and his respect because she is demonstrating her intimacy with the correct moral behavior.

Observing these fears of the men, I started asking myself whether the reserved behavior expressed by the women was not their most important strategy for dealing with men? An interview with a woman in Niamey, a *teegal* wife, supported most strongly this view of mine. She told me kindly that a woman should never make the mistake of loving her husband, or showing her husband that she loved him. He would only get high ideas of himself, and go and take different wives or girlfriends. By her showing indifferent behavior, however, the man would fear her, not knowing her feelings. If the woman makes her heart strong, and is just interested in her own work, she will not care even though he chooses to divorce her. My guest places her hand on my shoulders and tells me that she is sure that all men are the same, WoDaaBe, Hausa, Tuareg and *anasara*. I agree with her, feeling the strength and compassion of being a woman among women. In the context of the importance of being indifferent to men, she tells me that she went to another country with a few other women in order to make some money from the sale of medicines, and left her child behind. Men should be afraid; women should not make themselves vulnerable.

CHAPTER 8

THE RAIN STARTS TO FALL

The year 1997 was a difficult one, due to lack of rain and a long spring (*kokke*). The first rain came at the end of May. The second rain came one week later. Four days passed and then a heavy wind started blowing from the north, carrying a great deal of dust from the Sahara. It covered both the fresh new grass and the dry grass from last year, leaving the bush with basically nothing for the animals to feed on. The animals were thus dependent on people buying them fodder in order to survive, placing a heavy burden on the household. Many of the newborn animals died. At the end of June, it rained heavily in the area, preventing the situation from becoming disastrous. The *kokke* season, the time of the first rains, is thus a time of great physical and psychological stress. Many people lose weight over the dry season (*ceeDo*), especially those who are vulnerable, such as children who have recently stopped breast feeding, nursing mothers, and elderly people. For everyone, rain that fails to materialize carries the fear of losing one's means of livelihood.

One night at the end of June, I discuss the situation with a small group of men: Bermo, Hassane, Gidado, and Akali. We are sitting on blankets around a fire, which is not far from my bed. Close by, the *duDal* fire is lit in order to keep the insects from bothering the animals. The cattle gather around it and blend with the darkness of the night. The reflection from the fire glows on their skin and white horns, making them slightly visible.

Bermo shows me his hands, asks me to touch them in order to feel how old they are after the work of *ceeDo* and *kokke*. "I have pain in my hands because of my work. If I sit down and rest, I feel pain everywhere because of tiredness. [....] When it started to rain, things seemed to be proceeding fine. And then, a wind came from the north, it came, it covered the *geene* [dry grass], it covered everything. I woke up in the morning, and saw that there was nothing. I was just left with nothing because there was nothing that my animals could eat."

Bermo continues, "The cows could not stand up. They could not stand up on their own. They were only able to when people helped them. In the morning, I did *dimdol* in order to find grass. Then God took me to this place, where the grass was not covered completely." He looks down, is silent for a moment: "We were really suffering this time when the wind covered the grass, because this was right after the *ceeDo*. But today, I thank God because the situation is better."

Gidado adds, exaggerating a little, "And today we have much more milk, because now you cannot see the porridge in the calabash because it is so full of milk!"

"Still, people even today have to help their cows to stand up," says Hassane seriously, "The time before was really difficult, and now I thank God that the situation is better."

Bermo continues, "All the animals were suffering, both the cows and smaller ruminants. This wind came eight o'clock in the evening. It was over the day after around six o'clock in the morning." Akali explains to me that the disaster was caused by the wind because of lack of grass cover. He gives me an example in order for me to understand this better, telling me that the dry grass (*gene*) is like a house. If the house is good, the wind will not be able to enter and damage it. If the house is weak, the wind will enter it and be able to blow dust everywhere. He explains that it is the same with grass, if there is no vegetation cover and wind arrives, it will blow up large amounts of dust.

"It rained someplace," Bermo adds to his explanation, "then the wind of the rain continued to us but without the rain. It came here and it covered everything with sand. We did not really spend so much money to buy millet for ourselves, but to buy fodder for our animals." Gidado tells me that it was so difficult to find *sa'anjo* (the by-product of millet which is used as fodder),[48] that one day he and his father had to go separately in order to try to find some. One time, he went to one place and bought two sacks of *sa'anjo* and his father bought two sacks at a different place. Bermo adds, that these four sacks did not last longer than three or four days.

"Sometimes, when I was feeding the cows on *sa'anjo*", Gidado says, "they did not want to eat it, so I had no other options except feeding them millet. I had to pound the millet and then feed it to the cows!"[49]

---

[48] During a period of drought, *saánjo* is in very high demand, making it expensive and hard to get.
[49] He literally says: "*Mi duufa gawri*". Millet has to be pounded a couple of times; the first time separating the *gawri* from the *saánjo*, which is the animal fodder; then the *gawri* is pounded again and these two products coming from the pounding (*gawri* and *sondi*) are used to make the porridge. He is talking about that they feed the cows on *gawri* and *sondi*.

Akali explains to me that the cows could not eat this *sa'anjo* because it was the by-product of wheat, not of millet, and thus of very low quality.

"Until we got *huDo* [new wet grass] I had to feed our cows millet. I did not count how much *sa'anjo*, I had to give." Gidado adds.

Bermo states: "It was impossible to count how much they ate, because we had to feed big cows, cows with calves, and the calves themselves, the castrated bulls, sheep and goats. I had to give all these animals fodder. At one place we stayed, the animals got *giitii bali*.[50] We had to buy *sa'anjo* three times and each time two sacks."

I ask if this year was more difficult than last year.

Bermo replies: "This year was dangerous. We had a lot of problems this year. I think it was three times more difficult than last year."

We turn to discussing briefly the year called *kunsiter*, which was the drought of 1984, when many in the lineage lost most of their animals.

"*Kunsiter*'s really a two year period when it did not rain," Bermo tells me, "thus it was a more difficult time. After *kunsiter* there were three years which were not very good, and this time was thus more difficult. One year was similar to this one. Some people also lost their cows in a year called *gol Dadge*. That was three years ago. People then went north, not very far to *singiigaran*. All of these people's cows died that year. For some there were five cows left, for others three, for others one. That year was not very good. And then last year was not very good, and now this year. I do not know if this year will bring rain and give a great deal of grass, maybe, I do not know. Today at least, there is not very much grass."

"How do you think the grass will be this year?" I ask him.

"I do not know", he tells me, "Perhaps the rain will fall and perhaps the earth cover will prosper well and the *huDo* grow well. Perhaps it will rain and the grass (*huDo*) will be plentiful. I do not know. Until now, I do not know. If the rain will stop falling, you know it is the water that creates *huDo*,[51] if it will not fall then the grass will become dry. This year has been difficult for us herders, very difficult. This year, cows died, sheep died, goats died, the offspring of sheep died, the offspring of goats died, all people had problems this

---

[50] According to Akali, the sudden rains and their coldness cause this illness, in combination with the animals being half starved. In order to prevent the animal from dying, people build a fire and carry the animal to it. This illness is never a problem during the *ndunngu* season, because the animals are better nourished then and thus better able to tolerate the coldness of the rain.

[51] I find it interesting that he says "*diyam geii huDo*" i.e., literally, the water owns the grass.

year. Until this day, if my cows sleep on the ground, they cannot stand up by their own effort" (February 1997).

I am not a true herder, a true BoDaaDo, because deep inside my heart I dread the time when it rains. It has rained once, and as much as I desire the rain, I still fear its coming. My feelings are thus conflicting, pulling me into the darkness of guilt over fearing the rain, so needed by the people taking care of me. The first rains are always accompanied by great thunderstorms, unlike the gentle rain arriving at the end of the rainy season. The night becomes yellow, because the wind unleashes a great deal of sand, and then it starts to rain heavily with the wild wind. Some WoDaaBe own tents, which they place as shelters over their beds. They protect against the sun in the dry season and the rain in the rainy season. This kind of tent is the same as the Tuaregs use, and it is expensive.[52] The tent is fastened to several poles, buried in the ground around the bed, to prevent the wind from blowing it away. Those who do not own tents, such as I, have to lie down flat on their beds with nothing more than a plastic sheet to cover them. Sollare and another woman place the plastic over my bed, tucking the ends under the poles of the bed to prevent the wind from pulling it away. I tried to help but it is hard to see because of the sand. Their movements are quick because of their long training in this task. They have to hurry because the air is already dark from the dust, but the wind pulls the plastic that struggles in their hands. I crawl into the bed and lie down flat under the black plastic in the complete darkness while they fasten the plastic carefully on three sides. They leave one side open for me to enter and go out. I have to hold the plastic down on this side because of the wind. I feel like I'm buried in a grave of complete darkness. There is no sound except the loud marauding wind. My eyes are open but I see nothing. In the past, people used a similar method of protecting themselves from storms. They stacked a great number of straw mats on top of one another in order to protect themselves from the rain. Today, the thick black plastic has replaced the mats for this purpose.

The wind blows with incredible force, followed by thunder and lightning. The smaller animals, such as snakes, scorpions, and spiders, arise from earth. The risk of a snakebite is never greater than just after rain fall. But the rain is a valued force and so is the thunder and lighting. How could they not be? In

---

[52] When I stayed in Niger, one tent was more than 50,000 CFA.

the morning, I see smiles on people's faces because it has rained, meaning nutrition for their animals and themselves. It has perhaps also to do with more intimate embodied experience. The air is fresh. The coldness that the rain brings with it is a relief and there is a sense of a cycle being renewed, of a new year slowly unfolding. According to Akali, the WoDaaBe say that each raindrop has a *malaa'ika* (angel) inside. How could it otherwise fall down from such a distance and be so gentle? All other things, which would fall down from such a height would harm or even kill someone. It would be painful if people poured a large amount of water down from a great distance. Thus, water itself can be destructive but a raindrop coming from the sky is not. The thunder (*riggaango*) is sometimes called *njadago malaa'ika'en*, which translates as the command of the angels. The thunder is the voice of the angels, when they direct where the rain will fall.

The lightning is still a dangerous force of nature, regularly killing people and animals. Everyone knows several people that have been killed because of lighting striking close to them. Akali tells me a story of man of his lineage group, who was visiting a different house when a storm started. He was with his young daughter, and they hurried back to their camp holding hands. On the way to the house, lightning struck him down, killing him but leaving the child unharmed. "*Aeki Allah.* the act of God" he adds, because acts of God are hard to understand sometimes.

I found it interesting that the rainbow, which is so valued and mystified in my own culture, is conceptualized rather negatively among the WoDaaBe. The rainbow is disliked, because it prevents the rain from falling, especially if there is not a lot of rain in the clouds. "Why?" I ask, and I am told that the rainbow is like a fire, the rain cannot fall close to it. However, if there is potential for a great deal of rain in the sky, the rainbow sometimes moves away from it. The bad affects of the rainbow are not only manifested in its negative effect on rain, but its ability to poison the water in the wells. If a rainbow's end comes to the waterhole area, it can make the place unsuitable for human use, because wells cannot be made there. When someone attempts to dig a well there, the hole can suddenly be without air to breathe, thus making its construction impossible, even killing the person stuck inside the well.

The composition of the *wuro* keeps changing throughout the span of the year, people coming and leaving for different reasons. The one thing affecting me the most is the absence of my friend Jumare for several months. She leaves her three children with her parents. Her youngest boy is only about three years old and missed his mother badly. The older boy, Njunju, is around five or six years old, and does not say anything (as far as I was aware) which is well in accordance with the appropriate behavior of the WoDaaBe. However, I see the expression on his face become strange every time when he is asked, "Where is your mother?" Usually he does not reply, and people would always continue, "Your mother left! She went far away." Jumare had not wanted her *kobgal* husband, she had refused to follow him when he claimed her. She had tried marriages with men from other lineages but now was back at her parents' house with her children. WoDaaBe women do not have claim to their children in cases of divorce, but often if the child is very young, the father will leave it with the mother and claim it later. In some cases the father does not claim the child. Jumare had all of her three children living with her for reasons that will not be discussed here. However, even though Jumare was not married, she had a boyfriend. She left with this boyfriend in order to "follow" him to Burkina Faso where he was seeking out opportunities as a migrant worker. "I travelled far", she told me when she came back to Niger, to continue to live with her parents, "To Mali and then all the way to Mauritania."

Akali laughs when I discover that the father of little Gabidi who likes to sit down at my bed is a man from another lineage.

"Yes, this little boy is not a Gojanko'en. He is not one of my people", he tells me. "This is a Bii-koro'en boy. If his father wants, he could just take him." The thought is strange and somewhat alien to me.

"But he would surely not want to go?" I ask Akali, "You are the only people he knows."

"Later, when he is bigger he will want to know his father." Akali tells me, "Perhaps someone will tease him, let him know that he does not know his own father, and then he will want to leave in order to go to stay with his people."

I have bought a black cloth and thread because I want to learn the handicraft of the women. I am not sure why. I have never done this kind of work except as a child in school. A great deal of my time is spent waiting to go to places, waiting for the day to pass, and I feel that something like embroidery could be a positive distraction. I suspect that perhaps the reason that I want to learn it, is also to prove to others, and even more to myself, that I am in fact capable of doing something useful. Embroidery implies patience (*munyal*) and I want to be patient. Thus, perhaps my desire to do embroidery connects to my desire to learn the *munyal* of the WoDaaBe. I go to Jumare for assistance, having previously expressed my wish to learn how to do the embroidery. I have seen her work many times, and the beauty of it always impresses me. I ask when I am sitting with her and her mother Fatima, and two other women, "Can you teach me to do embroidery?"

"You want to learn the work of WoDaaBe women", she says, "then you need cloth and thread." I have all that with me and hand it over to her.

"You see, the red thread and the green ones are the first ones", she tells me and puts red thread into the eye of the needle, "and only later do you put the white, the yellow and the orange." She looks at the cloth, and then starts in the middle of it. She works slowly but easily.

"Can I try now?" I ask after a while, and she instructs me while I try to continue her pattern. I have understood the logic of it, but despite trying I can see that I do not impress anyone. My small hands are almost as if they are too big for the needle and the thread. One of the women says, "Embroidery is very difficult." Fatima tells me that I should just give this to Jumare, and she will make me a beautiful cloth.

"No", I protest. "I want to learn how to do it." I add in order to make my claim more justified: "I want to learn the work of women." Jumare smiles, understands what I mean but tells me that she will do a little more work on it and then later hand it over to me.

It surprises me how much interest people show in my embroidery. Every visitor wants to see it and many want to help me with it. Sollare wants to help and she almost begs me to let her do a little. Her mother tells me that the child does not know what she is doing and that she will spoil my cloth, but I cannot forbid her to help me, so she gets to embroid my cloth a little. My embroidery also helps me in communicating with the women, creating something we have in common and can discuss and analyze. Everyone needs to belong, even the anthropologist who is studying elements of belonging. Thus, even though I had not realized it when I asked Jumare to teach me, the embroidery was an opportunity to sit down with the woman and talk. It felt different somehow to be working on something just like the other women, when staying among them in the middle of the normal day. My disability in participating in conversations became more tolerable. Thus, instead of not doing anything other than writing and drawing, the embroidery gave me a different kind of activity which others, especially the women, could relate to and discuss with me, thus helping me as well to relate to others.

During this time of the year, the shallow ponds have formed and we stay quite close to them. The structure of the work and the social interaction is different. The camps are close to each other, meaning that every day there are interactions between people, both from my own lineage group and other groups. There is no need of going very far to get water but it is urgent to find nourishment for the animals. Dadi, one of my friends from the city who works as a migrant laborer, is back to stay at his mother's house for a few weeks. He is a little older than I am, and our relationship has developed into a kind of a joking relationship, almost as if we were cross-cousins (*denDiraaBe*). I find it is refreshing to have him so close by, and wish almost every day for his visits. His father is in Nigeria, and had left soon after Dadi was born. Thus, even though Dadi is over thirty years old, he has only seen his father a few times. His mother had attempted to do a *teegal* marriage several times, but now she is back with her own lineage. She lives with her oldest son and his family. They have almost no animals, and thus make their house (*wuro*) with the brother of the old woman, who helps them with necessities.

Dadi helps me with my embroidery, mainly through commenting on it and encouraging me. He helps me a little, his work being so much more beautiful than I suspect mine will ever be. Even though embroidery is not as common among men as among women, men seem to know how to do it well. "*Mariyama, debbo WoDaaBe*. Mariyama, the WoDaaBe woman", Dadi teases me when he sees me working on my embroidery. He knows a little English, and thus our conversation sometimes takes place in a mixture of Fulfulde and English. He stays at the house of his mother and brother but comes almost every afternoon in order to visit me.

The day turns out to be hot. I have arranged an interview with an elderly man at his house. I usually have to make appointments with people in order to not disturb them too much with their work, and also in order to reach them before it gets dark. I tell Akali that I really want to bathe, and perhaps he can help me to find place where there are not many people. I go with him and Dadi to a large pond not far away. It is long like a stream, breaking into sections that stretch in all directions surrounded by trees and bushes. He finds me a small place located by one such branch of the pond, where the high leafy

CHAPTER 8 THE RAIN STARTS TO FALL

Watering the animals is a difficult and time-consuming task, carried out in the hot sun.

bushes create almost a circular wall between the bush itself and the edge of the pond.

"Dadi and I will go to another place to bathe while you bathe here" Akali tells me when he hands me an empty container to pour the water, "and you have to bathe really well now. You have to remember to brush your skin until you feel pain, not just to stroke it a little. Bathing here in the bush is supposed to be painful."

When I am sure that he has left, I slowly start taking my shoes off. I am standing at the edge of the water. It almost touches my toes. "I can't take of all my clothing off in the daylight", I think to myself. I am used to bathing in complete darkness and even then I try to take off only a few articles of clothing. The reason is not only the fear of someone seeing me, but rather the foreignness, which I develop in the bush, towards my own body. It is pale even for a white person. Now it looks odd to me and almost repulsive. My body looks like something dead, raw, like something that has been lying under water for a long time. I have started to imagine my body to be like the white flesh of a fish. I find this a strange comparison myself and speculate that perhaps it has something to do with the WoDaaBe finding the flesh of fish very repulsive. I take off my clothing and it feels wonderful to be able to stretch out, to bathe properly and feel clean again.

Next day there is *dimdol*, the movement to the north in search of pasture. Kala'i announces late in the morning that we will do *gonsul* and everyone starts packing and preparing for departure. Kala'i had left on his son's camel the day before, accompanied by his brother, to search for pasture for the animals. He comes back and discusses the situation with other men. There is nothing. The earth is dry, lacking vegetation. The place where we stay, however, also lacks grass and thus there is no option other than to move. My own packing does not take a long time, and while the women finish packing their own houses, I help with the smaller children. Several homes leave at the same time. I ride with Akali, on the back of the camel called Azarif. We move slowly, stay close to the herd and the other people. In front of us, Njunju is herding a flock of goats, thus helping his mother's brother. The cattle are a little further away guided by Kala'i and his other sons. The landscape changes gradually, and instead of the steep hills around us, we arrive at a long depression, which is woody in contrast to the landscape that I am used to. "Do you know where we are?" Akali asks. "This is the Tadis valley." I have seen

Tadis, the long valley on a map. Observing the other families that have gradually joined us is more interesting to me. Women riding with their young children on their donkeys. By their side, an older child in the middle of baggage loaded on the donkey. A young man is riding in front of the herd on his white camel. A boy is holding the herder's stick on his shoulder, following the cattle. The sounds of the different animals are soothing to my ears, and the dust unleashed by these different creatures carries the smell of earth and life. I look around me, never before having seen so many people migrating at the same time. Our own family is not visible any more, just the streams of people in the large riverbed. Occasionally we greet people who ride close to us, some are part of our family but others are from different lineage groups.

Two elderly women ride past us on their donkeys, one carrying a calabash on her head. By their side is a child riding a castrated bull, which also carries some of the livestock items. The women observe me with curiosity, greet us as appropriate, and then continue talking, not taking their eyes of me. It is too far for me to hear what they are saying. Akali laughs and says without turning around, "Did you hear what they were saying?" "No" I admit. "They were talking about you", he says, and I see that he is smiling. "They were talking about this being a very curious sight, a white woman riding behind a BoDaaDo man!" He adds. "They were discussing how well you ride the camel, just like a BoDaaDo woman, and then when you greeted them in Fulfulde they were even more surprised." I try to sit the camel exceptionally well, pretend to be holding casually to Akali's saddle, now more aware of their eyes observing me. "You do ride the camel very well. You know bush now." Akali continues more talking to himself than me. I try to hide a smile, treasuring the rare compliment.

We find our family again, and Akali's father tells him that the sheep have got lost. Akali has to go looking for them, and thus I have to walk. I walk with Dadi and Kala'i following the herd. The walk is pleasurable at first, Dadi and Kala'i telling me about the herd and individual cows. After a few hours, however, I have become very tired, and so are the rest of the people. The women remain expressionless, but the tiredness can be read from their faces, and the children are crying from thirst and exhaustion. There is no grass anywhere and late in the day we stop on a hill which is almost deprived of vegetation. When I arrive with Dego and another man, the baggage has been taken off the donkeys. One goat collapsed from exhaustion, but it was killed before dying and can thus be cooked and eaten. I had met Akali a few miles back. He had found the sheep far away and had just arrived back with them. The camel was tired, but Akali had to continue in order to search for grass for the animals. I am sitting on my blanket, helping reassemble my bed, when he comes back. There is no pasture anywhere, we probably have to move again tomorrow even though it is the fifth day of the moon cycle and there is thus a taboo on movement.

I walk over to Bermo's homestead in the evening, which is just a few feet away. He makes his house with his father-in-law, Djuri, who has been of great assistance to me. We sit down on a mat close to the house and I do an interview with Djuri to clarify a few things. I feel guilty to be taking his time, after such a difficult day, but the last few days have given few opportunities for interviews. He tells me it is fine and speaks slowly as usual so I can understand his narrative. His wife brings us a bowl with meat from the goat that had just died. The men, being of different ages, are not able to eat together and thus separate the meat into smaller portions. "With whom shall I eat?" I ask Akali quietly, and look at the women who are working, and think that perhaps I should just join them. "You eat with Djuri" Akali tells me. I whisper back, "I cannot eat with him… that is not appropriate!"

"No, it is fine" Akali assures me, "He wanted the two of us to eat with him, but I have *semtuDum* regarding that because you know my people do not do like that… but it is fine that you eat with him."

"Come here, Mariyama" Djuri tells me, and puts his hand on his straw mat. I obey and sit down close to the small plastic lid where the meat is put. I feel shame, even though I am used to eating with the younger men. He picks out the good pieces, takes them apart with his fingers, and places them on my side of the bowl. I avoid looking into his eyes, eat little. *SemtuDum* is embodied. I have been breathing it with the air since I came, and I discover now that it has, to some extent, become part of me.

The day after, we have to return to where we came from. There is no grass in the area, and even though there was not much where we came from, the situation is still somewhat better at our old place. In the morning, Kala'i and others search for pasture, but without success. Because of the taboo on the day, the herd leaves around noon and the people leave four at o'clock in the evening. To migrate during a day that has a taboo is never good, but to leave when the day is almost finished makes it less bad than otherwise.

WoDaaBe sell goats at the market to buy millet for everyday consumption.

When it starts to rain and the grass of the *kokke* grows, thus bringing nourishment to animals and pleasure to people, it is easy to forget the hardship of the spring. Ponds have formed in various places, and we have moved to the north where other families of the same lineage group join us. Unlike in the dry season when the next houses were at a great distance, the houses are now very near to each other. Akali tells me that I can safely go out and walk around.

"Are you not afraid anymore that I will get lost?" I ask him.

"No", he tells me. "You just have to be careful not to go far, and you have to look where you are going. But it is no problem if you get lost because my people are everywhere in this area." It is wonderful to go out for a walk, without the fear of getting lost and dying from dehydration. Our camp is close to a large waterhole, surrounded by trees and vegetation. I walk to the water and sit down on a fallen tree next to it. Birds are singing which is relaxing and beautiful. I look at the light brown water, watch the reflection of the sun dancing on its almost immobile surface. The pond itself is full of life. It is brought to life by the buzzing of flies, bird song, the whispering of the grass, and the black insects surfing on the immobile water. I treasure the silence, close my eyes just listening to the sounds around me. I wake from my thoughts, when a large cow splashes into the water not far away. I do not move, just look around, and see that a young boy has arrived to water his herd. I do not say anything, just observe the animals satisfying their thirst. I know this boy because I have been to his house several times. He is the son of Bermo. His front teeth are missing and his hair is short with small braids. Finally, he notices me and I see him looking at me open-eyed from a distance where he stands in the water.

"Mariyama, is this you?" he calls.

"Yes, it is me" I tell him.

"Are you here alone?" he asks.

"Yes."

"Why are you alone? Where is Akali, where are your friends?"

"I just wanted to be alone."

"Are you sad?" he asks, and in fact I am surprised that he would ask me so straight out, because the subject is usually not talked about directly among those I know. He is, of course, only a child and is clearly very concerned about my well being.

"No, I am fine", I tell him.

"Why are you alone then? Why are you sad? Do you want me to get someone for you?" He is looking at me with surprise and I do not know what else to say. I just stand up and tell him that I am going to walk for a short while. "Yes, go back to the house", he says with his sincere eyes, and goes back to attending to his cows. I am worried that he will tell people that I am sad, but still decide to walk a little further. I walk slowly along the lake, following a small path, which has been forming for the last weeks around the trees. I see the remains of a cow lying on the path, its empty eyes looking in my direction. There is nothing left of it except the skin, which covers the pile of bones. The bones are sticking out everywhere so it looks too small for this cow. It is not the first dead animal that I have seen lying around, so I continue. I have not gone far when I see a woman with whom I am familiar. She is at the pond with her donkey to fill a leather sack (*sakji*) with water, in order to bring drinking water to her house. She greets me, and I greet her. We shake hands, and she asks me, "Where is Akali? Where are your friends? Why are you here alone?"

"I just wanted to walk around a little."
"Does Akali know that you are here just by yourself?"
"Yes, he knows."
"It is not very good that you are alone, you could get lost. Why do not you go back and ask someone to go with you?" I do not know what to say, but she pushes her donkey to continue and probably just assumes that I will follow her advice.

I continue with my walk only to meet another woman, telling me the same story. I decide to hurry away from the pond and enter the bush where there are fewer people. I walk in the sand with sparse patches of grass, enjoy the freshness of the air and just being by myself. The pond is out of sight, and I walk into nowhere trying to keep track on how to get back. Finally, it is as if I have reached my destination. The rather flat surface has ended and I am standing on a gently sloping hill, which ends abruptly. Down by my feet, the Tadis valley opens up, a huge fertile depression in the Sahel landscape. In the distance, I see two camels grazing under a tree, appearing only as different shades of color. There is a great difference standing above everything, seeing things far away. The contrast is great from the rather hilly plateau that always prevented me from seeing things from a distance, to seeing many things at once. Suddenly, I feel like I have an overview of the way things are. I have only seen this surface on a map but then it was too far away to be realistic and meaningful. I have seen it by being a part of it, but then it was too close for me to grasp it as a part of a bigger whole. The long valley is beautiful. I can see no end to the bush on the other side. The hills and the woody shelter seem to go on forever. The landscape blurs together in a mist at the horizon.

THE BORDER TOWN

> I feel ashamed of having nothing. Sometimes, I want to go into the bush and disappear (Ali, a migrant laborer in a border town).

It is hot and the sun is high up in the sky. I am in a border town close to Nigeria and on my way to meet a WoDaaBe man who has agreed to give me an interview. Two WoDaaBe men walk past me. On their shoulder they carry a broad stick, on each end a heavy gasoline container hangs, wrapped in rags. They do not stop nor slow down. "Mariyama", one calls to me, "you see that now I am no better than a donkey." I know these young WoDaaBe men, having met them during the annual *Cure Sallée* festival held in the bush. Last time I saw them they wore colorful clothing and danced in the night. Their clothing now consists of rags, bought cheap at the market, "Western" style pants and T-shirt, torn and dirty from their work. They do not seem like the exotic WoDaaBe I had seen photos of in the United States or as the proud pastoralists I saw in the bush but more as poor people living very much at the margin, gaining their livelihood largely through smuggling. Most of the smugglers make one trip per day, carrying between 58–70 liters on each trip. They are not able to keep their backs straight under the weight and they are half running in order to get to their destination as fast as they can. It is ironic that the stick, which lies so heavily on their shoulders, is the *saaruu*, the herder's stick, which stands as a symbol of freedom in the bush. They are among many WoDaaBe who have started earning an income by migrant work, only staying a part of the year in the bush.

I had not planned to stay long in this town situated on the border of Niger and Nigeria. Its closeness to the border being expressed in various ways: Nigerian bread, numerous stereos and televisions, big bottles of Coca-Cola, Nigerian candy, and inexpensive gasoline smuggling over the border. Some people speak English; many originate from Nigeria. The smuggling and selling of gasoline has certainly put its mark on this town in more than one way.

Several times fire has broken out and because of gasoline being stored at all kinds of places, the fire was hard to control, burning down a large part of the town.

I have been here several times, and as earlier I stay with a Fulani family known to assist WoDaaBe people when they need a place to stay. Things are not going well in Niger at the time. In this town, already well known for high crime rate, violence was growing. People had been beaten or even arrested at nights without any explanation. My consultant did not even consider it safe for me to sleep any longer with the other WoDaaBe in the courtyard of the Fulani family. He got permission for me to sleep inside the locked house, sharing a mattress with one of my hosts' children.

I arrive at my meeting place, which is a spot out in the open where a few WoDaaBe men sell gasoline. It is located on the main street and some men stand by the street waiting for business opportunities with the gasoline containers by their side, while others rest on a bench in the shade of someone's house. I am offered a seat on the bench and given a soft drink, observing their interaction and work. The two men I saw earlier have put their load down at the lot, and with the assistance of the buyer of their gasoline, who is also a WoDaaBe, they empty the several small containers into large 40-liter containers. He is a middle-man, selling the gasoline further. Many of the large robust containers have lost their tops, but the rubber of a cheap sandal has been formed to fit the opening, and seems to work well. All these interactions take place in the daylight on the street. The colorful hose used to pour the gasoline into the container has multiple uses. People wave the hose while standing along the main road. It is a symbol of gasoline for sale.

According to my informants, around 53 WoDaaBe are in the border town, a great majority involved in the smuggling of petrol. 37 of those are from the same lineage and all my interviews were conducted with people from this lineage group. Many of them are related, which provides a network of security, as no one will be hungry because his relatives will provide him with food. Some, if not most, of these men bring their wives to stay with them. The women earn a small amount of money by braiding the hair of other women, receiving around 250–300 CFA from each person. They also do embroidery for shirts or tops, either for themselves or someone in the family. Those men who are lucky get a job as a night guard because it gives them a place to sleep, to keep their things, and a place to stay during the day. Those

A WoDaaBe man is pouring gasoline into a another container, and will later sell it to his customer.

who do not have work as security guards usually sleep where their friends work as guards.

My first interview is with Ali, a young man around 32 years old. I had met him in the bush several weeks before. We played cards with a group of people but did not talk much. After that I had met him a few times, always within a large group of people. He looked like a serious person, as he did not smile often. I was shy and nervous when I asked him if I could interview him. He was very pleased and he seemed proud to be asked to talk about himself.

Ali and his extended family had lost all their cows in the drought of 1984. He went to Nigeria at that time, working as a security guard for a few years. Then he came to the border town and has since then been smuggling petroleum for 12 years. Ali has not been able to collect money to buy livestock but sustains his wife and child as well as his extended family who are all in the bush. His father has no cows of his own, and Ali has only been able to buy two calves with the money he has earned. His family tends cows belonging to Tuaregs and receives milk as payment. Ali buys all that his extended family needs, such as clothing and millet. He used to live in the city with his wife, but his young child (around 2 years old) became ill last year and thus his wife and child stay at his father's house. His younger brother, who works as a petroleum dealer (buying and selling) has, however, been able to buy seven cows with the money he gets for working in the same border town. The cows are a welcome addition to their father's cows in the bush. His narrative tells his personal story but reflects well many of the frustrations and desires embodied in migrant work.

What led to my arrival here is that one year all my cows died. This is what led to me coming here to this town. I had no opportunity to stay in the bush and that led me to this place. Allah gave me a possibility of some work with gasoline. I have done this work for a long time and I am still doing it today. I go to Nigeria and I carry gasoline over the borders. Then, I sell it here. The money I get for the gasoline supports me and buys food for my family and parents. My children [. . .] for this money that I receive for my work, I buy clothing and food for them.

I carry gasoline between the borders of Niger and Nigeria. Sometimes, I run into the police. Some of them take all my gasoline, some just leave me alone. Sometimes, they give me problems, sometimes not. Sometimes they see me, sometimes they do not see me. This work is difficult; it is really difficult. This place I stay now is not the same as my home *[in the bush]*. Where I am now, I think about my children, I do not know what time they wake up in the morning, I do not know if they have all they need. This is all I wonder about when I am here. I do not know what time they wake up or where they sleep. I think if I get any money to send to my house to buy food. This is my purpose of staying here. I do not have any cows; I do not have anything. Allah is powerful, and he gave me this work here so I have a possibility to support myself, this work is my subsistence. What I want, if I will get some money, is to buy animals and leave this place, I want to leave this difficult work, because I am really tired. But I do not see a way because I do not have any animals. I do not get anything beside what I need to buy food, so because of that, I do not see that anything will change. Today, I want an opportunity to leave this work and if you look at me you see why, Mariyama. From the time I started until today, all these twelve years, I still have not got anything. Today I have no animals, and now I am old. I have done this work for twelve years but I still do not have any cows, all I get goes into basic subsistence. But what I want is that God takes me out of this work, this work of gasoline. I do not have anything, and if I get something I want to finish this work, because it makes you old fast, you start when you are still young but slowly it destroys all the joints of your body.

[…]

Sometimes the police see me from afar, they take my gasoline; some will accept one thousand CFA for letting me leave with my gasoline. In Nigeria, I have to give 20 neira. For some I have to give 50 neira, and others 100 neira. Sometimes the Nigerian police will spot me, they see me and they will beat me, some will just leave me, but they have been beating people for many years. One year they beat me badly, my eye got hurt that time. Another year when I left *[name of town in Nigeria]*, I was carrying gasoline, I went a different way in order for them not to see me, and I fell down, and when I fell down, I hurt my tooth. It hurt until it fell out. It is like this every time. You do understand how difficult this is? Because you are afraid of the police, because of that this is really difficult. You understand?

[…]

I take care of my home in the bush, I take care of all those people, and everything I earn I send to the "house." I have to provide for seven people. I take care of these people with the money I get for the gasoline. As you know I do not have any cows, thus I have to take care of them like this, this is what is difficult. One day, I will get some money, then I will go to the house *[in the bush]*, I will buy millet. One day, I will buy a donkey because it is a donkey that carries the water from the well and the children use them to ride. They do not die from thirst because the donkey does this work. A donkey is necessary for migration in the bush. Every time when the rainy season starts, I leave the border town and I go to the bush and then come back here. My father is in the bush and I take care of all these people. When I arrive to the bush, I do not have the opportunity to stay there for a long time, because it is difficult for me to stay there. If I go to the bush, I do not stay for longer than a week because of my work. My work is difficult. I run, I run until I reach here. I buy petroleum for 8,500 CFA, and then when I come here I sell it for 8,500 plus 250, so my profit is 250. But you know 250 is not any profit. I show patience but 250 is not any profit. I have to be patient (munyal) because only like that do I get something to eat, maybe later things will be better than today. Perhaps patience will lead to me getting something.

You know, the people at my house [in the bush], they think I have received a lot of money, but I know that I do not have any money. As you know, by the time their millet is finished, they expect me to send money to buy more. I have some money, but it is little. If I receive some money, I will keep some of it. If I get money for this month, perhaps I can send 15,000, because the people in the bush must have money to buy millet. If, however, I get something in the next two or three months, if I get something good, then perhaps I will go to visit my hose in the bush [...]

What I want is to stop this work, I want to go to the bush and do herding, I want to have the opportunity to be a herder in the bush. But you see I do not have anything, I do not have any chance to stay in the bush, because I do not have any cows. There are people who are able to stay in the bush, but I do not have a chance, because I do not have anything, only those who have animals can stay in the bush. I have close to nothing. I want to sit down in the bush with my family, all my people are in the bush, but I do not have the opportunity of staying there. I am sad and I feel shameful towards my people because I have nothing. I feel shame because I am here and a lot of people in my age group stay in the bush. Those my age are in the bush and have animals, and I do not have any animals. Like this is shameful for WoDaaBe. Only by working with the gasoline do I get something to feed my house. Perhaps some day, when my house thinks that I am working here, perhaps if I do not get anything I will leave, I will be lost. They will not know that this is because I feel ashamed, because I do not get anything to give to them. And yourself, you know such a thing is shameful" (8 February 1997).

Some of my other interviews were conducted in a place where one of my friends was a guard. The place had a large fence around a small garage and a mechanical workshop. In one corner a small shelter had been constructed, where the guard's wife slept with her belongings. When I arrived, three men and three women were in the shelter making tea. The shelter was so small that I could fit inside but my consultant had to sit in the doorway. After the tea, I conducted an interview with one of the WoDaaBe middle-men, Buuda, who sells gasoline within the border town. He buys it from other WoDaaBe and uses his connections to sell it to drivers. We got permission to sit in privacy in the little storage space inside the mechanical workshop. We carried a mat and a blanket and made ourselves comfortable on the floor. The only problem was the sounds of repairs from outside, that sometimes became so loud that I found myself close to yelling in order to hear my own voice. Buuda came first to this town as a small boy; his father's job at that time was selling petroleum, and from him Buuda learned a great deal. The work of those who deal in gasoline within the border town is different in many ways from the work of those who smuggle it. It seemed to me as if the former were better off financially, despite their work not being as difficult and physically consuming. They are free of the dangerous and difficult task of smuggling the gasoline itself, but have to be active in the border town to make connections and find buyers for the gasoline. In many cases they have steady clients to whom they even give credit if necessary. He tells me:

"I know this work. I came here first when I was young. People got to know me, I get clients, and I sell fast. Sometimes people ask me for credit, and I grant them that. Later when they have money, they pay me back... Sometimes still, people do not pay me back, and that money is as good as lost" (February 1997). When he came first to the border town, he smuggled like the others: "What I did first was to go to [name of town in Nigeria] and carry the gasoline here, but then I decided to buy it within [name of the Nigerien border town] and sell it here." When I sat down at their selling spot, I seldom saw Buuda sit down. He was always actively seeking out clients for the gasoline. He knows how to drive a motorbike, and even a car. He is a businessman, relatively well-dressed, attractive and self-confident.

The other men I talked to had, however, all similar stories to Ali. Most of these men lost all or most of their cows in the drought of 1985–1986, and either have been making a living by smuggling since that time or done migrant work in different places before arriving at the border town. The number of cows that these men own today is low, and in almost all cases, far from sufficient to survive upon alone. Most have four or five cows (including calves), but there are exceptions. One man had 15 cows, another 17 cows, and another did not have a single cow. All of them desired to get back to the bush, felt the life in the border town was difficult and hoped to gain enough cows to be able to go back. As stated by one smuggler, "I came here the first time four years ago. I came to try to earn money to buy cows, but today I have not been able to buy any cows. The first years after I arrived here, I bought seven sheep and a donkey" (6 February 1998). One person had gone to Tabalak after the drought and was given a little piece of land by the government to cultivate millet. The first year he got nothing from his fields, the second year he got two sacks of millet. The government gave him food and sometimes his relatives if they had something, but there were times when he had no food for himself and his family. He gave up on this work and decided to go back to the border town and smuggle.

WORKING IN THE CITY

I came here four years ago. I came here to attempt to earn money to buy cows, but I have not received anything (February 1997).

There are some people who have not been able to get any work. They are here in Niamey doing nothing. These people have a great deal of problems. Others get really good jobs because they get to work for *anasara*. These people are lucky because they get money for food (4 April 1998).

WoDaaBe migrant work is generally a response to extensive loss of livestock. Those who go to the cities searching for work are mostly young people, usually still suffering as a result of the drought of 1984. The men have few animals and many support their parents in the bush, either by leaving their small herds with them or by sending a part of their income to them for millet. Their absence from the bush is a strategy that is not only directed at gaining enough money to buy more animals but also allows the animals they own to reproduce instead of being sold for basic subsistence items. As many migrant workers claim, "If I stay in the bush, I will 'eat' my cows", referring to the fact that they would slowly have to sell parts of their herd in order to buy millet and other necessities for the home. A large herd is capital; individual animals can be sold without harming the reproduction possibilities of the herd as a whole.

Migrant labor is not the only possibility for those having lost their animals or whose herd is not sufficient for basic subsistence. Some men become hired herders (*jokkere*), taking care of other people's animals (see interview in Marty and Beidou 1988:39). Others have cultivated for a few years, either sedentarizing then or practicing nomadic life along with the cultivation. Cultivation usually provides the herder with a few sacks of millet for his own consumption, allowing him to refrain from selling his cows for basic consumption. The sense of obligation to one's own kin also provides people with the option of staying in the herding economy. Akali told me that a BoDaaDo never has to go hungry because if he has cows, he will follow them, and if he has no cows, he can follow his brother. Akali is referring to the strong social obligation of helping one's own kin. A man who has a very small herd can establish a household (*wuro*) with his more affluent brother who will share his resources with him. However, even though it is socially accepted to have your brother provide for you, it is shameful in the long run.

Most of the migrant workers are men between the ages of 17 and 35 years old. They leave the bush for the crowded and noisy cities and often travel with their wives, young children and/or girlfriends. The WoDaaBe lineages maintain close networks within the city, staying together in rather large groups, thus forming large households, not unlike the house in the bush. The household composition is different, of course, constituted more of cross-cousins than of fathers and sons. Sometimes, older people from the bush come to the city for a short period of time, bringing news and messages, linking the migrant laborers to the larger community of WoDaaBe. The migrant workers return to the bush once a year, usually during the rainy season, spending a few months there. People often go to the bush for various other reasons, spending a short time there. This constant movement of people moving back and forth from the bush creates a steady flow of information, creating a bridge between bush and town. Gossip, news, and information travels between these two spaces during most of the year This constant flow generally prevents individuals engaged in migrant work from breaking away from the social network of their lineage group, or being without control and supervision from the elders or the lineage as a whole. If a WoDaaBe seeks to sleep in a place where there is no one from his lineage group or no other WoDaaBe, he becomes the subject of gossip and talk, suggesting that he wants to become something other than WoDaaBe.

By going to the cities to seek employment, young people try to create opportunities for themselves, hoping to gain something that enables them to return to the bush in the future. Obviously, with an increasing number of people without herds, it becomes increasingly important to seek employment elsewhere. In the late 1980s, only about 10 percent of WoDaaBe families had a herd that was sufficient for their basic subsistence (Bonfiglioli 1985; White 1990). Bonfiglioli estimated in 1985 that around 65 percent of WoDaaBe households have members engaged in migrant work (Bonfiglioli

1985:32). The numbers of people engaged in migrant work probably differ considerably for different lineage groups, because lineages adopt different strategies to survive. Bonfiglioli points out, for example, that among the Bii-Hamma'en a more predominant strategy is to work as a hired herder (*jokkere*), while the Gojanko'en have turned more to migration work (Bonfiglioli 1985:32; Marty and Beidou 1988:23). Women are usually conceptualized as "following" the man into the city, as WoDaaBe in general phrase it.[53] This is probably due to the view in WoDaaBe societies that the man's role is to provide for his wife or wives and girlfriends. In most cases women are engaged in various occupations in a city context. Often women visit their parents in the bush for a certain period of time, and in some cases women come to Niamey alone (unmarried, divorced) to seek employment. These women stay with their kin, usually under the protection of male relatives.

The goal of most male migrant laborers is ultimately to earn enough money to buy animals, enabling them to return back to the bush with their families. If they have a small herd in the bush, the goal is to wait until the animals have reproduced, thus enlarging the herd. During formal interviews, individuals describe their existence in the city as difficult and demanding. Two friends, Akali and Higi, draw a contrast between the bush and the city in strong binary oppositions, oppositions I heard repeated by many other migrant laborers. The bush is sweet as sugar, while Niamey is the place of corruption; the bush is a place of freedom for individuals while in Niamey they are constantly observed; in the bush people eat food that makes them strong and healthy, while in Niamey they eat food that lacks power and is unhealthy; in the bush people are surrounded by family while in Niamey they are without their closest kin. Asking both men and women whether the bush is better than the city, the answer was almost without exception: life is better in the bush. In fact people never seem to tire of telling me how much better life is in the bush, especially when I had never stayed there. When I was in the bush, the same people who previously had idealized the bush complained about how hard and dull the life in the bush was most of the time. They complained about the hard work, lack of money, extensive heat and dust, charac-

---

[53] As Dupire points out, the concept woman (*debbo*, pl. *rewbe*) is derived from the root *rew*, which means "to follow" (1971[1960]:50).

terizing the bush. One day, I am with Dadi, visiting his family. During a long migrational movement, we walk together just the two of us. We have been walking for two hours, it is around noon and the sun is extremely hot. I feel my face burning and my body is wet with sweat. Finally, there is an opportunity to stop and we place ourselves in the shade of a single tree. "Are you tired Mariyama?" he asks me, and I reply as is polite, "No, I am not tired." He laughs at this rather obvious untruthfulness and says, "I know that you are just following the *mbodagansi* (politeness in this context) of WoDaaBe. You know, if someone asks me I would say the same. The truth is, however, that I am tired, my clothing is dirty and I wish I was just back in Niamey and could take a shower and get clean clothing." The bush is sweet, as people tell me on my initial arrival, but it is also demanding and difficult.

Thus, many migrant laborers get used to other ways of living than they know in the bush. They get accustomed to the consumption of expensive clothing, to more extensive tea drinking, having money in their hands, and owning various "luxury" items. People who have grown accustomed to such a lifestyle may take longer to re-establish their herd and it is also possible that the longing to "return" will become more nostalgic than actually something they will act out. Some WoDaaBe who have been able to gain the means of returning to the bush have chosen not to do so, but have preferred to stay in the city, envisioning going "back" in an unknown future. I suspect that for some people, the desire for the bush will lead them back eventually, while for others it is only a nostalgic longing, more desirable because the bush is seen from afar. I know, however, many people who have gone back, either because their herd had reached a minimum size or because they simply gave up on their life in the city, decided to become hired herders or to "follow" their brothers. For most people it is probably a mixture of both, reflecting conflicting notions about the bush when people have lived another kind of life. I can understand such a notion, because during my stay in Niger I experienced the bush as being both a very difficult and a very "sweet" place.

Most migrant workers return to the bush for several months, and it is interesting to note that the majority return at the end of the rainy season when the bush is most prosperous. During all the other times of the year, work is more extensive and their labor more needed by their extended families. However, as noted by White, this pattern of migrant work could be the consequence of acute food shortage, which is more acute in the dry season than in the rainy season. Thus, ironically a small herd does not in general require less labor than a large herd, but can feed much fewer people (White 1990:99). By arriving at the end of the rainy season migrant workers have the best of the bush. They get the opportunity to meet many people of their lineage group (the camps being more scattered during the dry season), and can participate in annual gatherings such as the *Worso* and dances of various kinds. Their returning at this time of the year probably helps them to maintain extensive relations with their own lineage group.

Migrant Work in the Past

Even though people have always traveled to cities and towns to some extent, extensive migrant labor among the WoDaaBe started only in the aftermath of the drought period 1968–74. WoDaaBe have historically cultivated fields as a fallback activity, usually in order to rebuild their herds (Dupire 1972:44–55; Dupire 1962a:340: Stenning 1959:8), even though there are also examples of WoDaaBe cultivating during times of prosperity (Bonfiglioli 1988:96; Stenning 1959:8). During the nineteenth century, WoDaaBe were mostly situated in Hausaland.[54] The unstable political situation there caused many WoDaaBe to lose their herds, thus making them turn to agricultural activities (Beauvilain 1977:176; Bonfiglioli 1988:67; De St Croix 1972 [1945]:14). The years of 1890–1922 constituted a great crisis for the pastoral communities in the Nigeria-Niger area. During 1890, rinderpest killed many animals in the area, as did a long period of scarce rainfall that ended in a drought during the years 1911–1914. The military occupation also coincided with this same period (Bonfiglioli 1988:87; de St. Croix 1972 [1945]:13). During the period 1890–1920, WoDaaBe, who were then further to the south than today, lost most of their animals because of rinderpest. The remaining animals were not sufficient for basic subsistence, and thus cultivation became their most important subsistence strategy. After having acquired sufficient animals again, many WoDaaBe could return to their herding life (Bonfiglioli 1988:93–94; de St. Croix 1972 [1945]:13–14). Writing in the 1960s, Dupire says, furthermore, that in the Ader region some Gojanko'en and Njapto'en families cultivated due to special circumstances. These families

---

54 Hausaland is situated in present day northern Nigeria and southern Niger.

had lost most of their herds, and thus cultivated in order to prevent food shortages and avoid selling their remaining animals for millet (Dupire 1962a:129). WoDaaBe women trade milk for millet in market towns but during difficult times they have also been paid for repairing calabashes, pounding millet, and braiding other women's hair (Dupire 1962a:127; Wilson 1992:21). Perhaps these activities, performed by women and not related to herding activities, were the first signs towards a development in the direction of migrant labor in the cities. WoDaaBe women were then, as today, well known for their skills in repairing calabashes.[55] These historical references underline the complex relationship between agriculture and herding, and that these two economies must be seen in relation to each other. The sedentary sector is capable of absorbing excess labor in the pastoral society, providing various diversified occupations and thus minimizing risk in pastoral societies (Park 1993:310). Migrant work and working as a hired herder[56] seem to have increased considerably during the droughts in 1968–1974 while agriculture became less dominant. The increased population in Niger had considerably reduced the access to good agricultural land. From 1950 till 1975, Niger's population had increased from 2.4 million people to 4.2 millions (Hamidou 1980a:31). Population pressures in the south led to increased cultivation in the pastoral areas, as well as many former herders turning to agricultural activities. Some WoDaaBe went to the cities of Nigeria or the Ivory Coast. Rupp's report regarding the general situation after the droughts states that it was not uncommon that a third or even a majority of families making up one lineage faction were forced to leave the pastoral economy to search for paid work (CIDES: Rupp 1976:14). Moreover many WoDaaBe earned money by the selling their traditional medicines, WoDaaBe being known all over West Africa for having vast knowledge in this area. This general acceptance of their abilities thus probably led to many WoDaaBe finding clients for these products rather easily based on their ethnicity as WoDaaBe. Many people began alternating between the bush and various countries. Some individuals earned an income in Nigeria by working as

---

[55] This skill is an important one because many WoDaaBe have a taboo against drinking from anything that leaks.
[56] Being a hired herder has a somewhat negative status. Bouzous in the Tahoua area have traditionally worked as hired herders for the Hausa (Dupire 1972:63), but the Bouzous used to be slaves in the Tuareg society, and hence the WoDaaBe could have felt it degrading to be associated with them by working in the same profession. The increase in hired herders does in any case point toward the increased marginalization of the WoDaaBe.

guards for the houses of wealthy people or for companies, in addition to hard physical labor. Rupp's discussion does not distinguish between occupations done by Tuaregs and WoDaaBe, but in addition to those mentioned here, she argues that women pounded millet, collected firewood and fodder (CIDES: Rupp 1976:15), and also continued braiding hair and repairing calabashes. Migration work seems to have increased considerably after the droughts of 1984. Young men left in great numbers for Nigeria and took with them their girlfriends or wives, searching for employment mainly as security guards, some as manual laborers. The exchange rate between the CFA and the Nigerian *naira* was during this period quite beneficial to Nigeriens. When it deteriorated, many migrant laborers migrated back to Niger to search for work there.

Elderly WoDaaBe in the lineage group with which I stayed mostly in the Tchin-Tabaraden area tell me that their lineage originated from the Ader area where their families had stayed for several generations, being pushed further north with increased cultivation in that area, stating that the bush there had "died". As stated in chapter one, pastoral land has been decreased considerably with the emphasis on cultivated land. The group migrated to the Tchin-Tabaraden area, probably in the late 1950, but at that time rainfall was unusually high. The fact that the area is much further north makes it much more prone to drought, making the pastoral economy there much more risky than further south as also discussed in chapter one (see more detailed discussion in Kristín Loftsdóttir 2002). Not surprisingly this group suffered heavy livestock losses when rainfall fluctuated and was below average.

Migrant Work Today

It is difficult to estimate the extent of WoDaaBe migrant work in the present due to lack of statistical data.[57] People go back and forth between the bush

---

[57] I made two estimations of the number of WoDaaBe in Niamey. In September 1997, I estimated that 146 men were in Niamey and 67 women. In April 1998, however, during the dry season I estimated that there were 504 men and 372 women. These estimates were conducted by asking people from particular lineages to estimate the number of people from their own lineage, as well as to point out other informants from other lineage groups. Usually several people did the counting together, estimating the number of people from their lineage group until they agreed on a number. Children under 15 were not included. The estimates were supervised by a man from the Gojanko'en lineage. Most of those who were consulted were men, thus making the number of men more likely to be accurate. Here I only present this information in regard to the two main lineage groups, even though I also counted the number of people from each lineage faction.

and the city and thus the number of people differs at any point of time, even though it is to some extent dependent on seasonal variability. Some indication of the extent of migrant work is given in a report conducted in relation to the Niger Range and Livestock Project published in 1984, which estimates that the group studied most extensively by me in the Tchin-Tabaraden area is in the middle range when compared with other WoDaaBe lineages. The report states that for a 12-month period, about a quarter of the adult population left the pastoral economy at least once for migrant work, and furthermore estimates that 65 percent of households in Tchin-Tabaraden have household members who are migrant laborers (Swift et al. 1984:493).

WoDaaBe men sell tea on the streets, work as water carriers, make and sell ropes or find manual labor on a day to day basis. The migrant laborers themselves identify these as difficult occupations with small revenues. Many men also work as night watchmen, then often along with other types of occupations that can be conducted during the day. Women get income by various kinds of work as well, especially hair dressing in addition to making "traditional" WoDaaBe clothing to be sold to tourists (see also Wilson 1992:57; Bovin 1990). Women in the city are, of course, also responsible for the same tasks as in the bush; taking care of the children in addition to other general housework that has to be conducted on a daily basis. Groups of women have, occasionally, gone together to Burkina Faso and Nigeria for a few months, working at hair dressing, selling medicine and repairing calabashes (see also Rain 1999:182).

WoDaaBe are traditionally not known as craft producers, the various crafts are usually bought from other ethnic groups (Dupire 1962a:127) even though some forms of art-craft production have always been present. For the last few decades a growing number of WoDaaBe have, however, been engaged in handicraft production and selling. According to one consultant from the Gojanko'en lineage, the engagement with handicrafts started with a group of people that regularly went to neighboring countries to sell medicine. They went through Niamey and there they seem to have befriended an American woman who bought items from them. These items were personal items such as jewelry, and various kinds of decorative items. Each time they went through Niamey, the woman would buy some things from them because, as the man tells me, these were traditional WoDaaBe items. After the drought of 1984, individuals from yet another lineage arrived in Niamey, attempting to base their income on this activity, making objects for the sole purpose of selling them. These entrepreneurs mark the transition from occasionally selling personal items to a purposeful commercialization of identity-related products. Some of these individuals got in contact with the American woman and organized a co-operative where some of the goals were the development of the handicraft industry, emphasizing jewelry making (Wilson and Legesse 1990:6). The co-operative seems to have perished quickly even though the jewelry making did not. When turning to commercialization WoDaaBe were possibly influenced by Tuaregs who have been engaged in tourist related activities for a much longer time. But also, it is interesting to observe as discussed in chapter two, that in the 1980s images of eco-indigenism appear, the popular and greatly influential book the *Nomads of Niger* directly discussing the WoDaaBe being published in 1982.

These activities can be characterized as migrant work based on sedantarization in the city but some types of work involve transnational trading, requiring movements between several places. The occupations that can be classified as transnational trading are of several different kinds. Some import goods that are valued in Niger or can be sold at a higher price such as gasoline from Nigeria, as already mentioned. Turquoise turbans and swords are bought in Nigeria and sold for a higher price to Tuaregs and WoDaaBe in Niger. Others sell goods in neighboring countries such as medicine or crafts such as their own handiwork and handmade Tuareg jewelry. Since the Tuareg rebellion, fewer tourists go to Niger, resulting in deteriorating markets for craft products.[58]

For some, however, sedentarizing in the city to work as a guard can be desirable because the guard is often provided with a small shelter or hut where he can stay with his family. Working as a security guard is also a popular occupation because it provides a steady income, in addition to allowing time for other types of work. Some patrons will help their guards and their families if something unexpected happens, such as buying medicines for them. Yet this is a dangerous occupation and many WoDaaBe have been killed or attacked in the line of duty. Many guards sleep during the night, finding the

---

[58] The Tuareg rebellion is, as earlier stated, usually seen as starting in 1990 with the execution of Tuareg civilians in Tchin-Tabaraden sharpening the resentment that had been accumulating against the government due to the Tuaregs marginalization within the nation state (see Ibrahim 1994).

obligation to stay awake unjust and impossible. Those who hire the guards, however, find the claim just and rational, stating that the risk of attack is much more if the guard is asleep. A sleeping guard knows that if caught it can cost him his job. Most guards have to have a second job because their income is not sufficient to provide for the family, and tell me that they need to sleep in order to be able to attend to that job. "A guard is only like a photograph", one guard told me, "he is not a true threat to the thief. If a band of thieves arrives what is he going to do? He does not even have a gun to protect himself and the house." As a result of this vulnerable feeling, the guards want to have many people around them (wives and friends) because as they see it, it is the best protection against thieves. More people will be more able to alert the neighborhood if something happens. Presumably, the WoDaaBe and Tuaregs are popular as night watchmen in northern Nigeria, because they are conceptualized as ferocious due to their warrior image of turbans and swords (Swift et al. 1984:489).

Different lineages have some specialization in regard to the type of work conducted in Niamey, new migrant workers thus making use of the experiences and networks of their kinfolk already in the city. The selling of turbans is, for example, done almost exclusively by Japto'en and Ji'jiiru are more engaged in selling tea than other lineages. My study did not include a survey of what lineages were most involved in migrant work. The study conducted in connection with the Niger Range and Livestock Project, suggests that members of the following lineages leave the bush in greatest numbers; Bii Hamma'en in the Dakoro area, the Bii Korony'en (Bii-koro'en) Yisaw from Abalak, the Jiijiiru from the Tanout area, and Yaamanko'en from around Aderbissinat and Tamayo. The study argues that the Gojanko'en in Tchin-Tabaraden are moderately involved in migrant labor (Swift et al. 1984:492–493). In Niamey at the time of my research, Gojanko'en were, however, quite numerous, which could be due to the years that had elapsed between the study related to the Niger Range and Livestock Project and my own study or simply reflected that people from different lineages and areas work in different cities.

Relations with the Bush

WoDaaBe migrant workers generally state that they are engaged in migrant work due to necessity, expressing a desire to rebuild their herd. Many claim they try to send money to their extended families in the bush, intended to buy corn and other necessities for their family. Most have, however, usually hardly enough to feed themselves, and thus in fact only occasionally send cash. In addition, many migrant laborers get used to different consumption patterns during their stay in the city, making the cost of living somewhat high. Studies have furthermore shown that migrant work is in the long term not an efficient way of reconstructing herds. The study, conducted in relation to the Niger Range and Livestock Project, claims that only one of 13 migrant workers (making 21 trips during a period of 18 months) was able to buy a bull with his earnings (Swift et al. 1984:489; also reported in White 1997:99). Similar results were confirmed in my own survey among migrant workers in Niamey, where only seven individuals out of 37 surveyed had been able to buy animals since they started working as migrant workers, most of them having done several years of migrant work. In some cases, parents leave their young, non-breastfeeding children with their grandparents in the bush. Women often stay with their children for a few weeks or months among their birth family. In the city, several WoDaaBe families usually live in the same area and despite interacting with members of other ethnic groups, associate mostly with other WoDaaBe families, preferably from the same lineage group. A single homestead in the city thus usually incorporates individuals from the same lineage group, even though not necessarily from the same extended family.

Migrant workers are generally absent from the bush during the dry season when labor requirements are most intense and their labor in fact most needed. C. White suggests as noted earlier that this contradiction can be seen as due to the acute food shortage in the dry season. Even though a small herd requires similar labor to a large herd, it is not able to feed the same number of people (White 1990:99). As other studies have shown, this can be seen as a constant feature of migrant work in the cities; it drains the most valuable working force from the pastoral society (Arnould 1990:341; White 1990:99). It can however be suggested that the relatively flexible household organization, where one camp (*wuro*) can be constituted and reconstituted by different families, is able, to some extent, to respond to this labor shortage which occurs when the most valuable part of the labor force leaves for migrant work. In such situations, a few households will form one camp thus allowing for cooperation. The benefits of migrant labor can thus be seen as reducing the cereal consumption and occasionally bringing earnings, both leading to a reduction of animal sales during the dry season. The migrant worker, even though not earning enough to rebuild his herd, is at least able to refrain from selling the animals he already has, allowing them to reproduce. It is, however, somewhat ironic that the migrant workers flock to the bush at the end of the rainy season, i.e., at a time of prosperity and low labor requirements, when food and milk are abundant and social activities at their peak.

WoDaaBe migrant work can be seen as corresponding to some extent to what David Rain refers to as "circulatory movements", characterized by "people moving from their places of residence for varying periods of time but ultimately returning to them" (Rain 1999:3). Not all WoDaaBe migrant workers will necessarily return to the bush, but the fact remains that they see themselves as only staying in the city for a limited time, and return regularly to the pastoral economy for a few months or weeks per year to engage with their larger lineage group and the herding community.

THE MAKERS OF HANDICRAFTS

The handicraft work of the WoDaaBe can be seen as a commercialization of identity related products because these products are marketed and sold as traditional WoDaaBe items. This manufacturing of identity becomes clearer when one realizes that most of those doing handicraft work today are often engaged in the selling of other identity related products than WoDaaBe jewelry, such as traditional WoDaaBe clothing, Tuareg jewelry, and dance performances, which have been popularized in the general media of the West.

WoDaaBe produce several kinds of jewelry, mostly necklaces and bracelets. There are various models available for sale, and while some people are imaginative and creative in finding new ones others simply copy what has already been done. For many of the objects cowries are used, which were a currency in West Africa for many centuries. Ibn Batuta, for example, who visited the Mandingo Empire of Melle, in 1352, mentions that at that time cowries were used as currency (Meek 1925:65). The production of jewelry is divided into a number of steps, many items being made at same time, and is thus similar to an assembly line. The most common items of clothing sold are the woman's skirt (*wudere*), young woman's shirt (*henare surbadajo*) and a cloth used by men during dances. This clothing has extensive work in the same embroidery style that I learned in the bush, a style that is considered distinctly WoDaaBe. Recently, the styles of the embroidered clothing have been expanded somewhat to adapt to what tourists are more likely to buy. These new items include trousers, blouses, and shirts that are shaped like T-shirts. One English-speaking woman I met was wearing a shirt, shaped like a T-shirt, decorated with embroidery. It was clear to me that this was a WoDaaBe product bought at the *Village Artisana*, and I think that I could even have identified the person who made it. I asked the woman if she had bought it at the *Village Artisana*, and she told me that my guess was correct. I asked her if she knew that the WoDaaBe made this, and she told me that it had not been the WoDaaBe because the man at the store told her that a Fulani made the

Many WoDaaBe women do traditional embroidery to sell to tourists in Niamey.

clothes. I tried to explain that the WoDaaBe were often considered to be a group within the Fulani, but the information seemed irrelevant to her. "This is traditional clothing for a Fulani man", she told me firmly. Many of the handicraft makers sell, along with their other products, silver jewelry that they buy from Tuaregs. These are various pieces of jewelry, necklaces, earrings and bracelets, which are made and used by Tuaregs but not by WoDaaBe themselves. WoDaaBe only buy them to sell to tourists or other Westerners. The possibilities of profit are great because these objects are popular but the investment cost is high and the merchant has to have access to a large group of clients in order to earn the necessary profits from the sale of silver.

In addition, it is relatively common in Niamey that groups of WoDaaBe are hired to show dances, either by development organizations or foreign cultural institutions. Groups of WoDaaBe have gone abroad to show dances, most frequently to France, Belgium or Holland. These dance exhibitions are usually not well paid, but include the possibility of selling "real" WoDaaBe handicrafts or the Tuareg jewelry. Such dance-trips are simultaneously sales trips selling handicrafts and everyday items such as clothing, swords, jewelry, hats, and dance decoration items. Silver can bring great profits if taken on such trips.

WoDaaBe can be seen in the "tourist streets" of Niamey and even though not as numerous as Tuareg craft makers, they can be no less aggressive in seeking clients. Several co-operatives have been formed in relation to the handicraft work. The non-governmental organization of WoDaaBe jewelry makers called *Cooperative Artisana Bororo (WoDaaBe)*, established in 1994, was probably the first one.[59] The cooperative built a small house for their craftwork with the aid of a Belgian development organization, also getting a donation from a white person they had befriended. Such houses make a great difference, making the craft objects more visible and accessible to tourists and are thus greatly desired by most handicraft makers. At the time of my fieldwork six small houses were operated by the WoDaaBe, all crowded on the same popular tourist street in Niger, which is also close to many development institutions. WoDaaBe own five of these six houses, the sixth one is rented on a monthly basis. In most cases, several members of the lineage group formally own the house, but in some cases, I have been told that one person takes charge of it and also most of the profit. Others own their houses indi-

---

[59] This is according to my informants, but it is very possible that other lineage factions had formed co-operatives prior to this time which my informants are not aware of.

vidually, having earned money themselves to buy them. These houses differ greatly in size and quality, and most are perhaps more accurately described as shelters, being so small that there is hardly room for more than three people inside. The space is often economized by leaving one side completely open. The walls are made either of sheet metal on a wooden frame or wooden planks. These houses have generally been bought through profits made by the handicraft work, or in one case by direct assistance from a development institution. Moreover, two WoDaaBe rented space at the time of my research in the *Village Artisana* establishment, where small spaces are available to work on one's crafts. They can also sell their crafts in the *Village Artisana* store, which along with the working spaces is a popular place for tourists to visit. Most WoDaaBe, however, sell their objects on the street, offering them to other WoDaaBe, Hausa merchandisers or selling directly to tourist. Those who have houses sometimes buy jewelry from those without a house, other times they give them an opportunity to sell their objects within the house. These possibilities are still dependent on social relationships, such as lineage affiliation, the status of the persons in question, and their personal relations.

As with migrant work in general, the handicrafts have made very few WoDaaBe well off. One friend told me that those who earned money from them were not those who did the craft work, but those who sold them. He is making a reference to WoDaaBe who have developed strong sales networks and no longer make the jewelry themselves but buy it from other WoDaaBe. They buy the product at a relatively low price and sell it for a much higher price because they have access to better markets. This indicates an interesting internal dynamic within the WoDaaBe society, a dynamic that has created a division within it, between those who are primary producers and those who "process" the product, reaping the benefit of it.

WoDaaBe migrant workers have generally no means of protecting themselves and their belongings. Most people sleep in straw huts in the city, which cannot be closed and locked. Those handicraft makers who have sales places are fortunate to have a secure place for their objects. At night when people sleep in their homes, thieves arrive, often taking whatever there is, including people's clothing and personal items. During my first year in Niger, I did an interview with a young man who had organized a co-operative in Niamey. He was different from most other WoDaaBe in the respect that he spoke French well, and was familiar with quite political concepts such as those re-

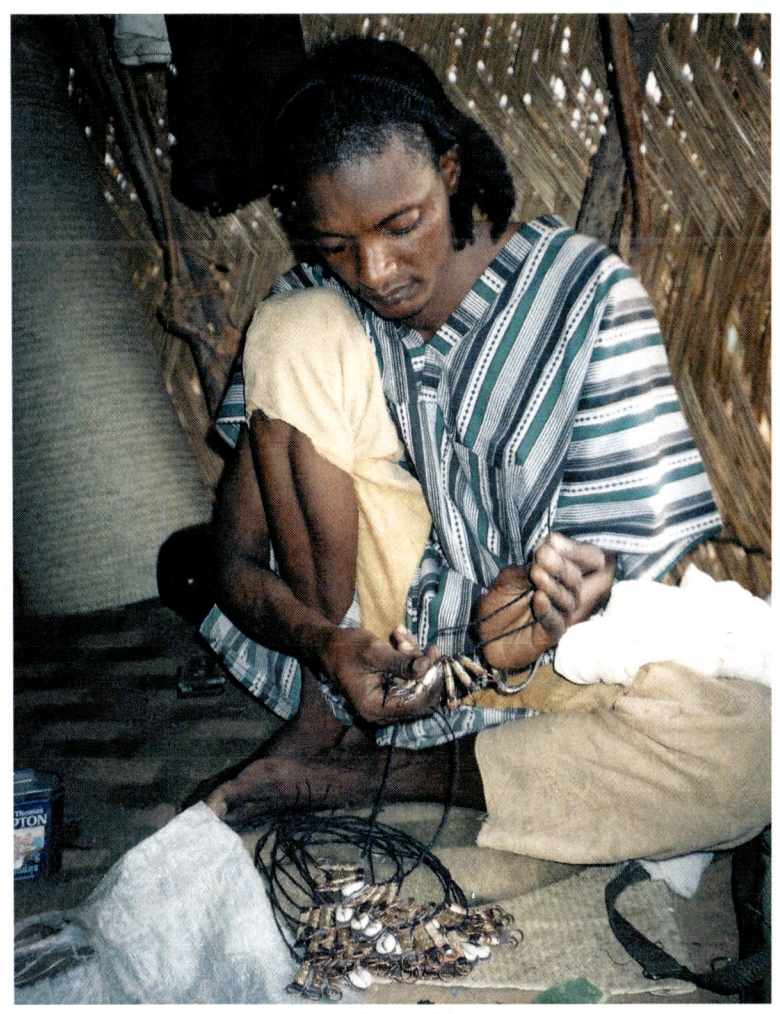

Work in Niamey is to some extent dependent on lineage affiliation. Many men have in recent years become engaged in handicraft production and selling.

ferring to indigenous people and allocation of resources. He was polite and gentle, but contrary to most other WoDaaBe I have known, he stated nothing in the context of how much he liked white people. Most other people, who I had interviewed, frequently expressed how "good" and generous white people were and how much they as WoDaaBe liked to be associated with them. This young man said nothing of the sort, and in his talk, there could even be heard criticism pointed at the development community and whites in general. I liked him, perhaps for his critical views, which were much more similar to my own than those of others I got to know, but probably also for his patience with me and my questions. When I left, he gave me a bracelet, signifying his friendship.

I never saw him again. A few months later, I heard that he had been killed during a silver sales trip in a neighboring country. He was in the company of a large group of people from his lineage group, who were in the process of organizing themselves to build a sales house in Niamey. They had taken a great deal of silver with them and had good prospects in town. A white person, with whom they had made an appointment previously, bought all they had for sale. In the night, a large group of thieves attacked the group, seriously injuring and harming several of the people. The other people in the group suspected that somehow the attackers had heard that they were carrying a great deal of money. They killed him by beating him to death.

Shame and Survival

In her writings, Dupire indicates an element of shame associated with being engaged in other occupations than herding one's own animals (Dupire 1962a: 126–127). Contemporary WoDaaBe engage in various activities that have no relation to herding or to life in the bush. Several more recent authors emphasize shame as experienced by WoDaaBe migrant laborers due to their work in the city (Swift et al. 1984:492; White 1997:100; Bovin 1990:38). Swift et al. suggest that WoDaaBe preference after the drought period 1968–74 to do migrant work in far away cities in neighboring countries – thus having to pay high transport costs – as opposed to finding work in Niger's cities, could be related to the feeling of shame (Swift et al. 1984:492). One informant confirmed this stating that when the handicraft work initially started people felt shameful (*be nani semtuDum*) selling items in the city. People would hide the finished products inside their clothing when taking them to the market so other people could neither see nor guess that they were going to sell them. In my own research, I did not find WoDaaBe migrant workers being generally ashamed of their work in the city. Some individuals I interacted with were on the contrary relatively proud of their work in the city, emphasizing their importance in providing a security net for those in the bush. Those who expressed shame in relation to their work were not ashamed of having an occupation outside the pastoral economy but more of their inability to rebuild their herd or send money to their extended family in the bush (Loftsdóttir 2004b).

Even though I did not experience shame being associated with migrant work per se, shame seemed to be associated with failure to earn enough in the city. This association of shame with failure was reflected in how WoDaaBe generally discuss different kinds of job, shame association with a certain occupation thus seems related to its economic possibilities. One elderly migrant worker tells me that the handicraft is not shameful but rather the work in relation to selling tea and rope or carrying water. WoDaaBe generally state that these occupations do not provide a great deal of income, that those engaged in these tasks usually only earn enough to eat and would prefer other kinds of occupations. The handicraft work and the selling of turbans have, however, the possibility and hopes of earning some income but both these occupations need starting capital. Shame seems thus today to be more connected to the failure of earning income from one's activities in the city rather than with working as a migrant laborer. Some occupations, such as tea selling, rope making and water carrying are associated with failure, and thus shameful. The feeling of shame for not having anything was clearly expressed in Ali's words quoted earlier in relation to smuggling when he stated that he was ashamed in relation to his family for having nothing. Possibly, migrant labor was considered shameful in the past because migrant work was associated with a failure to adhere to the right way of being a WoDaaBe (lack of *mbodagansi*) in addition to be associated with inability to provide for oneself. Today, the migrant workers associate shame not so much with their work as with their inability to fulfill their goals in the city and their becoming more economically dependent on others. Instead of associating shame with being a part of migrant work, the migrant workers themselves emphasize it as important in creating new diversification strategies. This need for diversification is not only an individual strategy but conceptualized by the migrant workers as a strategy of reducing risk for the family or lineage group as a whole, thus in a sense creating continuity with other strategies of risk management, such as agriculture. As argued by de Bruijn and van Dijk (1999:135) pastoralists reduce risk by exploiting various resources. The emphasis on risk management is clear in the following quote from an interview with a WoDaaBe man:

If there is another drought, another time that the majority of the cows will die, I will have some skills to help my family in the bush. I know different types of work, I know different languages, and I know what to do in the city. What does my brother who always stays in the bush want to do then? (18 January 1997).

To some extent WoDaaBe migrants thus associate their work with new survival skills. Several migrant laborers tell me that the WoDaaBe need to know new skills to make a living, in order to survive during difficult periods. "Now all WoDaaBe are engaged in commercialism", an elderly migrant worker tells me. He continues:

Those WoDaaBe who have foresight are engaged in commercialism, even though they also keep cows. If you see someone who is only thinking about his cows and has no other way of earning an income, he is not very aware of the present situation (15 October 1997).

Ethnic Relations in Niamey

Migrant work among WoDaaBe and the handicraft production and selling brings WoDaaBe into contact to greater extent with various ethnicities that are in Niamey. It is difficult to estimate the number of people generally in Niamey due to their numbers fluctuating along with general conditions in the country. Niamey's inhabitants are fewer when the season is good, only to increase during difficult times. The estimate which I heard most frequently is that 700,000 people live in the very spread out city. In 1979, the inhabitants were estimated at 300,000 (Hamidou 1980b:34). Contrary to many other large cities in the Niger area, Niamey is a recent city. Pre-colonial accounts do not mention Niamey, and Niamey was probably a small village during the early colonial time. The history and development of the town is thus tied with the history of colonialism in Niger. The city was established as the capital of the "Territoire Militaire du Niger" in 1905. The capital was then moved to Zinder in 1911, a more ancient city and by many considered more suited as the capital, but in 1926 Niamey became the capital again (Gado 1997:26, 37). The movement of the capital back to Niamey can be seen as a political act, aimed at preventing the evolution of the Hausa elite, who the French feared would ally with the Hausa in northern Nigeria. The Zarma and Sonhai (more predominant in the area of Niamey) were seen as more easily handled politically because they were culturally closer to populations in areas controlled by France (Ibrahim 1994:18). The transfer of the capital has also been explained by Niamey having a more stable water source than Zinder (Gado 1997:32). The population of Niamey grew fast after it was established as the capital for the first time. Prior to 1917, the inhabitants of Niamey did not have to pay taxes and were also exempted from forced labor, contrary to most other areas in Niger, thus drawing the population to that area. Also, land was made easily available for those wanting to settle there, and the French created a large livestock and corn market. To make Niamey look even more favorable in comparison to other markets, taxes in the neighboring towns' markets were made high. Dire famines during the periods of 1901–1903, 1913–1915, and again 1931–1932 led, furthermore, to massive migration to Niamey (Gado 1997:26-36).

The most common languages heard in Niamey are Zerma and Hausa. Most WoDaaBe men and women who stay extensively in the city master Hausa and those from Tchin-Tabaraden also speak Tamasheq. Zerma and Songhai are elites that have traditionally held strong positions of power in Niger (Ibrahim 1994). However, WoDaaBe generally use the term Hausa to refer to all these groups. Hausa are referred to in Fulfulde as *haabe*, but the concept has a somewhat ambiguous meaning. According to Lovejoy, during the 18th century *jihad*, the term *haaBe* became used somewhat simultaneously with the term non-Muslim, probably as a result then of the enslavement of non-Muslims and the domination of the Fulani of the Hausa states during that period. The term "Fulani" came to mean "free" as opposed to *haaBe* and slaves (Lovejoy 1981:210). Lovejoy claims that the ethnic label Hausa that had been used to refer to a specific ethnic group in the caliphate changed to signify the Muslim peasantry and merchant class, embracing a much larger population of people (Lovejoy 1981:211). Lovejoy does not use the term *haaBe* as a direct translation of the term Hausa, and it seems as if these concepts used to have different meanings in the Sokoto Caliphate.[60] However, for many WoDaaBe today the term Hausa is translation of *haaBe*,

---

[60] The same understanding of the term is used by C. S. Whitaker, Jr. Whitaker writes, "*haaBe* is a Fulani word meaning non-Fulani; Hausa, probably a linguistic and cultural designation, is commonly applied to the *haaBe* and Fulani collectively, for the Fulani rulers soon became assimilated to the culture and language of their subjects" (Whitaker 1970:19).

and used over ethnic groups that are according to them, "almost the same as the Hausa." According to Ibrahim, the term Hausa is today used to refer to all those who speak and dress like Hausa in Niger more than as referring to people of a common origin, (Ibrahim 1994). WoDaaBe use the term "Ndowi'en" to refer to the Fulani. According to the WoDaaBe themselves, this term is not looked upon favorably by the Fulani, causing them to use the term "Fulbe" when speaking directly to a Fulani person, but "Ndowi'en" when talking about Fulani

In Niamey most WoDaaBe associate with members of their own lineage group or with other WoDaaBe, living and working together, even though making friends as well with people from other ethnic groups. WoDaaBe use various physical markers to distinguish themselves from their neighbors, such as specific types of tattoos, jewelry and clothing in addition to domestic objects (IRSH: Bovin 1970). In a city context, such markers of identity acquire an intensified meaning being important in distinguishing the WoDaaBe from other populations. WoDaaBe openly state that their special kind of jewelry, clothing and bodily decorations distinguish them from other populations in the city. I have previously discussed symbols (*djelgul*) and marking of animals, and how Akali explained the meaning of the term by referring to belonging within a particular group. Just like cutting the ears of the animal to create that association, people wear *kodul* necklaces on themselves or a particular hat, and style their hair in a particular way, thus placing themselves within their ethnic categories by a conscious act of bodily expression. Life in the bush involves, of course, contact with various ethnic groups, mostly Tuaregs, Fulani, Hausa and Arabs. WoDaaBe men frequently make livestock transactions, buy millet and animal fodder at the neighboring markets. WoDaaBe women trade their milk with Tuareg women in the bush, and in the city they sell it for money. They braid women's hair from other ethnicities and repair their calabashes. The interaction can even be more personal. Akali tells me that when he was a young child, his grandmother used to go to a small town to do trading with milk (*sippal*). While she was selling the milk, she left him with a Tuareg woman, where he played with the other children and ate porridge with them. WoDaaBe men and women in the city interact, however, daily with people that are not WoDaaBe. WoDaaBe in the Tchin-Tabaraden area share, furthermore, the area with Tuareg herders and cultivators, thus being more influenced by Tuareg culture than WoDaaBe groups in other areas, often speaking Tamasheq fluently and in some cases having adopted some of the Tuaregs' cultural artifacts. The relationship between these groups is characterized by cooperation, such as in terms of well digging, but also of conflict especially because of the use of natural resources (Swift et al. 1984:342).

As in the bush, negative stereotypes of people from other ethnicities, are frequently expressed, such as that Hausa are dishonest and that Tuaregs are thieves and dangerous. It is generally an insult to say to another WoDaaBe that he or she looks or behaves like a member of another ethnic group. Young men, for example, who stand in culturally defined joking-relationships (either in the same age group or cross-cousins) often refer to one another as Hausa or Tuaregs, intended then as a friendly insult. Too much association with members of other ethnic groups in the city is furthermore generally criticized and mocked. If people of other ethnicities greet me while I am tagging along with WoDaaBe friends when they go places to do hair dressing, my friends firmly tell me not to reply, explaining "these are Hausa" or " Tuaregs" thus "not our people." WoDaaBe endogamous practices, the prefered form of marriage being with one's cross-cousins, show in themselves the strong emphasis on maintaining separation from those defined as ethnic others. WoDaaBe are of course not alone in holding stereotypical views of other ethnic groups. People from other ethnicities also express stereotypes about the WoDaaBe (Dupire 1971[1960]:48; Horowitz 1972:113). Interrelations with the Beriberi in Niamey are characterized by a joking-relationship, which is similar to that between WoDaaBe cross-cousins (Dupire 1962a:27).[61] WoDaaBe stereotypes of Hausa and Tuaregs do, however, not always correspond with actual relations between individuals of different ethnicities. At a name giving ceremony the mother invited several Hausa women who were "her friends." They were given honoree positions at the festival, and treated in all ways as honorable guests. My male friends also introduced me many times to Hausa and Tuaregs who had been their friends for a long time.

---

[61] Dupire mentions that the origin myth of theWoDaaBe lineage group Bi-utejo includes a narrative of the Beriberi. The Beriberi are said to have lived with the WoDaaBe, luring cows from water with fire and entrusting them to WoDaaBe, thus making the Beriberi and Bororo as close as cross-cousins (Dupire 1962a:29).

JUMARE'S ACCIDENT

When Akali arrives in the morning, we go through our formal greeting process as usual. It is almost a double greeting because we do it both in Fulfulde and English. When I ask for the third time, "All is fine?" Akali looks directly at me and answers, "No, actually there is a problem." He looks down again. "My sister Jumare had an accident yesterday. A car hit her. People told me this when I came home last night. They had been looking for me." There is tiredness in his face.

"Is she alright?" I did not even know that she was back in Niamey.

"Yes, but she is hurt, she received a hard blow on her head. She is in the hospital now." He briefly tells me what happened after he had left my place the night before. He had gone directly to the hospital after hearing the news, but it was almost eleven o'clock and the soldiers guarding the hospital did not want to let him in. He begged them to let him inside, told them that it was his sister who was hurt, and that he had to see how she was. After a while they realized that he was not leaving, and took pity on him and let him inside. The motorist had not driven away from the accident, as usually happens, and he even promised that he would cover the costs of medicines and hospitalization. The doctors gave him a list of necessary medications and the motorist left to buy them and had not been back. Thus, when Akali saw his sister, she had not received any medication. He asked the doctors to give him the list over the medicines needed, and he would try to find an open pharmacy to buy them. He took a taxi in order to find an open place and he managed to buy what was needed so his sister got some medical assistance. This took a long time and he was not back at his place until four in the morning.

Our first opportunity to go to the hospital for a visit is during our lunch break. The visiting hours start at 12:30. We arrive a little after noon, and there is already a large group of people waiting for the hospital gates to open. We wait with the others, a large mixture of people of all ethnicities. Akali tells me that last night he left 1,000 CFA for his sister, in case she needed something.

Other WoDaaBe arrive at this waiting place. They greet us and ask Akali how his sister is doing. I see many of the people I have learned to know, familiar with all their faces, most of the names. The gates are finally opened. The crowd of people moves fast through the opening. I feel the pressure from bodies, and I am almost pushed to the side, but I manage to stay in the flow. Akali has forgotten about me, he is far ahead and then suddenly stops, waiting for me to catch up. Many small buildings constitute the hospital. Akali knows where we are going. We approach one building and enter. The paint job on the walls is old in comparison with the hospitals I know, and everything is somehow empty, signifying Niger's poverty. The smell is the same as in hospitals everywhere. People rush by me. Akali walks fast and I try to keep up with him and the rest of the WoDaaBe. We enter a small narrow room, which seems almost like a hallway. A man with half of his face cut and bleeding is sitting at the left side in the room, being cared for by a doctor. There is blood on his clothing. Jumare is lying on a straw mat on the floor. An old blanket has been placed under her head, she is lying on her side, and her body curled up into a fetus position. She is fully clothed except for the upper part of her body, which is only covered by her headscarf. I do not see her face, because she covers it with her hands. Her body is thin and small. I kneel by her side, stroke her, people are coming and going through this hallway, and I feel the other WoDaaBe standing and kneeling by my side and back. I hear Banjo (Akali's mother's-brother), asking out to no one why Jumare is only given a straw-mat on the floor. A woman, standing by my side, shakes Jumare gently and asks her if she is in pain. Does she know her? "Do you know who I am, Jumare?" the woman asks firmly, trying to get the young woman to look at her. She receives no answer, no response. Someone comes in. It is a doctor handing Akali Jumare's X-rays. Akali wants me to look at them, which I do, even though the X-rays tell me just as much as they tell him. Things are confusing somehow, like everything is spinning. Akali is suddenly out of sight. I assume that he is asking about a hospital bed, or her condition, or both. A doctor arrives, shouting at the group of people in the room. "There are too many of you, I want you to leave, only two people are allowed in the room... you hear? Only two people..."

I pretend not to hear, continue to stroke Jumare's motionless body, wonder to myself why he has to be so angry at these people who only want this woman to be taken care of, who want to know that she is going to be fine.

From the floor I look around me, at the walls which have not been painted for a long time, at the old damaged benches, at the rusted table feet, and I feel sorry for the doctor. I still do not want to leave unless told to do so by Akali or Banjo, so I stay. Some of the other people leave, but a few remain with me. The doctor leaves us alone.

Akali comes back, he kneels by my side. His voice is tired and emotional. "You help me, Kristín. She must get a bed. They do not help her if she does not get a bed. I do not want to leave her like this. I am sorry, you help me for this money." He never uses my name unless he is very upset. I tell him to take my wallet and pay what is necessary. When he comes back, he tells us that Jumare has to be moved to her bed. The men in her family tell her harshly (as is appropriate) to stand up. "Stand up Jumare, you hear, stand up! We want to move you to a different place." Banjo says this firmly, but she does not move. I am the only woman left, so I put my arm around her, trying gently to move her, telling her that she has to stand up to go to her bed. One of the men sees what I am trying to do and helps me to raise her up. Jumare puts her arms around my neck, and rests her head on my chest. She tries to stand up and manages to do so with the support of this man and me. She is heavy, but when people try to move her away from me, I tell them I do not mind. Akali asks me if it is all right like this, and I tell him that I want to help her. I arrange the scarf so it covers her breasts, and then start slowly to move to the door. Her eyes are closed, and she is leaning heavily on my body. "You wait…" says Akali suddenly. Her nose is full of slime. He takes a cloth and removes it gently as if she was a baby. "Now, it's okay…" he whispers, and somehow this whole scene is so ridiculous that I am not sure whether to laugh or cry. She smells, and there is blood on her hands and feet, half of her hair is shaved off, and she is leaning motionless on my body. This small act of making sure that she looks "okay" is full of love and at the same time carries a feeling of powerlessness. It is the big brother taking care of his young sister, or at least taking care of the things he has the power to. We go slowly through the hallway, she leans heavily on my body, and I feel the sweat dripping down my forehead. Someone asks, "Is she too heavy?" I shake my head. Jumare moves her feet slowly but surely as if it is an automatic unconscious motion. Her arms are around me and my arms are around her. I cannot even look up to see where we are going, just following the feet of the people in front of us. I am not able to understand how such a delicate person can be so heavy. The sweat continues to drip down my forehead. Finally, we enter a room, and there is an empty bed waiting for us. She curls herself up in the bed, and another man helps me to position her. But it is hard, she is on the edge of the bed and I am afraid that she will fall off.

"Akali" I say. He is standing behind me, but does not answer.

"Akali" I call again, "perhaps we can move her further into the bed." He does not answer. She cries and mumbles, "My head, my head" putting her hands over her forehead. "Akali", I ask, "perhaps we can give her some aspirin or something...?" I turn around and I see that he is looking at a distant place, his eyes are full of tears. He does not even seem to realize that I am talking. He looks down and sits on the floor with knees bent up to his chin, I see the tears are flowing down his cheeks. As much as I want to put my arms around him, or say something to him, I do nothing. I have been in Niger long enough to know that I cannot do that. *SemtuDum* makes it impossible. He has to gain control over his feelings and I would make matters worse by showing mine. The other people in the room are silent as well, except Banjo who tells Akali harshly, "You stand up! You are not a baby, you are a full-grown man, stand up now! You hear me? *Ndotti'en* (older men) like you do not cry if they see something difficult. Everything is the same for them. Stand up and stop crying!" Akali does not move; he does not answer. He sits on the floor for a while longer. He wipes his eyes and nose and then stands up slowly. I look at Jumare's face, try not to look at him. I just focus on her fragile beautiful face that I have known for such a long time.

The emotional stress which is part of the fear of losing someone you love is something shared beyond cross-cultural boundaries, the paralyzing fear at the thought that one may be losing this person. The talking and sharing of the person, is part of a process of healing this fear. When we arrive back to the house, I tell Akali about one time in the bush, when I was sad, and did not want to eat. I was offered something to eat, and I did not want it. Then Jumare came with her calabash and said, "Now, Mariyama and I are going to eat together and talk." And she sat by my side, handed me the spoon, and smiled and I smiled back and felt the loneliness disappear from my heart. Akali tells me about how Jumare always wants to braid his hair, and how much more skilful she is than other women. "She made my *gadaruu* (braids on the back) last time I was in the bush" he strokes over his braids at the back. This sharing of memories is soothing and healing. We are silent in a comfortable way.

We go back to the hospital late in the night. The only people staying with her are her *semaruu* (fiancé) and his older brother. I have only met him a few times. He is around the same age as I am, handsome in a delicate way. I look at his face, and I see the face of his son, Njunju, whom I know so well from the bush. When Akali goes to pray, I talk briefly to this young man. He is sitting on Jumare's bed, leaning over her, I am on a straw mat on the floor by the bed. "Look", he tells me and at the same time he is watching Jumare. "Look at God's work (*ayki Allah*)." He repeats, "Work of God", and nods almost like agreeing with himself. "We just came here to Niamey a few days ago, and then this happens." There is no anger in his voice, no bitterness. I look at his face, he is just looking at her, and I try to find a trace of such feelings but find none. He is just stating a fact to me, which is beyond emotional stirring. People I know have died, and I have seen the same thing. I have asked Akali: "Are you not upset?" only to be told: "At whom? At God? Does someone have the right to be angry with God? How can someone be angry at God?" I look at Jumare and the only thing I say to the young man, is "*Allah laamiDo mawDo* (God is powerful)." He nods, not taking his eyes off her.

"This happened just yesterday afternoon" he tells me, "I was not with her, but was told about this right after it happened, and rushed to the hospital. She looked like she was dead. We all thought she was dead. We all cried. And then she did *fintii* (to die and wake up), she woke up. She vomited a lot of times. I really thought she had died."

Akali comes back from praying, his face is serious and tired. "The man in the next room just died" he says. "They were carrying him away." He sits down on an empty bed in the room and says almost like talking to himself: "If people's time is finished, it is finished. Only God knows everything." We are silent and then he continues talking, but looking at me, "White people know what to do about everything. They open people up, put in a new heart, they do this and that, different medicines, different operations, and they take a child out of its mother stomach in order to save it. But if someone has reached the time that he has to die, then there is nothing they can do. The person only dies. All is in the power of God."

Death is with us again the day after. We are leaving the hospital, Jumare is in a better condition. I can see life moving back into her, even though she is obviously in a lot of pain. When we go out of the building, a pick-up truck backs up to the door of the hospital. Pain and horror are strange things. Even though we fear them and wish them out of our lives, we tend to want to "look" at them when we are safely removed from them. We look without thought, with curiosity, without responsibility, like there is some important information to be gained. Accidents in all places I know draw crowds of people who just want to "look." When we walk past the pick-up, that is just what I do. I "look" without thinking. There are a few soldiers in the truck, and one man is lying on his back in the truck. I do not see his face, just the motionless body, rather strangely located, the opened shirt, and the blood on his chest. And still, held in the grasp of a naive innocence, I ask Akali: "Oh, do they sometimes use army vehicles to take injured people to the hospital?" Akali looks at me and answers drily, "He is dead. He was probably shot, didn't you see that?" Of course he was dead. I just did not want to see it. A picture flashes through my eyes, of someone dying with a bullet in the chest, bleeding, believing that he will not die, praying and dying.

I am a sheltered anthropologist. My friend Akali would prefer that I never see anything, hear anything, and learn anything that is ugly and cruel. I see sadness on his face when, for some reason, he has to tell me something sad and cruel, as if he feels old and tired. But he never wants to shield me from death. Once in the bush, when we are on our way to do an interview, we pass an encampment. We approach it in order to greet the people living there. Two people are working on something in the shadow of a tree. When we approach the tree, I see something is lying beneath it. It is a small calf, just a few weeks old, with soft brown skin, and a little tail, big eyes and a wet nose. But it is lying stiffly on its side and its throat has been cut. It has been cut so deep that its head, which is pulled back, is almost severed. The earth has absorbed most of the blood, leaving only a black irregular circle. The flies form a dark moving mass on the bloody neck, feeding on it. I stop, look away, feel sick. But Akali stops me.

"No" he commands: "You look, you take a good look." His voice is so firm that I automatically obey him. He walks to the calf, lifts the head, so its dull eyes look in my direction. He says: "You never knew something like this before, you have never seen death. But this is death, and it is better that you look, that you know it well. You do not want to because then you remember that later you will die as well. You do not want to look because you want to forget that death exists." I look at the calf and for some reason its death is more real for me than that of the man in the back of the pick-up truck. Perhaps because I saw its eyes, perhaps we only know death if we look it in the eyes.

Pleasure follows suffering, just as suffering follows pleasure (*GaDa belDum nawDum no warii, gaDa nawDum belDum no warii*). The difficult dry season comes after the pleasurable wet one, and if you suffer through it, you will again reach the wet season. I am sitting by Jumare's bed, and two days have passed. She still does not talk, just expresses what she needs and she has demonstrated that she knows people, that she has suffered no serious damage. I stroke her body as I have done before in a need to express my feelings toward her. I know that this is not what a WoDaaBe would do, and I am actually rather surprised that Akali has not remarked on it. I have accepted that my need for touching is not appreciated, is not appropriate in most situations. I stroke her forehead as gently as I can, and then I move my hand thinking that she is asleep and I am just annoying her. She opens her eyes, and says "*Beldum Mariyama*. This feels good Mariyama, you know I have such a pain in my head." I move my hand back onto her forehead, and she whispers "Yes, like this."

She will never realize how much this simple moment meant to me, but it does not matter. How could she understand? How could she understand my need to show the way I can that I like her, that I like others? I do not need her to understand; just the fact that she finds pleasure in what I try to express to her is enough. The fact that for a moment we speak the same language is all I need.

GENDERED LIVES

Life works in strange ways. After Jumare's accident, I felt a change in the attitudes of the women toward me. Perhaps this was my imagination, because the relationships had been developing slowly, but I felt as though those who did not know me well, began to trust me more after the accident. Jumare's situation became a starting point in most of their conversations with me. The women asked me how she was doing, and we would discuss how tragic this had been and that God had been merciful to us.

WoDaaBe women stay together. Even though the women had been kind to me, I was an outsider. I had always been treated differently by the women I had known for a long time and who were part of Akali's family than by those who were a part of the same lineage group but did not interact daily with me. The latter had always, I thought, treated me with some suspicion. The women, however, who had known me for some time and were from different lineage groups, were more casual with me. In Niamey, I had interacted with a greater number of women from various lineages. I was thus freer to deal with various groups of people, being more able to control my own movements. In Niamey just as in the bush, I had observed that one's activities are carefully noted and talked about. Women whom I had almost never seen knew various things about me. The women informed me, almost as if they wanted to let me know that they knew, that I had stayed by Jumare's bed when she was hurt, that they had heard that I had been there every night.

At the end of the day, I like to stay with Amina and the women associated with her household. I bring my embroidery with me when I can. Her house consists of an old straw hut and a huge fenced yard surrounding it. A house will be built by the owner one day on this spot, but until that time arrives, a few WoDaaBe families have received permission to stay in the yard. It is a large space and thus popular as a meeting place. The men usually stay in the hut, while the women are in the shade of one of the trees in the yard or the wall itself. Just as in the bush, the women's work is separate but complementary to the work of men. Women are responsible for the caring of children and the home, but they also try to earn income by various means.

I got to know Amina relatively late during my fieldwork and then only in the context of Niamey. As with many other WoDaaBe women, I met Amina because I became friends with her husband. Usually, it is a difficult way of starting a friendship, because in most cases the existence of the husband shadows the relationship and is accompanied by a fear that I will complain to him about something. But Amina was different. Perhaps it was her maturity, her easiness with me, her ability to understand what I was saying, her desire to be understood herself. We became friends when I asked her if I could draw the patterns of her embroidery. She told me the names of the patterns slowly, repeated them patiently, did not laugh and give up when I repeated them incorrectly. I had met her a few times before but this time I felt a connection to her, a link that I think everyone sometimes feels for a few people. I showed her my own embroidery, that I had learned from Jumare. Amina studied my patterns carefully, kindly complimenting me on how well my stitches were done and how elegant the pattern was.

Many women I knew made money by doing embroidery. Most made traditional skirts, but others adapted the craft of embroidery to various other kinds of styles that could be more popular with the tourists. Much work is put in each article, most of them taking weeks in the making. The more intense and tight the patterns, the more beautiful the article is usually seen as being. The younger people regard the intensity of the patterns as making the article more traditional, stating that in the old times people could hardly see the dark cloth itself because of the intensity of the embroidery. When I discussed this with older people in the bush, they had different stories to tell. They claimed that in the past most, if not all, the clothing was lacking embroidery and when people started to do embroidery, the patterns were few and scattered.[62] It is interesting that the lineage that is most involved in selling embroidery in the handicrafts market has in fact only recently started doing it.

The embroidery follows certain strict rules but leaves space for imagination and creativity. Many patterns have been used over and over, but many women also imitate ones they have seen done by other women. The patterns,

---

[62] I conducted no systematic study of the development of embroidery among other WoDaaBe groups, so embroidery could have an older history among them.

both old and new ones, come from their near environment. One *surol*, represents the house, another one called *dangalel*, refers to the leg of the table in the bush. When an article has been embroidered, it is lined with white cloth. Elderly people tell me that before people started to do embroidery on their clothing, the clothing was decorated with this lining. The cloth embroided on is imported from Kano in Nigeria,[63] and quite expensive (each cloth costs around 10,000 CFA). Many women have started to use less expensive cloth, new model cloth as they call it, for the items to sell thus making more profit on the finished product. The tourists are not able to see the difference anyway. Many of the women also do embroidery to give as gifts or on the dance shirt (*henare*) of men, usually their husbands, boyfriends or brothers. The men will use it themselves, but occasionally sell it if they get the opportunity. Women generally do not earn much money for their work. They lack access to markets and the kind of connections which men have. Most often the women sell their articles to Hausa art dealers or to WoDaaBe men who have stores or who travel to perform dances in other countries. Sometimes, the women sell directly to a white person, then getting a somewhat higher price. The material used for the embroidery is expensive. Embroidery is not exclusively women's work. Many men also know how to do it and often do it for commercial purposes.

Despite the women receiving meager payment for their work, they have more income possibilities in the city than in the bush today. In the past, when milk production was more, women had greater possibilities of earning an income in the bush. The milk was the woman's commodity, probably giving her bargaining power in the pastoral economy. In today's situation, however, the herd is not sufficient for basic needs, so for most families there is not enough tradable milk and it is mostly consumed in the house, thus not giving the women income (see Wilson 1992:21). In Niamey, a woman can earn income by the embroidery, hair styling, and other small jobs. Even though these tasks are also done in the bush, a woman has to travel longer distances to find her clients, and her free time is thus much less than in the city. In addition, they are free from the time consuming task of pounding millet because they usually either buy the millet (which is prepared by machine) or

---

[63] I am told that in Niger only WoDaaBe use this kind of cloth.

they cook rice and pasta. Women stay together in a group, talking and working, helping each other. I put my own embroidery aside, and another woman, not working on anything in particular, takes it up and starts working on it, as is customary.

Working in the City

I leave the house with Amina and Mama at half past ten in the morning. They are co-wives and are out most days to do hairstyling for payment. Amina is pregnant. I guess that there is less than a month before she gives birth. She has a small boy, Lemi, who is two years old and a girl, who is around seven years old. I find Amina beautiful, but she looks older than she is. Her life has placed heavy burdens on her. She has lost two of her children, boys who were twins. One died soon after birth, the other was five years old when he died. The small boy was healthy in the morning and then around noon he had some stomach pains. He was taken very ill to hospital in the afternoon, where he died during the night. Losing a child is an experience that many WoDaaBe women share. Amina is a *teegal* wife, meaning that she was an adult when she decided to marry her husband, contrary to Mama who was promised to him when still a child as is the custom with *kobgal* wives. Their relationship is special because Amina is from a lineage that is genealogically close to Mama's lineage, but as previously stated the *teegal* wives usually come from a distance lineage. Some people have even whispered that Amina's lineage is probably too closely related to her husband's lineage for a *teegal* marriage. Mama is childless (*surbaajo*). It was only a few months ago that her husband went to her father and asked for permission to take his wife to his house, thus concluding the marriage process that had taken many years. The husband had taken the long and expensive trip to the bush once before, asking for his wife, but at that time the father had refused. Under such circumstances the father does not have to give any explanation other than stating that the time is not good. The only thing the husband can do in such a situation is to accept the decision and try again later. It is not unusual that a husband has to go more than once to try to get his wife, but it is certainly more expensive when he lives in the town, and has to travel the long way to his father-in-law. People tell me that Mama cried; she did not want to go with him. I look at them and think about the difference in age and experience between her and Amina.

When we leave this morning, Amina's daughter wants to go with us, but she is not allowed to go. Some women at the homestead hold the little girl tightly until we are out of sight. She tries to struggle and her cries follow us long after we are out of sight. We follow a small path into the bush behind the fenced yard. I have my backpack stuffed with my book and embroidery, in addition to Mama's embroidery. Mama has offered to carry Lemi on her back, to ease the pregnant woman's burden a little. She places him on her back, puts a cloth around him and ties it above her breasts. Mama is a small woman and cannot walk completely straight with him on her back. It is the hottest time of the year, the sun is high, its light burning and powerful. Mama and I hold hands and she teases me that I could never carry Lemi on my back in this heat. She is probably right. We walk up the steep hill. We are on the edge of the Katako market. An American working in Niger with development told me that people call the market of Katako, "the market of thieves." The name derives from the fact that many items sold in the market are said to be stolen and when people go through the market they are at risk of being robbed. In any case it is a poor people's market, and the WoDaaBe women prefer to go there because things are less expensive than in other markets in Niamey. We are not at the market itself, just on the edge of human habitation. All the houses are adobe but old and decaying. As usual, small children call after us, and I can see some surprise that a white women is with two WoDaaBe women. We pretend not to notice it, as it is appropriate for WoDaaBe women to be indifferent to everything. A young man greets me, and I almost greet him back, but Amina, reading my thoughts, whispers: "Don't do it!" I am still learning how to behave in a proper way.

We stop on the street in front of the walls of one house. Amina asks Mama and me to wait, while she enters in order to explain my presence. The children gather around Mama and me, making us both kind of embarrassed. We hold hands and pretend not to notice it. Amina comes to the doorway smiling, and tells us to come inside. Right within the entrance of the house, a chair has been placed for me and for Mama. We sit down, and Amina is next to us, working on the hair of the Hausa woman. The woman has given a child a coin to buy me cool water in a plastic bag. The number of people that have gathered around us, in addition to those peeking inside the doorway is almost overwhelming. I try to follow the example of my friends and pretend that I do not notice it. Mama puts Lemi down, who has been asleep, and he starts playing with the other small children. Mama asks for her embroidery and I take it out along with my own. Mama and I work on our cloths while Amina braids the Hausa woman. We work almost completely in silence, just concentrating on what we are doing. Sometimes I leave the cloth in my hands untouched and just watch Amina working. She lets nothing distract her, neither the children gathering around her nor her own son who tries to crawl into her arms. Someone brings little Lemi a plate full of rice. He is told to sit down around the plate with the other small children and eat. He gets his own spoon and seems happy. Amina tells me to take some photos if I like, "Are you sure it is alright?" I ask her, and she smiles. "Yes Mariyama. This is the house of my friend, you can take photos of everything and everyone you want." I go around and take a few photos and sit down again. "Did you take all you wanted?" she encourages me, "You don't have to be shy."

When she is finished braiding the woman, Amina tells me that I had better use the bathroom before we leave, because "the bathroom in this place is without any problems." The bathroom is fine. It is composed of two enclosures, one around a little hole in the ground and another without a hole, intended for bathing. Amina pushes me into the one intended for bathing, after having asked me what kind of "toilet" I need to do. I tell her that I can just as well use the other one, but she shakes her head and tells me that this one is much better for me. Even though I as usual do not have much privacy regarding my bodily functions, her forethought and kindness are touching. She waits with me, so firm in her role as my friend and caretaker. When we come out, Amina yells surprised. It is Lemi that has caught her attention. Within the courtyard we are in, are several small houses, each one separated from the next with a low straw mat fence. Lemi, who was starting to feel tired and impatient, had walked unnoticed into the small yard of Amina's friend, and started spilling the drinking water. He is wet from head to toes, and his small pants are dripping with water. Around him and the big, now empty, water jar is a large pool of water that he has spilt.

Before we leave I thank Amina's Hausa friend for her hospitality. I thank her in Fulfulde, which everyone finds very impressive even though they do not understand it, but Amina translates what I am saying. It is hot outside, and we walk inside the Katako market. Amina tells me that this woman has been her friend for many years, and she regularly comes and braids her hair. "How much are you paid?" I ask. Amina shakes her head, "I don't let her pay me for this, she is my friend, I never take payment from a friend. Never!" She shows me coins in the hand of Lemi and laughs, "But you see she gave Lemi some money." Lemi opens his hand a little and shows me the treasure in his hand.

From the market we enter a little area full of small shelters, they are so small that they cannot really be labeled houses. I feel that the place is familiar, but cannot situate it in my mind. "I have to braid another woman here" Amina tells me, and we walk into a small square-shaped shelter made out of thick straw mats. It is attached to an adobe house. We enter and sit down within the small space. There are some other people there. The darkness in the hut is so striking after the bright sunlight, that I only see dark shadows.

"Do you want your embroidery?" I ask Mama.

"No, I am tired" she tells me. We are all sweating and hot from the sun.

"Do you want some Coca-Cola Mariyama?" Amina asks. I tell her yes and that I have money to pay for it, and that I also want to buy for them. They do not want it, just want to have some water. Mama sends a boy to buy Coca-Cola for the anthropologist. She goes out. I close my eyes and concentrate on the sounds around me. I hear Amina stand up, because Lemi has peed on the floor. She goes out, tries to find something to wipe it up with. She comes back in.

"It is so hot today", she says, her face dripping of sweat.

"Are you tired?" she asks me.

"No, I am fine" I tell her and smile, "just resting a little." Mama comes back, Amina had sent her to buy something to eat. She is bringing a bowl full of rice.

"*Bismillah*", Amina announces, "move here, Mariyma. It is time to eat. I am sorry, there is no meat." The three of us move our chairs around the bowl. We wait for a few moments as is customary.

"You start", I tell Amina, "you are much older than I am." Amina smiles (knowing as well as I that I am probably older) and we eat silently in the heat. The Tuareg woman comes back, the same woman whom I saw before. She starts searching the ceiling of the hut for some fake hair that she wants Amina to add to her own. I do not understand her conversation with Amina, because they speak Hausa together. Mama braids the hair of a young girl. The girl kneels in the dust in front of Mama. It is a painful process, and even though the child does not cry out, I can see tears in her eyes. She moves around, and

Mama tries to put her back in place, tries to make her sit down and stay still. I have many times seen young children in the bush being braided. They scream and cry, they are held between the knees of their mothers and aunts. Sometimes they are struggling and crying the whole time. The women are firm and determined and do not give in to the crying. My assistant told me that he remembers clearly when he was braided as a child. He did not want it, and often he was so angry, that after it had been braided he would cover his hair with sand and dirt. Mama uses the same firm technique with this Tuareg child.

The woman wants to have a WoDaaBe hairstyle. Amina talks to me while she carefully separates the hair of the woman in different areas to be braided. "You see Mariyama, she likes the hairstyle of a WoDaaBe woman. She thinks it looks better than the Hausa hairstyle." An old woman enters the house, takes water from a clay jar on the floor. I move a little to the side to give her room. The flies resting on the water jar move like a black cloud with a buzzing sound. Amina has stopped talking. The old woman leaves. We hear an angry cry, and it is little Lemi in a fight. He is sitting on the floor in the corner of the hut and eating a dish of beans with a little girl. Both of them have spoons, and have been eating quietly but all of sudden they will not share the food with each other. The little girl has the plate in her hand, and tries to move it out of Lemi's reach. He cries, but she is firm. Amina resolves the conflict by giving Lemi a plate of his own, and he is happy. The little girl leans over her dish, her serious eyes looking around as though she still does not trust that someone will not try to take the plate from her.

Amina resumes braiding the woman. "You look tired" she tells me, "when I finish here, we go back."

"Are you finished with what you were going to do?" I ask.

"No, I was going to go to another place, but that can wait until tomorrow." I try to protest but it is useless.

"I am also tired", Amina says. The woman whom she is braiding is young, but her eyes are dead and cold. A man comes into the hut to sell something. They talk, and again I do not understand the conversation. I hear the word *anasara* and guess that he is asking about me. The time moves slowly, and both Mama and I just sit down doing nothing, only watching Amina working. The man is still there. It is hot, I see pearls of sweat covering Mama's face and know that it is the same with my own. The flies cover the lowest part of my shirt and my backpack. The water jar and my backpack have black patches formed by the hundreds of flies occupying the place. I leave them alone, not wanting a cloud of flies around me. There is a lot of traffic in and out of this small hut, the old woman and another man come in, then go out. I feel tired and only look at them from the corner of my eye.

Amina has finished the hairstyling. "See how beautiful this looks" she says smiling. The Tuareg woman looks in the mirror that Amina has handed her, but without smiling. She looks at her sides and at the big pile of hair in the front, fixing it a little around, and I see that this is not the first time she has this type of hair style. Amina laughs and says, "You see people love WoDaaBe hair." She is correct, I have seen several times in down town Niamey, women wearing WoDaaBe braids, or some stylized version of their braids. It looks strange to me, and I have tried to ask some WoDaaBe why they think these women want to style their hair like this. They do not know of course. They guess that it is because it is beautiful.

When we leave the small hut, a man is waiting in the doorway for the Tuareg woman. It is refreshing to step out after having been in the hut for so many hours. The sun is lower in the sky and thus not as hot. I look at the place around me, and I suddenly remember when I was here last time. I was going with Akali to visit a group of WoDaaBe who rented a small adobe house not far away. The house was old and without electricity, but three men rented it together for their families. It cost only 7,000 CFA per month, and was thus easily affordable. During the day they could stay in the courtyard doing handicrafts work and at night they had a place to sleep. I also remember that Akali did not like to go with me there because there were so many prostitutes living in the same area. I remember walking this road with him. He was embarrassed, and rushed through because he felt it was not at all good to take me to that kind of place. Suddenly it seemed obvious to me that the Tuareg woman being styled as a WoDaaBe woman was a prostitute; the men coming and going, probably waiting for us to leave. Everything seemed to indicate this, but still I was not quite sure. I was curious to know if I was correct but I was not sure how to ask my WoDaaBe friends this question, afraid of being offensive and wrong.

"This woman is your friend?" I ask Amina.

"Yes" she tells me, "she is my friend, I have known her for a long time."

"She lives in this house?" I ask, "...this house is a little different from most houses I have seen…" Amina becomes a little distant, smiles, as if all of sudden she also does not know what to say to me.

"Does she have a husband?" I ask, and Amina gives me a response after a short silence, "No, it is only her one…" Her voice fades out, it seems as if she is leaving something unsaid.

"Is it not difficult for her not having a husband?" I ask, and Amina's distant look grows stronger in her eyes. She looks at me, asking, "Do you know what work she does? Or perhaps you don't know?"

I am hesitant, "Maybe… she is a woman who sells her body…?" Amina relief is almost surprising.

"Yes, that is what she does" she almost calls out, "You know that some women do this, don't you? You know that." I suspect that she had feared that I had never known that some women had such an occupation, and that she did not want to be the one to explain it to me. Her relief is great, and perhaps it has also to do with the feeling of our sharing the same world to some extent. We talk about prostitution and Amina's and Mama's reaction to it is one of pity and disgust.

"Her house smells", Mama says.

"Yes, it is dirty", Amina says. "The children are her sister's, she herself is not able to have children. Only God knows why. But the children are filthy too and they grow up in this environment. You remember, Mariyama, you asked about the camel whip?" I remember that I had wondered what it was doing there.

"She uses it on the kids, she beats them and scares them from entering the house when there are men with her." Amina feels that worst of all is the fact that the old woman, the mother, knows about the whole thing. She eats the food that her daughter earns by selling her body.

"You saw when her mother came in?" Amina asks me. "She knows about this, but she does not say anything." I am not sure if Amina is more shocked by the daughter letting her mother know about her occupation or the mother for not trying to force the daughter to change her ways. This connects of course to the WoDaaBe element of shame, *semtuDum*, which is so strong between parents and their children.

What evokes my interest is why the Tuareg woman wanted her hair styled as a WoDaaBe woman. I ask Amina about it and she tells me surprised but laughing: "Oh that is because she gets more clients this way. The clients just come and come if she looks like a WoDaaBe woman. If she has a Hausa hairstyle they do not come." I feel confused, finding this rather distressing and ask, "Do they think that she is a WoDaaBe woman, or do they realize that she just has her hair that way?"

"I am not sure." Amina responds, "I think they know she is a Tuareg, perhaps they don't care. Didn't you hear what the man who sold the jewelry said when my friend tried on the earrings after I had finished styling her hair?" I shake my head. "My friend asked him: 'Do I now look like a WoDaaBe woman?' and he said: 'Now you are a WoDaaBe woman'."

Dupire writes in 1960, that men of other ethnicities cannot possess a WoDaaBe woman. WoDaaBe women conform to endogamous rules of marriage within their lineage, and there is a great taboo on a woman having sexual relations with someone who is not a WoDaaBe.[64] "That kind of woman would be worth nothing", WoDaaBe men occasionally told me with disgust. Probably nothing would be as shameful for a lineage group as one of "their" women selling her body to ethnic others. Yet WoDaaBe women are independent, as previously emphasized, engaging in various sexual relationships prior to their marriage, traveling in groups – without men – to neighboring countries.

---

[64] It is seen as less significant if a man has sexual relations with non-WoDaaBe women although it would still be significant from what ethnic group the woman came.

DANCING IN NIAMEY

WoDaaBe dance performances have become an annual event in Niamey during the period at the end of *Ramadan*. The end of Ramadan is celebrated all over the city, people being generous and in a festive mode. One of my neighbors gives me fat sheep leg in sauce, sharing food as is customary.

The dance is organized by different WoDaaBe lineages outside Niamey's sports stadium. It goes on for several days, starting in the afternoon until the sun sets.

The different WoDaaBe lineages located in Niamey meet the day before the dance in order to discuss various aspects relating to the event. Prior to that meeting the heads of the lineage factions meet. The "chief" of dance, *Maj-samari*, emphasizes to the younger people that they have to be patient and not get into conflict with members of other lineages. People discuss payments that have to be offered by those who want to photograph the dance, those who desire photos usually being white people (*anasara*). The older men stress that the younger men should hand the money to them, for them to redistribute later. Afterwards, a WoDaaBe friend whispers to me that younger people frequently put the money away without telling anyone, because they know that the elders would also keep the money for themselves.

In the late afternoon, these different lineage segments gather in front of the sports stadium. Arriving mostly in small groups, they join their own lineage faction, forming small circles. The factions discuss among themselves and then join those belonging to the same main lineage, forming two groups representing the two major lineages (Degere'ul and Alidjam). The men sit down forming large circles and discuss the upcoming event. Even though no one protested when I participated marginally in the lineage faction discussion earlier that day, I am clearly not supposed to enter this discussion. My friend Bermo, from the Deger'ul lineage, asks me to sit down with him a few feet away and rest because after all, he explains kindly, they are only "talking." I understand his polite way of telling me that I am not welcome in this group, knowing that it would be almost impossible for him to include me because most of the men are strangers to me, and, importantly, belong to other lineage factions than he does. Bermo and I sit down by some hard rocks at the end of the asphalt, and another friend joins us. The three of us watch the people discussing a few feet away, talking among ourselves. After discussing for a while, the *Alidjam* group stands up and walks toward the *Degere'ul* who have also stood up. The men in their best clothing with turbans carefully wrapped around their heads approach each others. They shake hands and greet each other formally.

"I am afraid of these people", Buuwa confesses to me as we watch the two groups approach each other. I ask him why rather surprised. He looks as if he is stating the obvious: "Because these are not my people." My eyes flicker back to the group; the members of the two main lineages have greeted formally and merge into one large unified group. Their discussion is brief and the gathering soon breaks up. Buuwa and others explain to me that the dance directors, each representing a specific lineage group, will come together regularly during the dance performances to discuss problems and issues relating to the dance. These meetings are important, as they explain, for the dance to become a success, maintain cohesion within the group and avoid embarrassing conflicts between different lineage groups within the area of Niamey.

Going to the Dance

The dancing has already started and we are late for this second day of the dance. The men left for the dance a while ago and the sun is moving lower in the sky. One of the girls impatiently tells the others to hurry because we are late; we should go before the dance is over. The last women finish dressing while the others start arranging for our departure. The house is a straw hut, standing on a vacant building lot. All the valuables are placed in a small chest that a Hausa woman living close by has promised to keep while we are away.

We are in festival clothing, my companions wearing embroidered blue striped Nigerian cloth used for festivals occasions, wrapped around their waists. The embroidery on the cloth is their own work and they let it face inward to protect it from the dust and the sun. My clothing is arranged for me in order to make it look better and we are ready to enter the public eye. Inne, who is staying in Niamey for a few weeks for the first time, places her head-

At a lineage dance festival in the bush, a man carefully wraps his turban to prepare for the dance.

scarf around the upper part of my body. She is beautiful, embodying all the qualities that WoDaaBe value: graceful, proud and reserved when men are around. Our friendship started on my initial arrival to Niger one and half years ago, and being from the same lineage group that had welcomed me to their homes in the bush, she feels responsible for me even in this new context, the city. Her arrival in the city is due to her being selected along with a few other people by a team from a European Cultural Institution, to do dance performances in various European countries. Like the rest of the group she does not know when or for how long. She waits in the city for the European organizers to give them further information on the departure day. Her friend, Gintodo, is also there for the same purpose, though having stayed somewhat longer. The other women are younger, and some have stayed longer in the city.

The sports stadium is not far away. We walk fast, following the 'fragmented' road. The sun is hot and I feel the heat rising from the asphalt. The sounds of clapping and dancing are clearly audible from the stadium. A few young Hausa men pass us on the road and call out some remarks, some simply greeting us. My friends whisper in my ear: "Don't say anything, don't give them an answer." We pass them by; looking through them as if they were invisible.

Small groups of WoDaaBe men stay in front of the dancing area, talking, resting and dressing up for the dance. Further away the male dancers have gathered in a large circle dancing and singing. They are difficult to see because of the crowd that surrounds them. People of other ethnicities are present; some young men sell water and snacks. We stop a little away from the area before entering it and arrange our clothing for the last time. I continue at the same speed as before, but Inne firmly stops me. "Slowly", she tells me, jerking my hand firmly, forcing me to a complete stop. She looks me strictly in the eyes. I look down and we walk as appropriate, unavoidably passing groups of people watching us with curiosity. I can't help hearing Inne commenting with dissatisfaction, "Look at us, walking for everyone to look at."

We sit down in the shade of a tree side by side observing the people around us. "Would you like some water?" Inne asks me and buys me a small plastic bag with cool water. I bite the corner of the bag and suck the water. Several WoDaaBe women have gathered at a particular spot on the edge of the dancing area and we hear their laughter and occasional singing. "Come here",

Inne says, "they are going to dance." Inne is a talented singer and often leads the women's dancing and singing in the bush. I follow her hesitantly and she drags me into the center of the women's group, the majority of whom I do not know. Most of them are dressed in dark clothes, far from as spectacular and expensive as the men's clothing. Their shirts and skirts are often dark blue, sometimes colored by indigo, only their headscarves being in bright colors. Some have a folded cloth on their head, giving protection from the sun. Many carry their youngest child on their back; the older children probably playing around. It is hot; the sweat runs down my forehead. The women laugh and talk and then one starts to sing. The others clap their hands, creating a rhythmic music for the song. The fore-singer sings, and then other women, forming a chorus (*limtol*) repeating her words. Occasionally, one woman breaks away from the circle, entering into it clapping with a different rhythm, faster and stronger (*gamkii*). Her dance consists of moving her feet in abrupt, powerful movements, clapping in rhythm, not unlike the dance movements of the men.

Someone pushes my back encouraging me to enter the circle but I move closer to Inne. I feel shy and vulnerable, as if in a place I should not be. I have participated in similar events in the bush and it was natural there but this dance is taking place in the middle of Niamey. Inne and my other friends, who have never stayed in Niamey for an extended period, do not appear to perceive this as any different from our dances in the bush. I fear, however, that WoDaaBe women living in Niamey will find it rather strange if I, an *anasara*, am participating and I shy away from their gaze. I am at least sure that all non-WoDaaBe will see it as rather odd. Standing in the middle of the women's circle, I feel somehow rather foolish, dressed like a WoDaaBe woman and hoping that someone, Western, who knows me, does not walk by. All of sudden my clothing feels like masquerade, as if I am pretending to be someone who I am not. At the same time, I am with my friends and as such I do belong just as much inside the circle as outside it where I know no one, I lean closer to Inne, taking comfort and satisfaction in being with her.

The women's dance did not last for long and never became intense and powerful. After a little while the women seemed to lose interest and the dance dissolved. The day before the women also started dancing but that dance also dissolved quickly. During the following days, the women tried to dance a few times but always faded into the role of observers. WoDaaBe men do not observe them dancing, nor would they in the bush. Other spectators come and look at the dance for a few moments before moving on to see the men's dance, where people have to push their way around to see glimpses of the dancers; the audience being constituted mostly of WoDaaBe men and women, but also Hausa, Tuaregs and Westerners. I am with the women and thus the men generally do not approach me, with the exception of men belonging to the same lineage group as the women I am with. Inne, Nasara and I go to the circle of the male dancers and we push our way through so as to get closer. The dancers are doing a *rume rume*, where they form a regulated circle, standing side by side. The dance starts with a fore-singer (he is called *limtoowo*), who sings a *limtol*. He sings alone and then moments before his voice fades away, the whole group in the circle starts singing as well. Then the dance starts for real. The dancers start moving sideways (*gozul*), clapping (*hello*) to create a rhythm for the dance. Sometimes one or more dancers enter the circle, clapping in a faster rhythm than the other dancers. For those observing the dance there is a constant struggle to stay in their place, people push, try to get as close to the dancers' backs as possible. It is hot because people stand so close together. Inne never lets go of her hold on my hand.

The dance directors and a few other older men usually stand within the circle of dancers. Now there are three Westerners also situated in the circle. A man, with a dark mustache, wears a large WoDaaBe hat on his head and a woman keeps close to him wearing a WoDaaBe young girl's (*surbaajo*) skirt and having the same kind of hat as the man. The man and the woman look almost embarrassed standing there. The third person carefully places himself at a distance away from them. He is smiling, standing with his back very straight, full of confidence like I would imagine an explorer from the past. He takes endless numbers of photos with a camera and a video camera, which he has probably paid the fee for because no one protests. The two women accompanying me do not and would not suggest that I enter the circle. The previous day when accompanying my male friends – craft-producers making a living from selling objects to tourists and expatriates or for selling in distant countries – they suggested that I should go within the circle to get 'better photos.'

The dance is over when the sun sets. It is twilight when I walk home with the small group of people from "my" lineage. I am holding Inne and Nasara's hands. One of my male friends is teasing me, saying "Well Mariyama, let's now go home", meaning that we should go together to his place. The girls laugh when I say participating in the joke: "I don't have time now... you have to be patient...." It is dark when we reach the small hut. Dro draws out a straw mat for me, I sit down looking into the darkness while people change their clothing.

Classification of Dance Performances among the WoDaaBe

The *juulde* dance was one of many dance events I attended during my fieldwork, observing large formal gatherings of diverse lineage groups as well as small dance events participated in by a scattered group of family members. For some reason, this particular event described above, which I attended at the end of my research, drew out stronger the various conflicting issues that had interested and puzzled me before. The disjunction and flows of people and social locations – its enactment in the city, participation of WoDaaBe friends who had stayed extensively in the city and those who were not accustomed to it, Hausa and Western audiences – created a moment where these issues were better spelled out, if only for the ethnographer. By emphasizing its location in the city as important, I am not trivializing the array of changes that WoDaaBe identity and society have undergone, nor indicating that such performances take place in some kind of "purer" form in the bush. Performance enactment in real time, as argued by Fabian (1990b), is what always gives it meaning for those participating and observing.

Celebration of common ethnicity was clearly an important issue for WoDaaBe participants at the *juulde* performance. Ethnicity has been much emphasized in discussions of these dances in the popular press but, as argued by many theorists, performances can be seen as constituting one way in which groups express their ethnicity. Ethnic performances, along with other factors, can be seen as important in maintaining ethnic boundaries between groups in Fredrik Barth's sense (1969); affirming and establishing boundaries between self and others. My discussion here stresses the importance of identifying WoDaaBe dance performances in general as not only being about ethnicity but simultaneously constituting various other kinds of boundaries and identifications.

Ethnicity itself has to be understood within a broad political-historical framework and in this case it is important to acknowledge WoDaaBe increased economic marginalization within the Niger nation state. The performance identification as ethnic by participants could thus be intensified by the WoDaaBe general sense of marginalization, probably leading to a growing need for strengthening their difference from other groups. Changed political circumstances of a particular group can, as scholars have pointed out, lead to intensified ethnic borders (see Werbner 2001). The placement of the *juulde* performance in the city – the city not only constituting a sign of WoDaaBe increased poverty but also of negotiation of various relationships – could make the dance become particularly meaningful as a sign of WoDaaBe ethnicity to themselves and others. WoDaaBe men, many who seek work or clients for products on a day-to-day basis in order to feed their families, recreate themselves at the performance by colorful clothing that is identified as distinctively WoDaaBe, gathering together and demonstrating in a very visible way their presence in Niamey and within the nation state Niger.

Diversity and Factions within Unity

Yet the interpersonal interactions of WoDaaBe within the *juulde* dance reflect a more complex picture than only displays of ethnicity. When the lineage groups had no audience or interacted unobserved by the audience, the values manifested were not ones of unified ethnicity but difference and disputes, dance performances with both main lineages often conceptualized by WoDaaBe as war between these parties (see Paris 1997:73–74). In Niamey the preparation prior to the dance, i.e., the separate meetings of different lineage groups, aimed at creating cohesion and strength within each group, reflecting and reconstituting borders while simultaneously trying to create a bridge between the oppositional lineages. The preparation of the dance thus indicates that WoDaaBe conceptualize themselves as one coherent group in only certain contexts while in other contexts they see themselves as constituted by "different" people. The meeting of the two main lineage groups in front of the stadium the day prior to the dance, visualizes in a powerful way the differentiation between them. People grouped in two separate circles slowly approaching in a formal way. Buuwa's statement that he is afraid of these people because they are not his people, speaks of the dance not only as a demonstration and celebration of the ethnicity of WoDaaBe, of sameness, but as involving complicated interaction where the underlying themes are competition and "otherness." Thus, within the same performance elements of celebration of common ethnic identity (shown to the outside) co-exist with the strengthening of difference within that group (taking place through internal interaction).

Another example can be given in regard to this. A person I simply call Gorko, observed a wealthy white man who came to the dance. The man went to dancers preparing themselves, taking a few photos of them. The dancers requested payment for the photos. He refused, becoming angry, but after a brief argument he walked up to Gorko, standing next to the dancers and handed him 10,000 CFA (at the time of my study 500 CFA was about 1$) without saying anything, went back to his car and left. Gorko was from a different lineage than the dancers and had just stood there by coincidence. The dancers became angry with him for accepting the money they felt they had earned. Gorko, however, was very pleased with the whole incident, telling me that this man clearly did not like the other lineage, preferring members of Gorko's lineage group. I suspected that the man had simply not realized that these were individuals from different and rival lineage groups. It is possible, in my view, that when the man saw that he was in trouble, he sought out someone who looked as if he had authority (Gorko looked like a high ranking person) and gave that person the money in order to free himself from further disputes.

Gender constitutes other types of borders, interacting with ethnicity and lineage affiliation. WoDaaBe dances are, as my description indicates, gendered displays, where the roles of men and women are clearly spelled out. The *juulde* dances consist furthermore mainly of younger men and women, age being a salient feature of WoDaaBe social organization. WoDaaBe male dance performances generally involve the dances of young men. Older men have authority in organizing the dance performances and regulating them, as demonstrated in the meeting of the smaller lineage groups. Their demand to be "given" the money for photographs, to redistribute it later, tells of their claim to authority, and the younger men's actual not handing them the money tells of their non-confrontational resistance to that authority. Social actors seek to capture and appropriate authenticity to various ends. WoDaaBe themselves are, as previously indicated, actively involved in marketing their ethnicity by the handicraft production and simultaneously the

At the Niamey-based dance festivals, the spectators are outside the ring of dancers.

Niger State can be seen as having economic gains from marketing its "authentic" inhabitants, to increase tourist revenues.

Turning to the issue of gender, the *juulde* primarily privileged the cultural representations of maleness, because even though including women's dances, those performances were marginal, not drawing spectators or attention, nor taking a great deal of space in terms of time or location. Masculinity can be seen as expressed in dance performances, in combination with power and vitality as demonstrated in their internal dynamic of competition between different lineage groups. Men emphasized to me the physical difficulties of the dance, which requires endurance and strength. Even though the performances visualize WoDaaBe stereotypical views of maleness and beauty, those who are seen as good dancers do not, according to my information, automatically have high esteem in the group as a whole nor are they seen as beautiful without the context (and makeup and clothing) of the ceremonies. Men told me that some individuals who look impressive with their makeup were not seen as handsome without it nor were they necessarily popular among women. It is still likely that good performance in dances is important to increase a man's general prestige even though not necessarily translating into popularity among the opposite sex, but images in the popular press often imply dance performances are rituals of marriage or sexual relations. WoDaaBe marriages are much more complex matters than being reduced to encounters at such gatherings (see also Paris 1997:74). Even though seeing gender as an important aspect of the ceremony, I do not see the women as the main objects of the men's dances, but I find it more important to underline the competition between different men as crucial in terms of power and prestige, in connection with the ceremonies' importance in playing out internal differentiation and ethnic boundaries with other groups. Occasionally women still leave their lineage group of origin to marry someone from another group (*teegal* marriage). Anthropological discourses of lineage organizations have generally, in the spirit of Evans-Pritchard's classical study, privileged the male point of view of the system. On one occasion when I am at the dance with Inne, I state aloud – more speaking to myself than anything else – that most of the names I know are of people from two specific lineage factions. Inne looks at me and answers without interest as if stating the obvious: "That is because this is your house." Even though (and perhaps because) said casually, I feel a significant meaning to be attached to these words, and perhaps more so because they come from a woman, as women have different and more fluid relations to their lineage than men. Women are born into their lineage but can leave their lineage of origin, as well as (even though rarely) their ethnicity by marrying into other groups. Their children and families can thus become part of "others", be it different ethnicities or different lineage groups. Underlying Inne's comment is the assumption that these individuals at the center of my work are my "house." A house is not only a place where someone stays but space loaded with obligations and relationships. The house is a place that I belong to, a place that "owns", from a certain perspective, its members. I observed earlier that Inne almost pulled me away when men from different lineage groups tried to talk to me, not wanting me to speak to these "other" people. Being proud of her house, she knows that it is not considered proper for a WoDaaBe woman to stand in a crowd talking to a man from another lineage group. She pulls me away because in her view these people are not part of my "house" (lineage). Standing next to her and hearing her words, it strikes me that if I decided to study other WoDaaBe groups by living with them for extensive periods, she and probably many other female friends would see me as leaving my "house." I think that the action would only be comprehensible in the context that I was leaving my house, like a *teegal* wife, in order to belong to "other" people in another place. I find this comment important in this context because I think it both reminds us of how ethnicities or other kinds of groupings "recruit" individuals within their ranks in somewhat contradictory ways (even though my ethnicity was not WoDaaBe, I was still part of this 'house'). This "recruiting" has obviously gendered aspects, translating into the fact that men's and women's relationships to groups differ. Within the dance performances, gendered divisions of WoDaaBe social structure become evident in various ways, gender identities thus being confirmed and recreated.

Judging from people's interactions with me – not only being an ethnographer but a white Westerner – the dance furthermore seemed to be perceived differently by WoDaaBe migrant workers staying extensively in the city than those in Niamey merely for a few days stay. The longer people had stayed in Niamey, the more strongly they conceptualized the dance as an exclusive WoDaaBe performance, as having firm ethnic boundaries, in which an audience of other ethnicities had a specific role. WoDaaBe male dances in the bush have an audience as well, constituted by their families and lineage group, which have to some extent a different role than an audience of different ethnicity. As a part of the audience of the *juulde* dance in Niamey, individuals were supposed to have a passive role, and as an *anasara* one is expected to take photos and pay for them, even dressing in some articles of WoDaaBe clothing. The WoDaaBe (such as Inne and Gintudo) who had seldom experienced a dance in a multi-ethnic context saw the "audience" simply as a tiresome distraction rather than seeing them as having a particular role in the whole performance (i.e., the role of the audience), which was completely different to how they had talked about the WoDaaBe audience at dance performances in the bush. As their friend, I was welcome, and as a guest having stayed in their house, I was expected to participate in the gathering in a similar way as they did. I was expected to dress up as they would, i.e., they did not want me to dress that way in order to look like a WoDaaBe, but because they wanted me to look nice and they thought of course that their own way of dressing was nice.

For those WoDaaBe who had stayed in Niamey for a long time, with an extensive relationship with other ethnic groups in the city, the performance seemed to hold a positive and valuable opportunity to express the meaning of their ethnicity to themselves and to others. The performance demonstrates for them that being a WoDaaBe is to have distinctive traditions (*finatawi*), which attract the interest of others. Individuals, who regularly wander around the streets, selling tea, water, or jewelry, gather in their best clothing with their lineage group, experiencing a sense of belonging and self-worth through these performances. The *juulde* dance in Niamey constitutes a celebration of the common identity of the WoDaaBe, a demonstration of strength and the living tradition of the group.

DESIRE AND IDENTITY

"A harna belado amma a harnata mo koDei"

This proverb states that someone who is hungry can be made full, while someone who has *koDei* will never get enough. The term *koDei* can perhaps best be described as desire or even greed in English, it refers to the longing for something. Someone who has *koDei* can desire physical things, food or riches, but also power and prestige. In WoDaaBe society such feelings or desires are seen as a negative part of a person's personality. Someone with *koDei* is more likely to become a thief, cheater or murderer. In some sense, someone who has *koDei* is the antithesis to a person that follows *mbodagansi* and is thus characterized by sufficiency and reserve. For some WoDaaBe, an elderly WoDaaBe man tells me, the city has led to the strengthening of their *koDei*. The city has spoiled them, making some men develop a desire for objects and money. He tells me that these men do not share their wealth with other WoDaaBe – as would be proper for a WoDaaBe – but keep it to themselves. They do not care that some are poor and have not been as lucky as them. In addition, their methods of gaining clients are indecent because they follow *anasara* people down the streets trying to get them to buy their objects. Hence, they have adopted the way of "ethnic others" to interact with people, a way that is utterly non-WoDaaBe. What makes this observation even more interesting is the fact that the man telling this to me is a jewelry maker himself who has had various engagements with *anasara* (white people). I had observed him desiring wealth and trying to gain money through different means from his clients and myself. Yet, this does not make his comment invalid, since many share this thought. My friend Akali frequently expressed concern about the danger of corruption of WoDaaBe solidarity due to the element of money, and especially the development of lack of co-operation facing people during these difficult times. "WoDaaBe are few", he says. "We should stay together, share with each other, be happy for the success of each other because such is the way not only of *mbodagansi*, our tradition, but also the right conduct for God."

The city provides fertile soil for the development of *koDei*. Even though the WoDaaBe stay together, the city does mark a break with the life of the bush. Women are further away from their own families than when living with their husbands in the bush, and the men are separated from the guidance and authority of their fathers. Some men start aiming at *nganayka koltal*, the cultivation of their outer appearance, as expressed by Kala'i when reflecting on the young men in the city. The city offers new things and new temptations, along with a knowledge that is different from that of one's father. As Akali tells me, a man who respects his father and thus follows how WoDaaBe should behave, should never contradict his father even though the father is talking about something about which the son knows better. Only little by little without ever challenging the father's authority and experience, can the son try to inform his father.

KoDei is also the desire for power over other people, to stand above others. A young man tells me that he wants to learn new things, to learn to read and write, travel and see different things. He adds that he would still make his heart indifferent to it. If not, he could develop *koDei* to these new experiences, wishing for more, some things that would never be fulfilled.

The Dances

The colonial government and the present day African governments have requested the WoDaaBe to dance for various "folkloric" displays, as well as for tourists and visiting guests (Burnham 1994:xii). These performances are conducted for various occasions, such as cultural festivals, for development institutions or even private gatherings of the wealthy. At Niger's independence in 1959, a group of WoDaaBe performed dances at the festival. One European observer describes the dance in the following way: "All of those who were present, both black and white, agreed on pronouncing that these were the most amazing people they had ever seen."[65] (IST: Wenek n.d.:7). WoDaaBe are seen as attractive people, "good" to look at, and as decoration

---

[65] "Tous ceux qui étaient présents Noir et Blancs, ont éte d'accord pour déclarer que c'étaient les gens les plus étonnant qu'ils aient jamais vus" (IST: Wenek n.d.:7).

At a large gathering in the bush, the dancers have lined up in front of the spectators.

at a gathering having to do with "high" culture. It is impossible to say when the interest of the whites in the dances of the WoDaaBe started, but it probably dates to the early colonial period. An old WoDaaBe man tells stories of white people coming into the bush and asking for dance performances as well as vague stories of individuals that traveled to far away places to show dances. He recounts: "If white people came, they asked for the *hakkimidjo*, and people took them to *hakkimidjo*.[66] They would tell him that they wanted to take photos of people dancing. *Hakkimidjo* went and gathered people and then white people came and took all the photos they wanted and paid some money for it" (September 1997). Westerners do not seem to have been of particular importance for WoDaaBe in those times. Dupire describes in her research conducted in 1962 skin pigmentation with the terms *bodejo* (red), *bamalejo* (dark-red, a term generally not used by the ethnic group I studied) and *balejo* (black). Dupire mentions that the more sedentary Fulani use the fourth

---

66 *Hakkimidjo* has the same meaning as *ardo*, referring to the traditional authority of the WoDaaBe. In colonial times this was the highest authority found within the WoDaaBe group itself.

term *danejo* to refer to white skin color (Dupire 1962a:7), but her discussion implies that WoDaaBe did not use such a term. The minimal contact which WoDaaBe in Tchin-Tabaraden had with colonial powers at this time, can explain the lack of such identification at the time of Dupire's research.

Today, the interest in the dance has been growing, especially in the former colonial power France but also in other countries such as Belgium and Holland. In addition, an attempt has been made to take a large dance group to the United States but those WoDaaBe I talked to told me that that had been without success.[67] Often the same people, having established a connection with whites, go again and again on dance trips to different countries. Even though many WoDaaBe from various lineages desire to go on such a trip, most of those who participate in paid performances are those who have something to do with the handicraft work. This is probably because they have more contact with whites and are more accessible. Obviously, it would be harder for a BoDaaDo in torn, dirty work clothing, carrying water, to get such an assignment, than a BoDaaDo who has a shop selling distinctively marked WoDaaBe products, specially directed toward pleasing the client. For contemporary WoDaaBe, the category "white" (or Westerner) has thus become increasingly important since Dupire's research, and is usually referred to as *anasara* or, less frequently, *Turankedjo*. Interestingly, the use of the term *anasara* is not completely coherent, in some cases it implies Westerner and is even occasionally used about Afro-Americans, even though some WoDaaBe directly stated in interviews with me that the term could not be used about people with dark skin color.[68] The term is also often used about Asians, who are like Westerners associated with power, probably due to their similar kind of presence in Niger within the realm of development institutions and tourism. The concept *anasara* does not thus completely correspond to Western conceptualizations of whiteness nor to Westerners, even though it is most often used in such a way. The concept is, to some extent, used as an ethnic term, which was reflected when people talked about my "relatives" (*bandiraaBe*), referring to English or French speaking Westerners, or when defining my skin color as "red" like their own skin, which contradicts of course their claims of me being *anasara* and thus different from them.

---

[67] I have this information from the WoDaaBe themselves at the time when I did my fieldwork.
[68] In cases where people had interacted with Westerners, seen as people of color, it was somewhat inconsistent whether or not they were referred to as *anasara*. In some cases, WoDaaBe said to me when talking about someone: 'She is an *anasara*, but not a true one because she is black.'

The dances, both at home and abroad, are not well paid, but can provide an important opportunity to earn a considerable amount of money, the selling of handicrafts being a part of such performances. Many WoDaaBe, however, point out that they do not have enough money to buy things to sell. Individuals occasionally sell a few cows in order to buy material or artifacts to sell. Personal items such as clothing, swords, and hats are also in great demand. I saw men give up items that they had earlier told me that they wanted their sons to inherit and which they had inherited from their fathers. These individuals feel that they cannot afford to refuse the money that they can get for these items. A man of around thirty, showed me his *deDo*, the leather skirt that men use for the dance. He had nothing more valuable than this, he told me, because in it are embodied memories of his life as a young man. He wanted his young son to get it, but one year later he handed it over to a friend going to Holland for a dance performance, merely asking him to sell it for a high price. My young friend Sollare desired the beautiful top that young girls wear. Finally, she acquired one from her friend,[69] a half-made top that I helped her to finish once when staying in the bush. She was proud and beautiful in it, but after a month she gave it to a man going to Belgium for a dance trip. She did not want to but was pressured by her grandmother and her mother who desperately needed the money.

The dance itself has to be adapted to the needs of the market. Dances (except the *yake*) usually take place with the dancers forming a circle facing inwards. As I have previously described, the observers are located outside the circle. In a commercial dance, however, people perform the dance by lining up and facing the audience, in order to respond to the demands of those paying for such shows. Commercial dancing also involves the dancing of people who have children old enough to participate themselves which is not usually done. Women, furthermore, dance with men in commercial dances, which is generally not done among the lineage group in question. When asking people why they included both age groups and genders in the commercial dances, I was told that this was not a true dance and that the whites wanted it done like this.

---

[69] She had just become pregnant and could thus no longer use it. This top is only used by *surbaajo* (a woman without a child) because as the WoDaaBe explain, it is not beautiful for a woman with sagging breasts (i.e., one who has had a child) to wear them.

The younger boys look at the dancers with admiration.

Even though some of those who travel to dance performances in foreign countries are able to invest their money in things such as housing or cows, many do not seem to be earning much. It is hard to acquire information from people regarding how much money they earned and how they spent it,[70] but some patterns can be observed. Many dancers returning from such a trip were young men, suddenly wearing fancy shoes, pants and coats, with a large new radio. If lucky, they had earned a considerable amount of money, and should thus have be able to buy cows. People are of course generous with their relatives, but a great deal of the money seems to go into consumption items, such as tea, fancy clothing, expensive turbans, radio batteries and jewelry. The animal that I observed as usually being bought first for theswe earnings is the camel, i.e., an animal that is not of as great use to the home as many other animals but desired by young men as a source of prestige and to facilitate visits within in the bush. Finally, when the money is all finished the radio

---

[70] People are not willing to share this information with other WoDaaBe from the same lineage, and thus obviously not very willing to share it with me, even though some people gave me truthful information.

is sold at a small price. One man had three times in the recent past made such trips to foreign countries, every time buying radios and consumption items. His income had never been sufficient for anything else. It was only after the last trip that he managed to buy one cow, but had to sell it within a year to cover debts that he had accumulated.

Those who organized such trips during the time I spent in Niger seemed reluctant to give out information to those they recruited regarding simple factors such as when the trip would take place, for how long, when the travelers would return, how many performances would be conducted, etc. A friend of mine, whose home is in the bush, took his two wives with him to Niamey because he had not received information regarding when to leave or how long he could expect to stay in the foreign country. He waits a long time in Niamey before finally getting information regarding the group departure time. He then asks me whether he can tell his wives that they can come to me to borrow money for basic necessities, i.e., if he stays longer than he suspects. He has given them some money, but is afraid that perhaps the trip will take a long time, and they will not have enough for food. Other people from the same lineage are also going, and are thus in the same situation, and there is little extra money to borrow from the rest of the lineage because it has been spent on items to buy in the foreign country. "You should ask how long the trip takes", I tell my friend, but he is afraid to do so, both because he does not find it a polite thing to do, and probably also because he fears his question could be taken as a sign of dissatisfaction and that he could thus be dismissed from the team. When he leaves he still does not know how long he will stay.

When his group returns a month later, they look pale and very tired. The explanation is simple: they have been performing every day (except for two days) since they left. Sometimes there is one performance a day, sometimes two. "That is a lot of work", I say hesitantly. Another friend who did not go with this group, but has previously been on such a trip says, "Well this is nothing, once when I went, we were taken straight from the airport to perform at some place. Sometimes we had to perform two or three times per day." No complaints are directly verbalized. How can they be? Many people do not realize that those who recruit people to perform dances are highly paid individuals who do not have to pay the cost of the dance from their own pockets. WoDaaBe in many cases do not realize that it is not purely altruistic goals that are at work. Infrequently, some edge of criticism can be detected. One such incident had to do with photographs. Interestingly enough, those who organize the dance abroad also own the rights over all photographs taken of the performance,[71] selling such photos for a high price to the visitors. One man told me that he had seen a photo of himself and really wanted it. He offered to buy it from the organizer who said it would be given to him later. "But she never did" he tells me and smiles drily.[72]

In many cases, the WoDaaBe expectations of such trips are high, without accurate information about what the selling opportunities will be like. The group I previously discussed, returned a month later, many deeply disappointed. They had originally been told that the tour would take at least two months and that there would be plenty of opportunities to sell their handicrafts, but the trip took only one month and the selling opportunities were not as expected. The majority of the dancers came back with most of their items, especially their own hand-made jewelry and the silver jewelry they had bought. A great deal of time went into sorting the things out, since most people had taken with them objects to sell belonging to other WoDaaBe who did not travel. A huge pile of jewelry had to be separated and the owner of each item identified.

Extensive Western consumption is often being been seen as a solution for the survival of minority groups, thus "finding" them a place within a globalized world overshadowed by extensive consumption of people in the West. As Terence Turner points out, it has often been argued that the only way for indigenous people to survive and maintain control over their lands is by becoming connected to the free market system, and using their ecosystems to yield profit in an ecologically sustainable way (Turner 1995a). Cultural Survival has for example marketed various products, everything coming from the company's projects directed at indigenous people. Other examples of such an approach are Ben and Jerry's "Rainforest Crunch" ice cream and the cosmetic company Body Shop's "Trade Not Aid" (Turner 1995a:5). To claim that people can protest against environmental and human rights abuses by buying expensive cosmetics points again to the different dimensions of

---

[71] According to my understanding, photos are taken of the dancers by the team recruiting the dancers and then sold to spectators.
[72] This has changed very much since I completed my research. There are now many WoDaaBe from the area that I worked most in who have stayed extensively in various European countries, who take a critical stand toward Europeans, knowing that their goals are as various as their own.

power between the West and indigenous people, along with indicating the desire to consume that has become so characteristic of the West. This approach carries the implication that "we" in the West do not need to consume less, "we" only need to buy the right products.[73]

Indigenous people have, furthermore, a vulnerable position in relation to the international market. Various people come to Niger to buy WoDaaBe jewelry to sell in the West. The price that most WoDaaBe are paid for these products is not high, even though they sometimes manage to sell their products directly to individual tourists on the street. Foreign jewelry sellers buy their products at a low price, using the advantages of cheap labor in the Third World. In their own countries in the West these products are then sold in prestigious stores which place high prices on the items because of their handmade "indigenous" nature.

---

[73] The Body Shop is an example of the idea that indigenous people are empowered by connecting to international markets, because of Body Shop's strong public image as a "different" company, seeking to empower native people, and as an environmentally friendly business. Terence Turner has given an interesting criticism of their projects to empower the Kayapó in the Amazon. Turner points out that the more economically productive the natives can make their natural resources, the greater the incentives are for other more powerful individuals and groups to take over their areas (1995b:4).

CHAPTER 16

LIVED RELATIONS

Even though I would want it to happen, the anthropologist and the person who is me, never become completely separated and isolated from each other. I look into the fire, where I am sitting in front of my bed. The darkness around me is almost complete. The only things to be heard are the sounds of the bush surrounding me. These sounds are few, disappearing into endless space. There is no wind, just soft whispers of grass and trees reaching to the sky. The other people of my house, who had gathered around the fire like most other nights, have disappeared into the night. Most of them are getting ready to go to sleep and so should I. Akali is also sitting by the fire, encapsulated in his own thoughts. I have been less than a month in the bush, and am starting to know its people and daily rhythm. My environment is still new and confusing. I am not able to grasp it, not able to make it sit still, to classify it, to understand it. Every day I feel like there are new faces, new environments, as if the earth is moving under my feet and I just float and move with it, not sure where it is taking me. It is not an unpleasant feeling, just different from what I had expected. What is most difficult is my desire to be myself, to have people look at me and know me as a person, as Kristín. It is not that I resist my identity as Mariyama, in fact I like it. Mariyama is also someone, an individual. It is my other new name that concerns me: *Anasara*, white person. Sometimes people do not bother to call me by my individual name, just say *anasara*. Is that me? I am White, but I am something more. My desire is to be seen as something beyond that. These are my thoughts in the darkness, and it is easy to recall them because they have slipped into my mind so many times since then.

These are my thoughts as I look into the fire of the WoDaaBe encampment that I am a part of. I look up and observe my friend Akali. I interrupt the silence between us and ask: "Do you think you can ever forget that I am white?" He looks up, stares at me as if wondering if this is an honest question or not, and then starts to laugh. His laughter is genuine, almost cheerful. I am hurt, I do not understand: "Why are you laughing, what is so amusing?" His gentle laugher changes into a smile, and he says gently: "Kristín, how can I ever forget that you are White?"

I later understand the meaning of this interaction from a more painful and reflective point of view. Being White is the privilege of being able to forget one's Whiteness and to forget as well the color of others. It is a privilege which I wish that everyone in the world could afford, but the fact is that it is not so. I write in my diary while in the field,

> You can make friends with people who are so much poorer than you. You will forget the difference of power but they cannot, because the former is a luxury which you can afford but they cannot.

In the Western world-view, 'whiteness' has been constructed as a neutral, invisible social category, giving the privileged position of being able to 'forget' one's skin color (Frankenberg 1993; Hartigan 1997). Classifications into and ideologies of people as different races can be seen, in the words of Etienne Balibar, as representing "one of the most insistent forms of the historical memory of modern societies" (Balibar 1991:44–45).[74] Identity is, furthermore, fluid and contextual. I have previously discussed myself as a gendered person, but other dimensions of my identity are also salient. Even though my own ethnic identity is shaped by my origin from a small nation, both in regards to its population and in terms of world politics and power, my position in the world is still marked by my definition by the outside world as being 'White' and having an origin in a homogenous category, the "West." My country's small size, situated outside major world politics, strengthens my position in the larger world in some aspects. I can benefit from the privileges associated with an origin from the West, despite my native country not being so much associated with the negatives of imperialism compared to the more dominant players in world politics. My categorization as being 'from the West' gives me access to various resources, thus being from the 'West' constitutes a certain reality, giving one access to things merely because one occupies this imaginary space of identity.

---

[74] This is not only a question of memory but of a certain order of the world, where present generations are either reaping the benefits or suffering inequalities due to the 'making' of the world during the colonial period.

WoDaaBe Agency

"Today *ansara* [whites] come and have great interest in WoDaaBe. However, in the past they had no particular interest in us."

The man who speaks these words is old and is rather puzzled by this. He is a powerful man who has lived a long life. He is correct of course in that many of those from the West arriving in Niger, working in relation to development or as travelers, seek to observe and explore "the" WoDaaBe. Chandra T. Mohanty has commented that the world is only definable in relational terms (Mohanty et al. 1991:2), stressing the complex webs of relationship and interwoven histories.

Social science's influential writing on globalization has importantly refuted earlier assumptions that globalization works on passive subjects, globalization often seen as either leading toward increased homogenization or that non-Western societies are reduced to a set of responses to Westernization. This emphasis on creativity in relation to globalization has in spite of its merits been somewhat at the expense of exploring relationships of power entangled within processes of globalization. Anthropologists among other scholars have been crucial in counteracting this vision of globalization as working on passive subjects, but studies of resistance in general – as pointed out by Lila Abu-Lughod (1990) – can fail to fully explore the effectiveness of power when stressing the creativity of resistors. Furthermore, building on Abu-Lughod's insights, it can be claimed that the concept of resistance has often been based on a binary distinction between oppression and resistance. I find it important to highlight that people are creative and active, resisting and manipulating various conditions, but can simultaneously be oppressed within certain structures of power (see also Loftsdóttir 2004a).

In the following discussion, I focus on two interlinked points of globalization: development practices in Niger and the handicraft work, attempting to draw out the multiple dimensions of power in these relationships as well as focusing on how the idea and presence of "whiteness" as a historically constructed category, overshadows and informs the relationships between WoDaaBe and the Westerners they are in contact with through development institutions and handicraft work.

WoDaaBe and Development

Appadurai (1996) sees globalization as a process of disjuncture which creates different and to some extent separated "landscapes" of people, money, images, technology, labeling these ethnoscape, financescapes, mediascapes and technoscape. In a sense Appadurai's idea can be applied more broadly, making it possible to talk about development as a particular landscape, *developscape*, consisting of visual aspects such as signs advertising the success of different projects, buildings and cars associated with development but also ideologies of development. Within these particular landscapes relationships takes place which are informed by these histories and ideologies. The concept "developscape" underlines the global nature of development and the movement of people, desires and ideas that it entails, which influence localized settings and are appropriated and affected by them.

Most WoDaaBe I spoke to, men and women, saw development projects as deriving from white people. This means that they are in a sense "racialized", seen as belonging to the domain of "white" others not in the realm of Africans. The "developscape" of Niger thus reflects a picture of the world where the majority of those who receive aid have a different skin color than those giving it. Even though many exceptions are certainly to be found, the general rule has been that local Nigeriens working for development assistance are subordinated to white, Western supervisors. Nigeriens work as security guards, gardeners, drivers and secretaries for development institutions in addition to various specialized tasks relating more directly to the projects themselves. International development institutions are of course various, embedded in different power structures, have different power relations among themselves and have different policies. In recent years most institutions have furthermore, emphasized NGO's (Non Governmental Organizations) in the countries, bringing local people more directly into the development process (World Bank 2003). That does not, however, change the fact that for local people, such as the WoDaaBe, those who work in the low paying jobs in relation to development have for the most part a different skin color than those managing the projects and offices. This is enforced by the fact that for those WoDaaBe or Nigeriens who have not traveled to Europe or North America, skin color is strongly associated with prosperity. Many individuals were surprised to hear that in my native country my mother cleaned and cooked, as most women do. It was contradictory to their own life experiences, which are in no way localized to Niger, because many have traveled within West-Africa, everywhere observing white people being served by dark skinned people.

Speaking to WoDaaBe about development and then to those who are in Niger to initiate development projects also revealed a deep disjuncture in the way in which people perceive what development is. Recent development discourse has emphasized that a project's beneficiaries should see the project as benefiting their long term interests (various oral references, also World Bank 1991:21; Painter 1991:5). The development practitioners in Niger expressed their concern to me that the projects' beneficiaries seemed not to have much interest in the projects themselves, but rather looked for projects to provide them with free goods and services. A World Bank report raises the question of the sustainability of projects, and whether created structures will be maintained after a project has been terminated. It notes that the participants in the project, who should be getting the benefit from the project itself, are always paid in cash or goods for their work in relation to their wells (World Bank 1991:21). This issue has been raised in relation to wells and medicines, it is claimed, for example, that the local populations should have to pay some part of the well's construction in order to become more responsible towards it (for example, DANIDA: Dagois 1995). Some development practitioners that I talked to feel that local populations should bear some of the cost of medicines, which are often distributed free, in order to emphasize that medicines are expensive and valuable. One man stated to me in relation to his experience: "The whole area from Tahoua thinks that medicines are free and that they are just meant to be given away, [that] nobody pays for them." (May 1997). Another person working in international development states: "You have probably seen this, 'give me medicine, give me medicine.' If you don't give them medicines you have done anything (sic) for them." His words express deep frustration with the sustainability of the work that he had conducted in Niger for more than a decade. It was also surprising to me how little information many of those I spoke to who had worked in Niger for many years in relation to international development had about basic structures of WoDaaBe societies, or pastoral societies. Often it was stated to me that it was too difficult to do projects among nomads because they were very "difficult to find", a statement which was surprising in my view, as in the area of Tchin-

Tabaraden WoDaaBe go regularly to the Sunday market making it very easy to locate people. The lineage structure of the WoDaaBe, furthermore, facilitates this process. Karen Greenough in her M.A. thesis on WoDaaBe in the Damergou region of Niger also speaks about this view of development agencies, in addition to remarking that most funders have little interest in information from those nomadic postoralist involved in the projects (Greenough 2007:117, 122).

The projects conducted in the area of Tchin-Tabaraden are few and have been almost absent since the early 1990s, at least partly due to the political instability caused by the Tuareg rebellion. However, even a young WoDaaBe child in the bush around Tchin-Tabaraden knows what a project is. My friend Sollare, a child who had never been under a roof, or ever seen a town until recently, is familiar with the concept "project." "A project" she tells me, "gives people food, it gives medicines, and cows." Many WoDaaBe in fact express views of development projects that are somewhat similar to what is feared by the development workers quoted above. Development is simply called "*proje*" in daily talk, which is derived from the word "project" (or "projet" in French), and refers to the distribution of medicines and goods and the possibility of acquiring a well paid job. For most WoDaaBe I talked to, the meaning of development was thus not connected to building of infrastructure which could improve the situation of the WoDaaBe in the future, or some other kind of sustainable development. *Proje* is simply speaking a means to redistribute resources from anasara, who have plenty of them, to WoDaaBe who lack them. These extracts from interviews clearly express such views:

"I would like a well, I would like a project to help us [...]. Your brothers help us, they give assistance, and may God thank them for that" (January 1997)

"White people, they help the WoDaaBe, they help all people who have problems" (February 1997).

"I would like Mariyama who came to be with WoDaaBe, to find us assistance. Give us work [...] try to find help for us" (March 1997).

As the last quote indicates, *proje* were frequently identified as an action of a single Westerner, acting out of his or her good will. Most *proje* were thus seen as conducted by individuals who came to Niger with vast resources, and gave them out of kindness towards WoDaaBe. This view was also expressed by those who had worked for the larger projects and had been in direct interaction with development people. They, as well, saw the benefits of the *proje* as being the payment they had received for their work, and the contact person for the project as the one they should be grateful towards. This means that the projects should not be criticized because the WoDaaBe I spoke to felt that they as beneficiaries should be grateful for the person's generosity.[75]

This view of *anasara* as possessing vast individual resources naturally carries hopes of *proje* or extensive and expensive gifts. Clearly reflecting this was that one of my greatest difficulties during my fieldwork was to convince and explain to people that I did not have *proje* to give them, that I did not have enough money to build a well or distribute large numbers of animals. Even though people realized that I myself did not have these resources, they still believed that my "ethnicity", as a white person, automatically would give me the access to these resources. This means in fact that these WoDaaBe are unlikely to see development as "empowerment" of local people but rather view themselves as passive recipients of delivered goods. This view was perhaps best demonstrated in one interview, where I asked what WoDaaBe could do themselves in order to improve their conditions which I asked because I had constantly heard that *anasara* should help WoDaaBe and give them projects. The response of the person interviewed was, "to find *anasara* who can do a project." The WoDaaBe and those engaged in development have thus different ideas regarding what projects are supposed to accomplish, the former seeing it as free distribution of goods, while the latter visualizes projects as intended to be sustainable in the long term by the people receiving the assistance.

Most WoDaaBe did not identify in my interviews "livestock development" in the form of ranches as "projects." If they were in projects, some WoDaaBe suggested, the ranches were designed to benefit other people than the pastoral populations. These comments fits quite well with M. A. Mohamed Salih's distinction between "livestock" and "pastoral" development (1990, 1991), discussed in chapter one. In my interviews, ranches were asso-

---

[75] According to Greenough's research some WoDaaBe have a more critical view of development in the Damergou area (2007) and the same could be said today about increasing numbers of WoDaaBe in the area that I studied.

ciated with the government, which *proje* in general are not. However, in active discussion of these issues, people remarked that in fact the government had sometimes done good *proje*, such as after the drought of 1968–1974, when some families received animals from the government as a part of the reconstruction program.

The Handicraft Work

WoDaaBe handicraft work and the popular images of WoDaaBe in Europe and North America inform to some extent the relations between WoDaaBe and Westerners. As previously discussed, whiteness is for WoDaaBe a potent social category, which equals access to power and possibilities of improving one's situation. Arjun Appadurai speaks of imagination becoming an organized field of social practices (1996:31), a point aptly applied to the agency of the WoDaaBe who actively engage with economic income opportunities which their images in the West have fuelled and stimulated. In their relationships with Westerners, 'culture' becomes an instrument in the struggle to gain access to resources and power. The handicraft production thus shows local engagement with global phenomena as well as how the people actively manipulate everyday circumstances, which is a symbol of creativity and the WoDaaBe ability to adapt to an ever-changing world. WoDaaBe history shows, of course, that they have always been opportunistic in their strategy, taking advantage of new income possibilities when necessary. The presence of international development in Niger as well as tourism, creates the platform for the WoDaaBe to market and sell their cultural artifacts which the popular images of them have stimulated interest in.

Most WoDaaBe in Niamey cannot generally read the texts or place the images of the popular media in a larger context of Western representation and images but many have seen these images that emphasize young WoDaaBe beauty and dances. Pictures of beautiful young WoDaaBe women or painted males ready for a dance are frequently displayed in the brochures from travel companies in Niger and are common themes decorating post-cards, the main buyers probably being Westerners writing back "home." Many have also seen the book Nomads of Niger, previously discussed. The interactions of WoDaaBe individuals with Westerners in Niger also make them familiar with what kind of interest people in the West have in the WoDaaBe.

I was frequently told by various WoDaaBe that Westerners like myself are interested in aspects such as photos of themselves with a "real" WoDaaBe, the purchase of something old or hand made, to see some WoDaaBe dances and that they even like to receive WoDaaBe names. This rather static list of things that *anasara* are supposed to want is in many senses just as objectifying as the images that the popular press presents of the WoDaaBe, and leaves little space for diversity within the category *anasara*.

Many WoDaaBe men also know how to manipulate the desires of their clients for the exotic, as could be heard in interviews, by observing their relationships with their clients and friends from the West, and in their relationships with me. This manipulation takes place in regard to the adaptation of WoDaaBe handicraft objects to better fit the styles which are desired by Westerners at various times, marketing them as authentic and traditional WoDaaBe art. The commercialization also takes place in relation to their own bodies and images as is observed in that at the *juulde* festival WoDaaBe demand payment for pictures taken of them. The overall discussion concerning the *juulde* festival indicates that money has started to play an important part in it, the festival thus becoming to some extent part of survival strategies in the city. Most women do not show Westerners as open an interest but some are still quite active in seeking out clients, then especially other women.

Manipulations takes place on a more personal level, because WoDaaBe consciously engage with the desires of many Westerners to temporarily acquire a new identity. One man told me that I was truly a WoDaaBe and would become more so if I gave him money because, after all, that would demonstrate that we were from the same family. Also, I was told that the "natural" friendships between WoDaaBe and Whites should also lead to Whites distributing money to the WoDaaBe. These WoDaaBe fulfill a romantic dream of many Western tourists and expatriates, where one sees oneself as being able to acquire the friendship of native people and be the "first" to be a friend of this isolated and primitive people.

Relations of Power

The WoDaaBe relationship with Westerners is fraught with ambiguity, as was evident in WoDaaBe relationships with myself (see also Loftsdóttir 2003). *Anasara* are seen as the road to prosperity, and someone who gets friends from the West has much to gain, due to the possibilities of acquiring *proje* or for the handicraft makers, access to overseas markets for the products. When I ask if someone is doing well in his work, the reply I often get is, "Yes, he has lots of *anasara* friends." These issues of power and resistance are well put by Akali when he criticized Europeans and Americans (including me) by saying: "It is very good that the French and the Americans come and see WoDaaBe. But, they come and see the WoDaaBe and then they leave while we WoDaaBe are never able to go anywhere. We are unable to travel to America and see things there. Americans come and go, but we can never go anywhere."

Carmen Martinez Novo has claimed that anthropologists have not analyzed paternalism much, the term being used among other things to refer to positive or romantic representations of indigenous people where they are not seen as equals (2007:11). Even though WoDaaBe actively manipulate and make use of their relationship with Westerners, these are not relationships of equals due to the great disparity of power. The WoDaaBe emphasis on not speaking of power, the emphasis on WoDaaBe and Westerners as being the same can be seen as attempts to make such relationships equal, at the same time as they often try to emphasize their own powerlessness in the context of the Niger nation state. The most vivid expression of these differences in power is probably the silence surrounding this relationship. In my experience, most WoDaaBe do not generally express criticism within the context of formal interviews or in a hostile way, usually only rarely and within unordered and unexpected circumstances. Silence is of course no less important than what is said, constituting an important aspect in reflecting people's conditions (Chakrabarty 1988:179). The reason for this can be sought in the interaction of various aspects, such as the absence of extensive direct confrontation between white colonizers and WoDaaBe subjects, Westerners not being an important counter-identification in colonial times. Also, the moral rules of the WoDaaBe (*mbodagansi*), intrinsic to their ethnic identity, do not encourage confrontational criticism, especially not of visitors. In addition, the hope of 'gaining' projects, seen by the WoDaaBe and other Nigeriens alike as a ticket for future prosperity, is also probably a significant factor, obviously correlating with aspects previously discussed, i.e., Niger's dependency on aid and the visibility of aid institutions in the country.

Even my very close friends would hesitate to verbally attack my "white" position of power, unless under unordered, unexpected and very personal circumstances. A few examples of such disruptions can be mentioned. When WoDaaBe individuals who were only marginally acquainted with me arrived at my small apartment in Niamey, they had to be told by other WoDaaBe they trusted and who knew me well that they did not have to stay outside the house but could safely enter. It was not enough that I invited them inside. This hesitation at entering into this space associated with *anasara* has probably to do with the fact that many WoDaaBe fear being accused of theft, something people clearly identified with their interactions with Westerners. I also heard relatively often criticism that evolved around international development assistance. One man pointed out to me, for example, that the *anasara* living in Niger get high salaries and live affluently among the poor Nigerien population. He stated, "All this is done in the name of the project but hardly any money goes to the people they should be helping. Then afterwards they probably say that the money went into this and that." He and his friend pointed out to me the big powerful jeeps belonging to various projects, driving past us on Niamey's streets, demonstrating this point. Samari's interview with me, presented earlier, carries a similar kind of criticism even though it is subtler. "Is research the only work white people have?" he asks. "If they really want to help us, why don't they then just give us some money so we can buy millet and livestock?" Samari stresses right after this comment that he is only joking, as always when people give any kind of criticism of their relationships with Westerners, thus attempting to neutralize the effects of his words.

This lack of criticism of these relations can, as previously pointed out, be seen as a part of a strategy of some WoDaaBe to gain a better position and access to the resources of those from the West traveling or staying in Niger. The WoDaaBe men that I spent time with in the city who earned income by selling jewelry to tourists and expatriates, made sure that the texture of the experience of being *anasara* in Niger is generally smooth and gentle. One sitting down with the WoDaaBe and they are sure to enter into the Garden of Eden before the fall (as phrased by Taussig 1993). There is no evilness in this world. Instead of guilt-laden stories of colonization and power, one hears stories from WoDaaBe of how 'good' white people actually are, how much they have done to help other people. One hears how beautiful their skin and color is and how 'their people' are in fact the same as the WoDaaBe. And how much their friendship is valued and how much the friendship with all whites is desirable. Underlining the poverty and powerlessness of the WoDaaBe as a social group in this way is as strategy toward gaining monetary assistance, especially through projects, and even though it is probably not intended in such a way, it fits well with the Western conception of indigenous people as marginal minorities within the nation states. It separates the WoDaaBe from poor Nigeriens of other ethnicities, constructing assistance benefiting individual WoDaaBe as a way of assisting the WoDaaBe as a whole, as an ethnic unity.

The prospect of getting a good income from the handicraft work are as previously pointed out very much tied to the contact which individuals have with Westerners but some few WoDaaBe have in fact been able to make a living from the handicrafts. Several times it was pointed out to me by WoDaaBe themselves that these are not those who make the products but those selling the items. A few WoDaaBe have developed strong sales networks, not making the jewelry themselves but buying it from other WoDaaBe. They buy the product for a relatively low price from the other WoDaaBe and then sell it for much higher prices to Westerners. An important basis for this is owning a where clients can come to purchase these products. Those who arrive in Niamey with some capital have better prospects of being able to buy their own house, in addition to being able to engage in selling more valuable products that give greater profit. There are, however, other factors as well. Those who have been in good contact with Whites are in a better situation. They are more likely to get clients for their products because they can become more integrated into a network of "Whites", perhaps, making friends and business associates from the original White contact. In addition, they can have access to credit, and they are also more likely to be asked to do dances for private or public gatherings. In some cases the sales premises have been built with the financial assistance of Westerners working with development, as part of a small scale development program.

Desires and Power

The commercialization strategies discussed previously, intended toward improving the lives of indigenous people (i.e., that natives can be empowered by producing exotic commodities for the market and/or be a tourist attraction), have in common that the power relationship between the natives and the people in the West are not really being challenged or questioned. As has been pointed out in relation to tourism, it is seen as quite natural for some people to spend their holidays in areas which are inhabited by people who themselves have no means to travel (Rossel 1988:2). Within development, the power relationships between those receiving and giving aid are similarly not often discussed in a critical way.

Tourists who travel expect to see the people whom they have previously experienced in colorful brochures or books. Such a view was reflected in the views of one woman who had lived and worked in Niger for a couple of years. She warned me at the beginning of my fieldwork that my WoDaaBe friends were not "real" WoDaaBe because "real" WoDaaBe would not work in the city, would not be interested in money, would not accept that photographs were taken of them. This woman clearly had a strong idea of what constituted a "real" WoDaaBe. Those who failed to conform to her idea of real WoDaaBe were simply rejected as false or corrupt. I know an example of a white woman who especially sought out WoDaaBe who had never been to Niamey, to have them perform dances in an exhibition in various European countries. For a second group to perform for her organization, she requested new people also "fresh" from the bush. This indicates wanting to "display" WoDaaBe who are somehow "pure", who have never seen civilization, and are thus more exciting than those not conforming as well with the popular image of the WoDaaBe as timeless, isolated people. Another white woman, who sold WoDaaBe items in Europe, asked for traditional WoDaaBe clothing but she wanted it used and worn. WoDaaBe were paid to make it and to wear it for one year before it was shipped to her. Hence it was not enough for the consumers to posses "real" WoDaaBe clothing, but the body fluids of a "real" WoDaaBe had to be included in the product as well.[76]

I have mentioned previously that I have observed the WoDaaBe collect personal items to be sold, both those living in the bush and Niamey. To me, there is something disturbing about seeing people collecting their personal clothing and items to be sold in a distant country to a stranger. During one

---

[76] The effects of the popular representation were also visualized to me in another context. When I told Western men that I was conducting fieldwork among the WoDaaBe, I frequently got a lifting of eyebrows and "suggestive" smiles and comments, implying that a young woman must definitely be doing something else among the WoDaaBe than serious fieldwork.

collection of items to sell while on a dance trip, I asked Akali why people would sell things that they obviously cared about. He said harshly, "You think that someone wants to sell his tradition, something that he has had for a long time and loves? You think someone wants it to be like this? You only sell this something because you don't have another choice."

DEVELOPMENT AND IDENTITY: CREATING SUBJECTS

Subjectivity concerns the way individuals view themselves, and how others see them. Of no less importance, different subject positions create various sites of resistance and acting on the world. Louis Althusser (1971) pointed out that people are "always already subjects", meaning that individuals are assigned specific subject positions, these being historically formed. Ideology "recruits" subjects and "transforms" individuals into subjects through the process of interpellation, i.e., the process in which social representations are accepted and absorbed by individuals as their own representations (p.174). Through this process, social relations manifested in representations become 'real,' even though they are in fact constituted by imaginary relations. The concept "imaginary" refers here to the relationship of the individual within a subject position that he or she takes.

Lacan's rereading of Freud addresses the making of the self in relation to others. According to Lacan, the self is constituted through a world of images and representations, thus disputing the idea that subjects are fixed and have natural unified identities. Subjects are the products of social, historical, and cultural systems of signification more than fixed biological units. The application of Lacan's ideas in post-structuralist theories, sees subjects as made through discourse and discursive practices[77] (Moore 1994:25). Teresa de Lauretis has in her theorizing of gender combined these ideas of the subject with Foucault's ideas of embodiment. I find that her comments on gender are useful for subjectivity in general, and thus all subject positions can be seen as "the set of effects produced in bodies, behaviors, and social relations" (1987:3). Subjects can thus be seen as being made through social representations, producing real effects on individuals and their relations to the world.

---

[77] Lacan himself, even though seeing the subject as constituted through language, was not talking about social discourse, but referring more to systems of signs (Moore 1994:25).

In addition, subject positions are the products of various social technologies, institutional discourses and practices (de Lauretis 1987:2). Subjects are made through discourse and discursive practices, which provide various subject positions within different discourses. Major dimensions of difference, such as race, class, ethnicity, sexuality, religion, and gender, interact in ways that give a multiplicity of subject positions (Moore 1994:55–57). As pointed out by de Lauretis, as a result of the individual's various subject positions, the subject is multiple and contradictory (de Lauretis 1987:2).

Individuals are thus given different subject positions within society that are constituted through various social representations and institutional technologies. A single individual can have several subject positions, because the different aspects of his/her identity are given social and political meaning.[78] Philip Corrigan and Derek Sayer have discussed the way in which the State constitutes identities, by regulating the civil society into different subjects (such as voters and consumers). My discussion does not focus on the State apparatus in particular, but these ideas can well be applied to larger structures than the State. What is important, for my purpose, is these authors' awareness of how these different subject positions assigned to individuals, force them to speak in a particular way, playing these roles. Some identities are thus privileged and approved while others are suppressed. The self is categorized, by making individuals act certain roles, based on certain rules in particular situations (Corrigan and Sayer 1985:198). Thus, as pointed out by Roseberry, the power of the State rests not so much on the consent of the subjects, but on the way in which the State defines and creates certain kinds of subjects and identities while ruling out other subjects and identities (1994:357).

Creating the WoDaaBe Subject

As I have shown the WoDaaBe seem to take two somewhat distinctive subject positions within discourse in the West, even though both derive from the same historical roots; they are seen as a pastoral people (or livestock producers) and as an indigenous people. It is interesting to observe that the literature on pastoral herding peoples has not referred much to its subject matter

---

[78] This understanding also draws from Foucault, who has argued that the concept of the subject has two meanings, one referring to identity and the other referring to someone being the "subject of someone else by control and dependence" (Foucault 1983:212).

as "indigenous" on "native", and the literature of indigenous people does not really speak much of livestock producers.[79] This demonstrates the way in which these are separate discourses, creating to some extent separate subjects.

The herding discourse is a political discourse because it formulates and affects the development of orientation and planning of projects intended to affect people's lives. Politics are about the distribution of power in society, how resources are distributed, to whom and controlled by whom. Even though power is the subtext of various discourses, it is perhaps never as openly expressed as in development discourse. Development is about power in multiple ways, both because it aims towards distributing resources on a local level, and also because in the context of some of the very poor nation states, development organizations can have important effects on national policies. Development discourse is institutionalized and thus takes forms similar to that of the state discourse. The subjects that the development discourse addresses and thus constitutes are "underdeveloped" peoples, located in the space of the Third World. Those working on these subjects are predominantly white Western males, equipped with data and a specific kind of technology. The goal of the development has often been to transform these subjects into more "modern" individuals, at least to transform their economies in a way that is seen as making them more efficient thus counteracting poverty and hunger. This emphasis has been justified with references to repeated droughts as signifying that these economies do not "fit" into the modern world.

The subject of development discourse is predominantly a male producer of animals in an economic system which has been unchanged for a long time. People are thus primarily given the subject position of "producer." As my discussion has indicated development discourse works from a series of "subjects." Agricultural populations are usually treated separately, constituting different subject matters, calling for a different approach and different emphasis.

Again, I want to point out in this context, that I find a focus simply on subjectivity/power and the State to be too simplistic. The State is not autonomous and I believe that three agents of power can be identified here. The

---

[79] They use the concept "nomadic", and I think to some extent "pastoral."

State is to some extent, as discussed, subordinated to policy decisions made by large development institutions such as the IMF. In addition, there are also private multinational organizations, which are becoming more and more dominant agents of power. It is interesting to briefly explore the relationship between these three "agents" of power. In many Third World countries, the State needs the money development brings, simply to keep itself from collapsing. Large development organizations, however, work through the State, benefiting from various state institutions and information. The overall international economy depends on the State, whereas foreign debts would not be paid if the state was not maintained. As I have discussed, many development projects are aimed at the herding subject, but seek to increase the national revenues of the State, not necessarily to increase the well-being of the people in question. Many projects benefit urban populations by controlling prices and imports, thus directly benefiting the State. Large multinational corporations also need the State in order to regulate time and bodies of potential working subjects, but cheap labor and lax regulations regarding security are an important part of profit for these institutions. The increased cry for privatization in Niger from development institutions could – even though not intended to do so – serve the interests of these multinational corporations. Who will the privatization of ranches benefit? Unlikely it will be the herders even though some "livestock producers" will have a possibility of good revenues from ownership of land. Who will the privatization of vaccination benefit? Does increased production in herding communities necessarily make herding safer and increase the quality of life for those involved in it? Does not increased production simply reflect the interest of the State?

What is interesting is not only how institutionalized discourses regulate subjects, but also how they rule out certain subjectivities. Thus, the State works from particular kinds of subjects, while suppressing other kinds of subjects. In Niger, this is demonstrated by the subjects of official discourse being herders and agriculturalists, while the ethnic subject (i.e., people having specific ethnicity) is forcefully suppressed. This is not to say that ethnicity is not mentioned in development reports, most include a static listing of relevant ethnic groups, but ethnicity is more addressed as "technology" than identity. By this I mean, that identity is seen as a relevant tool of classification, indicating language and some static traditions rather than as a source of meaning and direction. This is coupled with herding not being seen as a "way of life" or an important part of identity and existing in the world. Herding is simply livestock production, and those who participate in it are simply livestock producers. This dismissal of ethnicity is also reflected in the discourse of the nation State's civil servants. During informal interviews with State agents, it was frequently expressed that ethnicity was not relevant in contemporary Niger and for the Niger State, ethnicity was not an issue. One civil servant told me that conflicts were never between different ethnic groups, only between herders and agriculturalists. Thus, perhaps not surprisingly, it is hard to gain access to statistics regarding ethnic distribution in various spheres of the economy, and according to my information, such data is not collected. Ethnicity has for a long time been seen as a threat to the cohesion of the State, and thus policies seen as increasing ethnic identification are traditionally not considered desirable. The policies of international organizations and the State seem to be closely correlated, aimed at maintaining the cohesion and power of the State (see also Ibrahim 1994).

I have discussed another kind of discourse, taking place in the popular press directed at the West. This literature in the line of eco-indigenism addresses indigenous people as clearly marked subjects, characterized by their attachment to tradition, their preservation of rituals, and their long settlement in the same place, invaded by alien cultures. The discourse of the "indigenous" has a global quality in the sense that it brings together ideas of the Other in Western media creating a sense of "global community." I earlier criticized the association that that the term indigenous has with nature. It is, furthermore, interesting to observe that the indigenous subject is generally not gendered, which again is also a dominant Western form of representation. Most representations of the indigenous do not speak of inequalities within indigenous society, or point toward the relationship of men and women in a critical way, nor do they focus on the way in which gender is constructed and experienced. However, the subject is in fact gendered because "the" WoDaaBe (or the Masaai, the Bushmen, etc.) are most often males. Feminists in various contexts (such as Moore 1994:59) have pointed out this trend of the unmarked subject being actually a male; the male subject is the unmarked, the norm, a point of reference. The popular press thus constructs the view of "the" WoDaaBe as a male, in addition to incorporating age, by representing "the" WoDaaBe as a young male around 20–40 years old. Focusing on WoDaaBe representations in the popular press, there is a silence regarding women's status within the society, their voices and difference within the society. The exclusion of gender becomes more striking in my view, in the discussion of the dance, which is framed within exotic sexual relations. WoDaaBe women appear as running away from their husbands during these dances for no reason. There is no mention that those who participate in the dance events at night are men (married and unmarried) and *unmarried* young women. The wives are excluded. There is no mention of how it feels for the wife to be left behind while her husband goes to these gatherings. Women are simply defined as the objects of men's desire.

The discourse of the indigenous, furthermore, can rule out other subjectivities, such as those who are displaced, those who live in small economies, on the margins and are not native to their lands, or at least not more native than others in the area. Terence Turner has noted that the general Western public was shocked when news reports revealed that some of the Kayapó in Amazonia were living a high lifestyle in the city as a result of their engagement with the environmentalist agenda, at the expense of others of the same ethnic group. This led to the conclusion that "these people" were "eco-villains" rather than heroes (Turner 1995b:6,14). Also when a few indigenous groups were permitted to carry out ecologically destructive practices, such as mining and logging, in exchange for payment from the companies involved, some environment activists argued that these people should be seen as enemies by the environmental movement (Turner 1995a:3). I want to recall the story of the woman who told me that my WoDaaBe friends in the city were not "real" WoDaaBe because they failed to conform to her idea regarding what a "real" BoDaaDo should look like (which consisted of being traditional and innocent). Both the discourse of the "indigenous" and of the "underdeveloped" seem thus often to assume a coherent, unhistorical and passive subject. It is an unmarked subject, thus excluding dimensions of gender and inequalities that exist within all societies.

The term indigenous has, however, also gained some important legal status. Concern within the United Nations with protecting indigenous people was seen in the *United Nations Working Group on Indigenous Populations* (WGIP) established in 1982 and in 2007, the United Nations Declaration on the Rights of Indigenous People was adopted by the General Assembly. Other general policy documents also increasingly mention indigenous people (see Saugestad 2001:45). For example, since 1991 the World Bank has increasingly recognized indigenous people, accepting a revised operational policy in July 2005 (labeled OP and BP 4.10) replacing the one of September 1991 (labeled OD 4.20). In the policy, it is stated that the "Bank recognizes that the identities and cultures of Indigenous Peoples are inextricably linked to the lands on which they live and the natural resources on which they depend."[80] Even though the term indigenous can be criticized, it has to be recognized at the same time that through the popular and the legal reification of the term indigenous, marginal and poor groups have been able to seek increased rights for themselves. June Nash (2001) has critically pointed out that scholars have to acknowledge that deconstruction of terms such as culture can undermine the fight of many groups defining themselves as indigenous, which are at last able to use legal rights to reclaim various resources. A similar point is stressed by John R. Bowen (2000) who acknowledges the difficulties embedded in the concept, but simultaneously draws out the fact that no matter what scholarly criticism has to say about the concept, it has been useful to ensure the rights of many marginalized people. Within anthropology, the concept indigenous continues to be debated and contested because of the issues mentioned, as can for example be seen by a relatively recent debate in the journal *Anthropology Today* (for example Bowen 2000; Barnard 2004).

The subject positions assigned to WoDaaBe in these powerful Western discourses can have also been used by the WoDaaBe to provide locations of resistance. The WoDaaBe's involvement with the tourist industry is recent and at the time of my fieldwork those WoDaaBe that I talked to were generally not familiar with terms such as "indigenous", nor were they familiar with the ideology behind the term. They did not seem to recognize themselves as "indigenous" subjects, having issues in common with other "traditional" groups. Many have experienced marginal people in Nigeria, who seem to have maintained some of their traditional clothing,[81] but these costumes, consisting of a cloth around the waist, were seen by my informants as ridiculous. They seem to observe no similarity between their ritual dress and those of other groups in this context. When I showed a picture book of indigenous

---

[80] See the World Bank website:
http://wblnoo18.worldbank.org/Institutional/Manuals/OpManual.nsf/B52929624EB2A3538525672E0 0775F66/0F7D6F3F04DD70398525672C007D08ED?OpenDocument, accessed 13 October 2006).
[81] I am unfortunately not aware of the names of these groups.

people to a few WoDaaBe men, their reaction was similar to my informants' reaction to indigenous people in Nigeria; ridicule and feeling that these were not people that they identified with (the book also included a photo of a WoDaaBe man who was evaluated in more positive way). The preoccupation of Westerners with tradition and rituals is conceptualized by the WoDaaBe as an interest in the WoDaaBe per se. This will, however, probably change with increased tourism and increased familiarity of the WoDaaBe with tourism as a cultural activity.[82]

The WoDaaBe recognize the subject position assigned to them by the State and development discourse, and they are both influenced by its ideology and actively try to manipulate it. Many WoDaaBe expressed to me feelings that they, as well, were subjects of the State, of Nigerien nationality. The men proudly showed me their identity cards, which confirm their nationality. This ideology forms the basis for WoDaaBe of why the Niger State should channel development assistance to them, and should integrate them further into the state system by building schools for their children, creating wells, and increasing security in the pastoral areas. Thus, they do not only formulate their own discourse to fit within their subject positions in the development discourse, but also recognize themselves as subjects of the State.

---

[82] This has changed since this research was conducted. Many of those WoDaaBe that I was most involved with, are now very politically engaged, in addition, as WoDaaBe indigenous organizations have increased extensively since my research was concluded.

CONCLUDING REMARKS

The bush is sweet, runs like a song refrain underlining all my research experiences. The WoDaaBe like the bush, WoDaaBe are the birds of the bush, so WoDaaBe like to tell me, young and old, male and female. It is true, but only partially. Many WoDaaBe have also started to develop a desire (*koDei*) for the city. In addition, the conditions of herding led to livestock losses, hunger and misery, making the statement sound rather nostalgic. In fact, the bush is barren and overgrazed. The harmattan wind blows away brown gray dust while the herders seek to find grass for their animals. Akali, probably like most WoDaaBe, fears the WoDaaBe will die along with the bush, that its end will signal their end as well. WoDaaBe migrant work is still not only a story of marginality, but of agency and adaptability. Even though many older WoDaaBe resist migrant work, seeing it as the "herding of clothing" like Kala'i does – emphasizing the lifestyle that many migrant workers adopt – migrant work still signals resilience and creativity within WoDaaBe society. Handicrafts play on new opportunities created by an increasingly global world and migrant work in general shows a new way of using mobility which has been so intrinsic to WoDaaBe lives for such a long time. I have stressed that a binary distinction between oppression and resistance is not useful, the WoDaaBe being marginalized people and simultaneously, creative agents manipulating processes of globalization and relationships with Westerners to their own benefit, using their own cultural properties as instruments in the struggle to gain access to resources and power.

Popular and development representations of the WoDaaBe tend to define them as unchanged over a long period of time. People who are alive today bear, however, testimony to a very different kind of "traditional" life, using different kinds of housing, clothing and material culture.[83] More deeply, the

---

[83] Kala'i's generation of WoDaaBe report the use of bulls instead of donkeys and camels for transportation of objects and people. They also tell me that their houses in the past were small huts made of straw mattresses, with beds and tables made of local materials, not purchased from the Tuaregs as they are today. Some house items like the water calabash (*jogirde*) and the *kaggol* (a large carrier) have disappeared, while other items have been introduced.

WoDaaBe "ethnic" appearance has changed. The beads presented to me as being really old, constituting the *kodul* necklace, are made of plastic, and embroidered clothing was not generally used in recent past.[84] The men wore a small cloth tied around their forehead, the turban being used exclusively by chiefs. An old woman says, "Look at these young men, they all look like Tuaregs", demonstrating how tradition itself goes constantly through a process of change.[85] Historical references indicate that the WoDaaBe did not conceptualize themselves as a separate group in the the 19th century and that if they were, their boundaries from the Fulani were much more blurred than today.

Through the interactions of tourists and WoDaaBe, WoDaaBe-ness is underlined as composed more of symbols that can easily be marketed. These symbols are transformed into commodities and include the dances, jewelry and clothing (note that all have been adapted to the needs of the tourists). This emphasis excludes what is more difficult to sell and buy. The abstract ideas of patience (*munyal*) and reserve, of morality (*mbodagansi*), are less likely to be emphasized as composing "the" WoDaaBe. Some of the jewelry sellers try to some extent to integrate hospitality into their salesmanship by offering tea to good clients, or small gifts. Some aspects of WoDaaBe-ness speak strictly against the behavior which salesmen adopt. Salesmanship is not modest; it is not characterized by reserve or shame. But how can someone sell his product without adopting the techniques that other salesmen use around him? A few individuals within the WoDaaBe who have managed to acquire an extensive network of "white" contacts have gained wealth, which according to gossips will lead to these WoDaaBe "buying" themselves positions of power within WoDaaBe society. How will that affect the relationship of power within the WoDaaBe society? How will it affect what will be dominant in defining what being WoDaaBe means? The contemporary world is full of contradictions, manifested in WoDaaBe agency through

---

[84] As I have previously explained, I am here only referring to the group where the research was conducted.
[85] Brackenbury writes that "Tattooing is not much done, a few horizontal lines are sometimes made at the corners of the mouth in both sexes" (Brackenbury 1924:217). Meek, however, states that pure breed Fulani have no such marks because they associate them with slavery (1925). It is, however, possible that there have been regional differences in tattooing, and thus the WoDaaBe in Tahoua practice them while these other groups do not. Today, tattooing still seems to be done among all WoDaaBe groups. The men several decades ago had leather skirts around their waist (*deDo*) and sandals made from cowhide. The extensive tattooing of WoDaaBe women could be a recent phenomenon, as Reed reports in 1932 that WoDaaBe as a rule do not have "tribal face marks", (Reed 1932:426) a claim supported by Meek (1925) and Brackenbury (1924).

handicraft production and their buyers' desire for the authentic. Like other ethnic groups, WoDaaBe thus constantly redefine their tradition and cultural identity, tradition being, as scholars have now shown for a long time, dynamic and flexible. Discourses taking place in regard to the city, of desire (*koDei*) and lack of proper behavior are signs of constant negotiation of WoDaaBe identities, and one could even say that they signal a "local fetishism" of ethnicity, where identities are reinforced due to rapid transformations (see discussion in Novo 2007:5). A teenage boy who cuts his hair, hangs out with Hausa boys, smokes and steals, is identified to me as someone who is no longer a WoDaaBe, as someone who is "lost" to his people. But the eyes of people are sad when they tell me this. His father is too hurt to speak of him and others attempt to show him the error of his ways, hoping that he will again follow the "road" of WoDaaBe. Perhaps, most ironically of all, this boy is active in town finding tourists who are attracted to him because he is "the" WoDaaBe, confident and willing to make friends and share exciting cultural information. For them he is definitely a true WoDaaBe, and he thus defines for them what it means to be a WoDaaBe.

The popular images of WoDaaBe in the Western media can be seen as creating certain touching points with globalization, these images informing relations between WoDaaBe and Westerners within the handicraft production and development. For many WoDaaBe, the *anasara* is a relatively recent categorization of growing importance. I have used my own relationship with WoDaaBe as a point of reference, objectifying myself as an *anasara*, thus using personal interactions as an indication of various issues of power and inequality. WoDaaBe manipulate their relationship with *anasara* in various ways, negotiating their own identities as pastoral people, craft makers, and WoDaaBe, resisting and underscoring the multiple subject positions assigned to them. The popular representation of the WoDaaBe as isolated and traditional draws many tourists to Niger to buy and explore the WoDaaBe. Ironically, the myth of the WoDaaBe as a "pure" indigenous people provides the cash for some migrant workers to stay in the bush a few months each year.

This ambiguity is expressed in other ways as well. Development is an important part of WoDaaBe lives, not only due to its role in Niger's economy and pastoral development, but because it creates a "developscape." This "developscape" is formed by the physical presence of development in Niger and the lived relationship between recipients and givers of development assistance. Development thus has to do with the social and visual reality which it becomes part of. Many clients for WoDaaBe artifacts work in international development, WoDaaBe work as guards for homes of development staff, familiarizing themselves with the fact that *anasara* need to be served. The lifestyles of the majority of those working in development underline the difference in power between those who "get" development and those who "give" it. The fact that many of those representing different development institutions are white people creates, furthermore, a disturbingly racialized "developscape". The relationship which WoDaaBe had with me, a researcher closely connected with the development community, shows clearly the ambiguity and power embedded on a very personal scale in these relationships. WoDaaBe identification of the *anasara*, their association with development and all the riches in the world is thus truly something international aid should be concerned about in regards to how international development institutions present themselves in their employees' everyday lifestyle and projects around the world.

The presence of development in Niger also draws out ironical truths. Sadly, development is an easy target for criticism due to the endless list of project failures. Yet, in spite of scholarly criticism of various aspects relating to development, development represents something which is desired by many people in the world. Thus, WoDaaBe criticism of development does not focus on its ethnocentrism, technocentrism, lack of participation or other aspects which are frequently criticized by scholars, but more on the failure to deliver "development." As Ferguson (2002) states, there are all too real inequalities "that leave most Africans today excluded and abjected from the economic and institutional conditions that they themselves regard as modern" (p.559). Development thus reflects an increasingly global world and various forms of global encounters, both having to do with uniform projects that are applied all over the world, flows of people and ideas through time and space, discursively creating a part of the world as being underdeveloped, with people experiencing themselves as such.

Life in the world is full of desires. I think of Sollare's desire to have a house in the bush, to continue her life as she knows it, to have a husband who treats her well and gives her children. I think of Akali's ambition that the WoDaaBe will not "die" as people, even though he asserts that they will change. I think of Ali's desire to earn an income from his work in the city and return to the life in the bush and of Dadi's desire to get back to the city to take a refreshing shower while he is in the bush. Of many young men's desire of "making it" in the *artisana* business, earning money to buy cars, radios and beautiful clothing. Of people's desire to get something they call "development." Desire has been an underlying theme in my research, interwoven with ambiguity. Even the anthropologist has been consumed by conflicting desires, between the naïve desire for acceptance and desire to accomplish her task of becoming an anthropologist. The idea of desire as expressed in the concept *koDei* is negative in the society of the WoDaaBe, as I have shown. However, to speak of *koDei* is only appropriate in certain situations, not in others. Desire is also manifested in the concept *yidugo*, which signals a desire that is appropriate and natural. Everyone desires to exist, to have something that will allow him or her to live with dignity. Kala'i is the person who left a lasting impression within me, an impression that almost rests like a shadow over my writing. I met him at the market in Tchin-Tabaraden, a short time prior to leaving "the field." The dry season has been difficult, and he has arrived at the market to buy necessities. He has been traveling for a long time and he is tired. I had admired this man, respected him through fearing him. He had never shown me anything but kindness and he was the only person that I never felt "white" around, more like a young person who he saw as a part of his house. A moment occurs when there are only the two of us. We are sitting on a bench in an empty Tuareg shelter, facing each other. The shelter has been full of people but suddenly everyone has disappeared in order to catch the last moments of the market that will soon close. We have exchanged courteous and casual greetings; we have talked about all and nothing. His hands rest on his knees; his clothing is dirty and torn. He looks old. "I am tired, Mariyama", he tells me without looking at me, "I really feel tired after this season. This old man is tired." He looks at me and there is urgency in his voice, "I have to take care of all these people but the bush has nothing. My sons have no interest in cows, they just want to be in the city, following their own interest." There is bitterness in his voice. People arrive and we say no more. When he leaves, he places his arm on my shoulder and tells me that I should come back to him, because after all, I am like his own child. He tells me that I should tell my parents that his child (i.e., me) has given him a cloth to protect him against the cold. I do not know it then, but after I leave there will be another wait for the rain to fall and a large number of his cows will die. Ironically, his sons' work in the city will make it possible for him to stay in the bush.

Appendix 1
TRANSFORMING EXPERIENCE INTO A TEXT

> Ethnography is a research process in which the anthropologist closely observes, records and *engages* in the daily life of another culture.
> (Marcus and Fischer 1986:18; emphasis mine)

It has been argued that one of the virtues of post-modernism has been to direct attention to dimensions of power, embodied in knowledge's development and use, as an integral part of knowledge content (Downey and Rogers 1995:269). As Fabian points out, anthropology is an activity that is a part of what it studies (1983:157), making the relationship between anthropology and its objects potentially a political one (1983:43). Ethnographic research does not simply involve data gathering: who we are, and from where we come affects what kind of information we seek and are given, and how we perceive and locate it. Ethnography is thus a dynamic process, involving the interaction of real people, interaction between those presumably being observed and those observing, implying social relationships and the blurring of boundaries between subjects and objects. I think it can be stated that no data gathering is "simple" in its nature; rather, all research activity, ethnographic or not, is affected by the particular methods used, and by the relationship or non-relationship of the researcher to his or her subjects. The methodological challenges embodied in ethnographic research do not end with the completion of the research but continue with the process of writing, ethnographic accounts being the medium in which experience, theory, and culture are made available to a readership (Marcus and Fischer 1986:18). My goal here is to briefly point out the challenges that are part of writing ethnography and my own stand on some of the issues that have been debated within anthropology in recent years.

The spring prior to going to the "field", I enrolled in a seminar called *Writing Culture* at the University of Arizona. The semester has finished and I am seated, organizing my notes. Around me are papers, printouts and notes from the class. I look at the syllabus and read the title of the class as if I am reading something for the first time. I read it slowly, as if it was a strange, foreign language: Writing culture. It does not say writing about culture or the writing of culture. Just two words are standing side by side in all their simplicity. Writing culture. Perhaps because I like to make pictures, I can visualize someone writing culture, as if he or she is drawing another person's face or body. The connection of lines and dots makes a complete whole, which is recognized and understood in one way or another by everyone. The lines and dots form something we call a picture. It is a picture of something because we see a whole when we look at it. The whole is formed by the composition of its different parts. And writing basically does the same things, only by using abstract symbols. By these small dark symbols lined up together, we communicate our words, and with our words we can create a world of smell, of touch, of sight, of feelings. By writing culture, we are drawing a picture of something we see, we draw it the best we can but it has our personal touch engraved in it, and just like the picture of someone, it is perceived differently according to who is looking. In the end it is not this somebody, it never could be that, but simply an image, a reflection that at the best manages to communicate what we want to express. Culture is not only something we write about, but also something we write.

With an increased acknowledgment that ethnographic writing and fieldwork experiences themselves are not bound in the realm of objective truths, anthropologists have paid increasing attention to the process of writing. Even though the ethnography can be seen as characterized by dialogue, involving an active communication process with another culture (Marcus and Fischer 1986:30), it is still the anthropologist who holds the pen at the end of the research, usually safely removed from his/her research subjects. The anthropologist is the one who represents, and others the ones who are represented, no matter how much effect they have had on the research process itself. Experimental anthropology is concerned with the anthropologist placing him/herself into the text as a part of the research process (Moore 1994). The text will give glimpses of personal experiences of people as well as making me present within the text. The writing about the ethnographer in the text thus helps remind the reader of who is "telling" the story, moving away from a supposedly objective, positivistic representation of "other" people. By writing myself into the text, I try to speak *from within* my subject position rather than *for* someone. This phrase derives from Chandra Talpade Mohanty, who writes in relation to Latin American women, but I find it applicable for scholarship in general. To speak from within one's subject position means that one does not ignore the anthropologist's location in a world of power and meaning. Thus, by including myself, I provide the reader with some basis for knowing from where this ethnography derives, in what social-historical context. Placing myself within the text underlines that ethnographies are gendered products but obviously, research and the practice of anthropology itself involve gender (Bell 1993:4; Callaway 1992:30), making the researcher and those who are the focus of the research gendered subjects.

The problem with such experimental writing is that in some cases the text becomes "author saturated", meaning that the anthropologist is emphasized at the expense of telling about others (Moore 1994:116). Barbara Tedlock makes a distinction between a memoir of the field experience and a self-reflective ethnography. She argues that the self-conscious shift away from writing a memoir of the fieldwork experience and a narrative ethnography is that in the former, the author is the only fully developed character, while in the latter the author intentionally becomes a secondary character (Tedlock 1991:81). She also points to the significance of experiences in fieldwork and of reflecting on those experiences as a part of the knowledge process, by stating that "fieldwork is not simply a union card but the center of our intellectual and emotional lives" (1991:82). Anthropologists are professionals, not only because they are serious about their preparation and engagement with people in the field, but also because they are concerned about the issues of representation of their own works (Tedlock 1991:82). There is no single "correct" way to write ethnography and different involvements of the author in the text can serve different purposes. Anthropology as a field engaged in such diverse subjects should in fact embrace the idea that ethnographic expressions and presentations can be carried out in various manners (Campell 1996:81). The problem of the "author saturated text" has to be seen as part of a general problem of power and representation in anthropology. As Feld points out in relation to first-person narrative, such writing alone does not guarantee that the work is self-aware or insightful (Feld 1987:90).

A first-person narrative can also been seen as a form of literary device that aims at making the reader more involved in the text. Moore has discussed the way in which anthropologists of the past tried to remove themselves from travel writings by using a remote, dry style, especially female anthropologists whose position was more fragile within the academic community than men's (Moore 1994:125). Pratt comments that interesting subjects are often transformed in ethnographic writing to become quite dull (1986:33). The use of one's self in the text brings the reader closer to the people talked about, the anthropologist being a mediator between the experience of the reader and the experience of the people represented in the text. As pointed out by Moore, a text often becomes more interesting for the readers if some identifications are built into the text for them (1994:121). Even though ethnographies are often read by the subjects of the study, the largest readership is still an audience not familiar with the people the ethnographer is describing. It is of intellectual interest for the reader to see how the anthropologist relates to and experiences "his" or "her" people. Since all information is acquired through certain interactions and within certain conditions, information is appropriately contextualized when it is possible for the reader to evaluate to some extent how the anthropologist came to a certain conclusion.

In addition to these factors mentioned, I include myself in the ethnography because I hope that in giving a personal account of my experience and interaction with people, the experiences of those involved become more alive and their desires are more clearly expressed, along with my own. Thus, I hope to be able to move away from giving only descriptions of types, of general somebodies, towards real human beings, complicated individuals with diverse desires and sufferings. I seek to give a sense of "race", gender and ethnicity as lived experiences, rather than presenting them as abstract categories.

There are, however, clear ethical problems that arise with placing real persons into the text, especially when research is conducted in non-literate communities among people who have not had much exposure to the printed word. There is a risk that they do not realize completely what it means to be integrated into the text. This involves the problem of other people being able to read and observe personal information about them. Today, people live in increasingly integrated communities where ethnographies can be read by the members and even authorities of the societies in question. Information about people is also entangled within various power issues (Akeroyd 1984:134–135), concerning some of which the anthropologist may be entirely uninformed. Disclosure of personal information about individuals can thus be unethical in some cases, dangerous in others. Most anthropologists give people pseudonyms in addition to sometimes changing names of places and locations. When working in small communities, however, such measures are not necessarily enough to "hide" the identity of people.

Many individuals mentioned in the text wanted me to include their real names in the text. I decided not to do that, for the reasons mentioned above, the fear that they did not realize the ways in which such a text can be used and for the reason that I cannot myself predict the use and reading of my own text. All the names, except my own, are thus pseudonyms. Only in places where I thank people for information have I kept the correct names. The names of the different WoDaaBe lineages are accurate but I have not identified the names of the lineage factions in question because I fear that the individuals could be too easily recognized.

My formal interviews were all tape-recorded as were many group discussions. A majority of these were transcribed in Niamey with the assistance of WoDaaBe consultants. Other discussions, however, were not taped but simply written down after they had occurred, based on my own memory. And still other discussions were written down in the form of notes while they were taking place.

Where I present transcribed taped narratives, I present the number and the date of the tape. Discussions, however, that I have reconstructed from memory do not have a reference to a tape. Thus, the reader should be able to recognize where I quote direct speech and where discussion was more based on my memory.

Appendix II
INTERSUBJECTIVITY

The Danish novelist, Peter Høeg, writes: "[N]ow and again the thought strikes me that perhaps I have never really seen other people's expectations, that I have only seen my own, and the loneliest thought in the world is the thought that what we have glimpsed is nothing than ourselves" (Høeg [1988] 1995:402–403). One of anthropology's goals is to move away from one's self, to be able to reflect critically on it, and to be able to "see" other people's expectations and lives. Self-reflective or experimental ethnography "fails" when the only thing it provides is a glimpse of the anthropologist's expectations, but not those of the people in question. During my fieldwork, moments arose where I felt I had failed to see anything other than myself. These moments were probably the most frustrating of my fieldwork experience. Ironically, the feeling of only-seeing-myself surfaced probably less because of my academic concerns but more from a need of being accepted. Even though these periods were many rather than few, in retrospect these periods of self-criticism were important. They turned out to be transformative for my academic development, because from their process I was able to identify with and understand people in my closest environment and thus gain deeper insight into my research matter.

Other moments which I treasured, even though not as emotionally involving, were when I felt a sense of what Fabian (1983) has called coevalness, the sharing of the same time and the same universe with my friends. I experienced this at various moments such as when discussing matters dear to my heart with people close to me, or when analyzing patterns of embroidery (mine and theirs) with other women. I also valued those moments where it was obvious that we did not share the same universe or the same way of thinking, but could laugh together and reflect on it. Such moments almost created a dimension in reality where things could safely be analyzed and reflected upon. I believe that the strength of anthropology is found in its combination of a passionate personal approach with a strict commitment to knowledge and theoretical responsibilities. Some whites and educated Nigerien people expressed surprise that I was also staying in the city, clearly not seeing that as "real" ethnography, reflecting both conventional understanding of what anthropology is about (primitive people in an "original setting") and demonstrating exactly some of the things which I find problematic with popular notions of indigenous people. The lives of many WoDaaBe are experienced largely in the city, making ethnography there just as important as in the bush. During my life in Niamey, I was cared for, controlled, and supervised just as I was in the bush. Even though I went to libraries and archives and conducted interviews with non-WoDaaBe, the center of my life and of my research was my WoDaaBe family. I was sheltered, informed, helped, trusted and guided with firmness but kindness. Being in the setting of the lineage group, I felt sometimes like a prisoner, or a difficult child, like the family was constraining my research and me. I was, however, also reminded that the bush was a place where people die simply because they become exhausted in the heat, become victims of crime resulting from the unsafe conditions in Niger, or die because they do not receive medical assistance. These were the times when I thanked for being led to someone who I could trust with my life.

Appendix III
EARLIER RESEARCH ON WODAABE

The Fulani were for a long time of particular interest to Westerners, an interest that was probably influenced by their powerful position in the area of the Western Sahel, being the rulers of the Sokoto Caliphate which the colonial powers fought in order to gain control over its area. It was not until the early 1950s that intensive research took place on their society and social organization. During that time the Council of the International African Institute started encouraging research on the Fulani in the Western Sudan area in collaboration with the Rockefeller Foundation, the British Colonial Social Science Council and the *Institut Français d'Afrique Noire*. In a relatively short period of time, these Institutions funded three young researchers to conduct ethnographic research on pastoral Fulani in the Niger-Nigeria region. The first research was conducted by C. E. Hopen on the western border of northern Nigeria, and his book, *The Pastoral Fulbe Family in Gwandu*, published in 1958, was his main contribution to Fulani research. His research was followed by Derrick Stenning, who with his wife conducted intensive research during the years 1951–1953, and whose main results were published in his work *Savanna Nomads* in 1959. The third ethnologist was Marguerite Dupire, who was funded for two years of research, spending January 1951 until February 1952 conducting research in several parts of Niger, focusing on the WoDaaBe, but then continuing among the Adamawa Fulani in Cameroon.

Stenning's and Dupire's monographs, combining detailed historical work and ethnographic observations, were the first to focus exclusively on WoDaaBe. Stenning died when only thirty-seven years old, a mere five years after the publication of his *Savanna Nomads*, cutting short a very promising career. Dupire continued her research on various Fulani communities. Her ethnographic material on the WoDaaBe and Fulani societies gave a detailed description of the social organization and economic dynamics of Fulani and WoDaaBe societies (see discussion Burnham 1994:viii–x; Dupire 1962a:vii; Tardits 1985:5).

Stenning's and Dupire's research incorporated detailed economic and social analyses focusing on the organization of the WoDaaBe kinship and economic systems from a structural-functional framework. Both also paid attention to history in their work (though Stenning's use of history is more integrated into his overall discussion and approach).

Paul Riesman's more recent work among the Fulani Jelgobe, published in 1977 as *Freedom in Fulani Social Life: An Introspective Ethnography*, was very influential in shaping and influencing other studies of Fulani groups (see discussion in Stoller 1998), which I will not go into here.

After the contributions of Stenning and Dupire, research directly relevant to the WoDaaBe was not conducted for some time. The next major research among the WoDaaBe was conducted in relation to the Niger Range and Livestock Project, funded by USAID. The major findings from this project were published in a volume edited by Jeremy Swift in 1984, entitled *Pastoral Development in Central Niger*. Angelo Maliki Bonfiglioli, Cynthia White, Wendy Wilson and L. Loutan conducted research in connection with the project. Bonfiglioli has actively published results in relation to the work in the project, focusing on herding techniques and history[86] (Maliki 1981; Bonfiglioli 1988; 1985), giving a detailed analysis of the WoDaaBe herding practices and tracing the history of a WoDaaBe subgroup from the 19th century to the present. White focused, among other things, on seasonality and animal ownership (1986; 1990; 1997) while Loutan (1982) conducted extensive research on the health status and the health problems among the WoDaaBe. Mette Bovin has also more recently conducted extensive research among the WoDaaBe in the eastern part of Niger, especially concerning ethnic performances in relation to WoDaaBe identity as well as symbols relating to ethnicity (Bovin 1985, 1990, 2001).

More recently, few MA and PhD thesis have been are being conducted in relation to the WoDaaBe including studies on WoDaaBe ecological knowledge (Schareika 2003) and on WoDaaBe cattle breeding practices (Krätli 2007).

---

[86] I have not been able to locate the history document written in relation to his work on the project but in my research I use a published book discussing the same issues (Bonfiglioli 1988).

REFERENCES

Abadie, Maurice. 1927. *La Colonie du Niger*. Société d'Éditions Géographiques. Paris: Maritimes et Colonials.

Abu-Lughod, Lila. 1990. "The romance of resistance: Tracing transformations of power through Bedouin women." *American Ethnologist*, 17(1):41–55.

—. 1991. "Writing against Culture." *Recapturing Anthropology: Work in the Present*. (ed.) Richard G. Fox. New Mexico: School of American Research Press, pp. 137–62.

Advisory Committee on the Sahel. 1984. *Environmental Change in the West African Sahel*. Resource Management for Arid and Semiarid Regions. Advisory Committee on the Sahel Board on Science and Technology for International Affairs National Research Council. Washington, D.C.: National Academic Press.

Agnew, Clive and Ewan Anderson. 1992. *Water Resources in the Arid Realm*. London, New York: Routledge.

Ahmad, Aijaz. 1994. "Orientalism and After." *Colonial Discourse and Post-Colonial Theory: A Reader*. (eds) Patrick Williams and Laura Chrisman. New York: Columbia University Press, pp. 162–71.

AID Policy Paper. 1982. *Women in Development*. Bureau for Program and Policy Coordination. Washington: U.S. Agency for International Development.

Akeroyd, Anne V. 1984. "Ethics in Relation to Informants, the Profession and Governments." *Ethnographic Research: A Guide toward General Conduct*. (ed.) R. F. Ellen. Research Methods in Social Anthropology 1. London: Academic Press, pp. 133–54.

Alexander, Lieutenant Boyd. 1908. *From the Niger to the Nile*. Volume 1. London: Edward Arnold.

Alidou, Ousseina D. 2005. *Engaging Modernity: Muslim Women and the Politics of Agency in Postcolonial Niger*. Madison: The University of Wisconsin Press.

Alonso, Ana Maria. 1994. The Politics of Space, Time and Substance: State Formation, Nationalism, and Ethnicity. *Annual Review of Anthropology*, 23:379–405.

Althusser, Louis. 1971. "Ideology and Ideological State Apparatuses (Notes towards an Investigation)." *Lenin and Philosphy*. New York: Monthly Review Press, pp. 127–86.
Amin, Samir. 1976. *Unequal Development*. London: Monthly Review Press.
Amselle, Jean-Loup. 1998. *Mestizo Logics: Anthropology of Identity in Africa and Elsewhere*. Translated by Claudia Royal. Stanford: Stanford University Press.
Anderson, Benedict. 1983. *Imagined Communities: Reflections on the Origin and Spread of Nationalism*. London and New York: Verso.
Anthropology Newsletter. 1998. AAA Statement on "Race". *Anthropology Newsletter*. September.
Appadurai, Arjun. 1996. *Modernity at Large: Cultural Dimensions of Globalization*. Minneapolis: University of Minnesota Press.
—. 2001. "Grassroots *Globalization and the Research Imagination.*" *Globalization: A Special Issue of Public Culture*. (ed.) Arjun Appadurai. Durham: Duke University Press, pp. 1–21.
Arnould, Eric J. 1990. "Changing the Terms of Rural Development: Collaborative Research in Cultural Ecology in the Sahel." *Human Organization*, 49:339–354.
Azarya, Victor, Paul Kazuhisa Eguchi and Catherine VerEecke. 1993. Introduction. *Unity and Diversity of a People*. *Unity and Diversity of a People: The Search for Fulbe Identity*. (eds) Paul K. Eguchi and Victor Azarya. Senri Ethnological Studies. No. 35. Osaka [Japan]: National Museum of Ethnology, pp. 1–9.
Balibar, Étienne. 1991. "Class Racism." *Race, Nation and Class: Ambiguous Identities*. (eds) Étienne Ballibar and Immanuel Wallerstein. London: Verso, pp. 204–216.
Barnard, A. 2004. "Indigenous Peoples: A Response to Justin Kenrick and Jerome Lewis." *Anthropological Theory*, 20(5):19.
Barth, Fredrik. 1969. Introduction. *Ethnic Groups and Boundaries: The Social Organization of Culture Difference*. (ed.) Fredrik Barth. Boston: Little, Brown and Company, pp. 9–38.
Beaumont, Peter. 1989. *Drylands: Environmental Management and Development*. London and New York: Routledge.
Beauvilain, Alain. 1977. "Les Peul du Dallol Bosso et la Sécheresse 1969–1973, Niger." *Strategies Pastorales et Agricoles des Sahaliens durant la Sécheresse 1969–1974*. (ed.) Jean Gallais. Travaux et Documents de Géographie Tropicale. No. 30. Paris: Centre d'Etudes de Géographie Tropical.
Beckwith, Carol. 1983. "Niger's Wodaabe: 'People of the Taboo'." *National Geographic*, 164(4):483–510.

Beckwith, Carol and Marion van Offelen. 1983. *Nomads of Niger*. New York: Harry N. Abrams, Incorporated.

Bell, Diana. 1993. "Introduction 1:" The Context. *Gendered Fields: Women, Men and Ethnography*. (eds) Diana Bell, Pat Caplan and Wazir Jahan Karim. Routledge: London and New York, pp. 1–18.

Bennett, John W. 1988. "The Political Ecology and Economic Development of Migratory Pastoralist Societies in Eastern Africa." *Power and Poverty: Development and Development Projects in the Third World*. (eds) Donald W. Attwood, Thomas C. Bruneau and John G. Galaty. Boulder and London: Westview Press, pp. 31–60.

Bétaille, André. 1998. "The Idea of Indigenous People." *Current Anthropology*, 39(2):187–191.

[The] Body Shop. 1995. *The Body Shop: Skin & Hair Care Products by Mail*. (A Catalogue), NC: Buth-Na-Bodhaige, Inc.

Bonfiglioli, Angelo Maliki. 1981. "Ngaynaaka: Herding according to the WoDaaBe." Rapport Préliminaire – Discussion Paper. République du Niger. Ministry of Rural Development. Niger Range and Livestock Project.

—. 1985. "Evolution de la Propriété animale chez les WoDaaBe du Niger." *Journal des Africanistes*, 55(1–2):29–37.

—. 1988. *DuDal: Histoire de Famille et Histoire de Troupeau chez un Groupe de WoDaaBe du Niger*. Cambridge: Cambridge University Press.

Boserup, Ester. 1970. *Women's Role in Economic Development*. New York: St. Martin's Press.

Bourdieu, Pierre. 1990. *In Other Words: Essays toward Reflexive Sociology*. Stanford: Stanford University Press.

Bourque, Susan C. and Kay B. Warren. 1990. Feminist Perspective on Women in Development. *Persistent Inequalities: Women and World Development*. (ed.) Irene Tinker. New York and Oxford: Oxford University Press, pp. 70–82.

Bovin, Mette. 1985. "Nomades "Sauvage" et Paysans "Civilisés" WoDaaBe et Kanuri au Borno." *Journal des Africanistes*, 55(1–2):53–73.

—. 1990. "Nomads of the Drought: Fulbe and WoDaaBe Nomads between Power and Marginalization in the Sahel of Burkina Faso and Niger Republic." *Adaptive Strategies in African Arid Lands*. (eds) Mette Bovin and Leif Manger. Uppsala: The Nordic Africa Institute, pp. 25–57.

—. 2001. *Nomads Who Cultivate Beauty: WoDaaBe Dances and Visual Arts in Niger*. Uppsala: The Nordic Africa Institute.

Bowen, John R. 2000. "Universal 'indigenous peoples' rights'?" *Anthropology Today*, 16(4):12-16.
Brackenbury, E. A. 1924. "Notes on the 'Bororo Fulbe' or Nomad 'Cattle Fulani'." *Journal of the African Society*, 23(91):208-217.
Breman, H., et al. 1986. *Analyse des Conditions de l'Elevage et Propositions de Politiques et de Programmes*. République du Niger. CABO, Wageningen Pays-Bas.
Brokensha, David W., Michael M. Horowitz, and Thayer Scudder. 1977. *The Anthropology of Rural Development in the Sahel: Proposal for Research*. Binghamton, New York: Institute for Development Anthropology, INC.
Brown, Michael F. 1998. "Can Culture Be Copyrighted?" *Current Anthropology*, 39(2):193-222.
Bruijn, Mirjam E. de and Han J. W. M. van Dijk. 1999. "Insecurity and Pastoral Development in the Sahel." *Development and Change*, 30:115-139.
Burger, Julian. 1987. *A Report from the Frontier*. Cultural Survival Report. Nr. 28. Cultural Survival.
—. 1990. *The Gaia Atlas for First People: A Future for Indigenous World*. New York, London: Anchor Books.
Burnham, Philip. 1994. "Introduction to Savannah Nomads." *Savannah Nomads*. (by) Derrick J. Stenning. Münster-Hamburg: LIT Verlag, pp. ix-xv.
—. 1999. "Pastoralism under Pressure? – Understanding Social Change in Fulbe Society." *Pastoralists under Pressure? – Fulbe Societies Confronting Change in West Africa*. (eds) Victor Azarya, Anneke Breedveld, Mirjam de Bruijn and Han van Dijk. Leiden: Brill, pp. 269-283.
Burnham, Philip, and M. Last. 1994. "From Pastoralist to politician: the Problem of Fulbe 'aristocracy'." *Cahiers d'études africaines 133-35* xxxiv:331-357.
Burns, A. C. 1929. *History of Nigeria*. London: George Allen & Unwin Ltd.
Callaway, Helen. 1992. "Ethnography and Experience: Gender Implications in Fieldwork and Texts." *Anthropology and Autobiography*. (eds) Judith Okley and Helen Callaway. London and New York: Routledge, pp. 49-30.
Campell, Alan. 1996. "Tricky Tropes: Styles of the Popular and the Pompous." *Popularizing Anthropology*. (eds) Jeremy MacClancy and Chris McDonaughs. London and New York: Routledge, pp. 58-82.
Camphausen, Rufus C. 1997. *Return of the Tribal: A Celebration of Body Adornment*. Rochester, VT: Park Street Press.

Chakrabarty, Dipesh. 1988. "Conditions for Knowledge of Working-Class Conditions: Employers, Government and the Jute Workers of Calcutta, 1890–1940." *Selected Subaltern Studies*. (eds) Ranajit Guha and Gayatri C. Spivak. Oxford: Oxford University Press, pp. 179–230.

Chesi, Gert. 1977. *The Last Africans*. Wörgl (Austria): Perlinger-Verlag.

Cloud, Kathleen. 1986. "Sex Roles in Food Production and Distribution Systems in the Sahel." *Women Farmers in Africa: Rural Development in Mali and the Sahel*. (ed.) Lucy E. Creevey. New York: Syracuse University Press.

Clifford, James. 1997. *Routes: Travel and Translation in the Late Twentieth Century*. Cambridge: Harvard University Press.

Comaroff, John L. 1996. "Ethnicity, Nationalism, and the Politics of Difference in an Age of Revolution." *The Politics of Difference: Ethnic Premises in a World of Power*. (eds) Edwin N. Wilmsen and Patrick McAllister. Chicago and London: The University of Chicago Press, pp. 162–183.

Conklin, Beth A., and Laura R. Graham. 1995. "The Shifting Middle Ground: Amazonian Indians and Eco-Politics." *American Anthropologists*, 97(4):695–710.

Cornwall, Andrea, Elizabeth Harrison and Ann Whitehead. 2007. "Introduction: feminism in development: contradictions, contestation and challenges." *Feminism in Development: Contradictions and Challenges*. (eds) Andrea Cornwall, Elizabeth Harrison and Ann Whitehead. London: Zed Books, pp. 1–21.

Corrigan, Philip and Derek Sayer. 1985. *The Great Arch*. Oxford: Basil Blackwell.

CRDTO. 1971. *Dictionnaire élémentaire, Fulfulde–Francais–English, Elementary dictionary*. Niamey (Niger): CRDTO.

de Groot, Johanna. 1989. "'Sex' and 'Race': The Construction of Language and Image in the Nineteenth Century." *Sexuality and Subordination: Interdisciplinary Studies of Gender in the Nineteenth Century*. (eds) Susan Mendus and Jane Rendall. New York: Routledge, pp. 89–128.

de Lauretis, Teresa. 1987. *The Technology of Gender*. Bloomington: Indiana University Press.

de St. Croix, F. W. 1972 [1945]. *The Fulani of Northern Nigeria: Some General Notes*. Hants (England): Gregg International Publishing Limited.

Douglas, Mary. 1966. *Purity and Danger: An Analysis of Concepts of Pollution and Taboo*. Baltimore: Penguin Books.

Downey, Gary Lee and Juan D. Rogers. 1995. "On the Politics of Theorizing in a Postmodern Academy." *American Anthropologist*, 97(2):313–323.

Dunbar, Gary S. 1970. "African Ranches Ltd., 1914–1931: An Ill-Fated Stockraising Enterprise in Northern Nigeria." *Annals of the Association of American Geographers*, 69(1):102–123.

Dupire, Marguerite. 1962a. *Peuls Nomades: Etude descriptive des WoDaaBe du Sahel Nigérien*. Paris: Institut d'Ethnologie.

--. 1962b. "Trade and Markets in the Economy of the Nomadic Fulani of Niger (Bororo)." *Markets in Africa*. (eds) Paul Bohannan and George Dalton. Northwestern University Press. Northwestern University African Studies. Number 9, pp. 335–362.

--. 1971 [1960]. "The Position of Women in a Pastoral Society." *Women of Tropical Africa*. (ed.) Denise Paulme. Translated by H. M. Wright. Berkley and Los Angeles: University of California Press, pp. 47–92.

--. 1972. *Les Facteurs Humains de l'Economie Pastorale. Etudes Nigeriennes*, No. 6. Niamey (Niger): Centre Nigerien de Recherches en Sciences Humaines.

Eagleton, Terry. 1991. *Ideology: An Introduction*. London: Verso.

Eddy, Edward D. 1979. *Labor and Land Use on Mixed Farms in the Pastoral Zone in Niger. Monograph III. Livestock Production and Marketing in the Entente States of West Africa*. University of Michigan: Center for Research on Economic Development.

--. 1980. "Prospects for the Development of Cattle Production on Mixed Farms in the Pastoral Zone of Niger: A Summary." Discussion Paper no. 83. Center for Research on Economic Development. Ann Arbor, Michigan, The University of Michigan.

Edelman, Marc and Angelique Haugerud (eds). 2005. *The Anthropology of Development and Globalization: From Classical Political Economy to Contemporary Neoliberalism*. Malden: Blackwell Publishing.

Englebert, Victor. 1971. "Assembling Each Year for a Season of Dances, Bororo Herdsmen of Niger Celebrate the Rains." *Nomads of the World*. (ed.) Gilbert M. Grosvenor. National Geographic Society, pp. 172–195.

Englund, Harry. 1996. "Culture, Environment and the Enemies of Complexity." *Review of African Political Economy*, 76:179–188.

Escobar, Arturo. 1995. *Encountering Development: The Making and Unmaking of the Third World*. Princeton, New Jersey: Princeton University Press.

Ezeomah, Chimah. 1989. "The Conditions Governing the Schooling of the Children of Nomadic Peoples in Nigeria: An Approach to Solutions." A paper prepared for the meeting of National Specialists on the Conditions Governing the Schooling of the Children of Nomadic Peoples held at Conflans-Sante-Honorine (France), 11–15 September, 1989.

Fabian, Johannes. 1983. *The Time and the Other: How Anthropology Makes Its Objects*. New York: Colombia University Press.

—. 1990a "Presence and Representation: The Other and Anthropological Writing." *Critical Inquiry*, 16 (Summer):753–772.

—. 1990b. *Power and Performance: Ethnographic Explorations through Proverbial Wisdom and Theater in Shaba, Zaire*. Madison: The University of Wisconsin Press.

Feld, Steven. 1987. "Dialogic Editing: Interpreting How Kaluli Read Sound and Sentiment." *Cultural Anthropology*, 2(2):190–210.

Ferguson, Anne E. 1994. "Gendered Science: A Critique of Agricultural Development." *American Anthropologist*, 96(3):545–552.

Ferguson, James. 1994. *The Anti-Politics Machine*. Minneapolis: University of Minnesota Press.

—. 1999. *Expectations of Modernity: Myths and Meanings of Urban Life on the Zambian Copperbelt*. Berkely: University of California Press.

—. 2002. "Of Mimicry and Membership: Africans and the 'New World Society'." *Cultural Anthropology*, 17(4):551–569.

Finlay, Hugh et al. 1998. *Africa on a Shoestring*. Hawthorn (Australia): Lonely Planet.

Fisher, William. 1997. "Doing Good? The Politics and Antipolitics of NGO Practices." *Annual Review of Anthropology*, 26:439–464.

Foucault, Michel. 1980 [1972]. *Power/Knowledge: Selected Interviews & Other Writings 1972–1977*. (ed.) Colin Gordon. New York: Pantheon Books, pp. 109–133.

—. 1983. The Subject and Power. *Michael Foucault: Beyond Structuralism and Hermeneutics*. (eds.) Hubert Dreyfus and Paul Rabinow. Chicago: University of Chicago, pp. 208–226.

Franke, Richard W. and Barbara H. Chasin. 1980. *Seeds of Famine: Ecological Destruction and the Development Dilemma in the West African Sahel*. New Jersey: Rowman & Allanheld Publishers.

Frankenberg, Ruth. 1993. *White Women, Race Matters: The Social Construction of Whiteness*. Minneapolis: University of Minnesota Press.

Fratkin, Elliot. 1997. "Pastoralism: Governance and Development Issues." *Annual Review of Anthropology*, 26:235-61.

Friedman, Jonathan. 1990. "Being in the World: Globalization and Localization." *Global Culture: Nationalism, Globalization, and Modernity*. (ed.) Mike Featherstone. London: SAGE Publication, pp. 311-328.

Gado, Boureima Alpha. 1997. *Niamey: Au Cœur du Sahel*. Miroir du passé (tome 2). Niamey (Niger): Nouvelle Imprimerie du Niger.

Galaty, John G. 1981. "Introduction: Nomadic Pastoralists and Social Change Processes and Perspectives." *Change and Development in Nomadic and Pastoral Society*. (eds) John G. Galaty and Philip Carl Salzaman. Leiden: E. J. Brill, pp. 4-26.

Galaty, John G. and Pierre Bonte. 1991. The Current Realities of African Pastoralists. *Herders, Warriors and Trade: Pastoralism in Africa*. Boulder, San Francisco: Westview Press, pp. 267-292.

Geertz, Clifford. 1973. *The Interpretation of Culture*. New York: BasicBooks.

Gefu, Jerome. 1992. *Pastoralist Perspectives in Nigeria: The Fulbe of Udubo Grazing Reserve*. Research Report no. 89. Uppsala: The Nordic Africa Institute.

Goudie, Andrew. 1981. *The Human Impact on the Natural Environment*. Cambridge: The MIT Press.

Gramsci, Antonio. 1971. *Selection from the Prison Notebooks*. New York: International Publishers.

Grayzel, John Aron. 1990. "Markets and Migration: A Fulbe Pastoral System in Mali." *The World of Pastoralism: Herding Systems in Comparative Perspective*. (eds) John G. Galaty and Douglas L. Johnson. New York and London: The Guilford Press, pp. 35-68.

Greenberg, Joseph H. 1949. "Studies in African Linguistic Classification: II. The Classification of Fulani". *Southwestern Journal of Anthropology*, 5(3):190-198.

Greenough, Karen. 2007. "Development Agents and Nomadic Agency: Four Perspectives in the "Development Market"." *NAPA Bulletin*, 27:110-128.

Guichard, M. 1990. "'L'ethnicisation' de la société peule du Borgou (Benin)." *Cahiers d'études africaines*, 117:17-44.

Hall, Stuart. 1981. "Notes on Deconstructing 'The Popular'." *'Peoples' History and Socialist Theory*. (ed.) Raphael Samuel. London: Routledge and Kegan Paul, pp. 227-240.

--. 1990. "Cultural Identity and Diaspora." *Identity: Community, Culture, Difference*. (ed.) J. Rutherford. London: Lawrence & Wishart, pp. 222-237.

Hamidou, Sidikou A. 1980a. "Population." *Les Atlas Jeune Afrique: Niger.* (eds) Edmond Bernus and Sidikou A. Hamidou. Paris: Editions Jeune Afrique, pp. 30–33.

—. 1980b. "Urbanisation." *Les Atlas Jeune Afrique: Niger.* (eds) Edmond Bernus and Sidikou A. Hamidou. Paris: Editions Jeune Afrique, pp. 34–35.

Hannerz, Ulf. 1992. *Cultural Complexity: Studies in the Social Organization of Meaning.* New York: Colombia University Press.

Hartigan Jr., John. 1997. "Establishing the Fact of Whiteness." *American Anthropologist*, 99(3):495–505.

Henderson, Helen Kreider. 1995. Introduction. *Gender and Agricultural Development: Surveying the Field.* (ed.) Helen Kreider Henderson. Tucson: University of Arizona Press, pp. xi–xvi.

Herskovits, Melville. 1926. "The Cattle Complex in East Africa." *American Anthropologist*, (n.s., 28):230–272.

Hoben, Allan. 1982. "Anthropologists and Development." *Annual Review of Anthropology*, 11:349–75.

Hobsbawm, Eric. 1983. *The Invention of Tradition.* Cambridge: Cambridge University Press.

Hopen, C. Edward. 1958. *The Pastoral Fulbe Family in Gwandu.* London: Oxford University Press.

Horowitz, Michael M. 1972. "Ethnic Boundary Maintenance among Pastoralists and Farmers in Western Sudan (Niger)." *Perspectives on Nomadism.* (eds) Williams Irons and Neville Dyson-Hudson. Leiden: E. J. Brill, pp. 105–114.

—. 1986. "Ideology, Policy and Praxis in Pastoral Livestock Development." *Anthropology and Rural Development in West Africa.* (eds) Michael M. Horowitz and Thomas M. Painter. Boulder and London: Westview Press, pp. 251–272.

Horowitz, Michael M. and Thomas M. Painter. 1986. "Introduction: Anthropology and Development." *Anthropology and Rural Development in West Africa.* (eds) Michael M. Horowitz and Thomas M. Painter. Boulder and London: Westview Press, pp. 1–8.

Hunwick, John O. 1965. "Islam in West Arica, A.D. 1000–1800." *A Thousand Years of West African History: A Handbook for Teachers and Students.* (eds) J. F. Ade Ajayi and Ian Espie. Ibadan University Press and Nelson, pp. 113–131.

—. 1997. "Sub-Saharan Africa and the Wider World of Islam: Historical and Contemporary Perspective." *African Islam and Islam in Africa: Encounters between Sufis and Islamists*. (eds) David Westerlund and Eva Evers Rosander. London: Hurst and Company in co-operation with the Nordic Africa Institute, pp. 28–54.

Høeg, Peter. [1988] 1995. *The History of Danish Dreams*. Toronto: Seal Books, McClelland-Bantam Inc.

Ibrahim, Jibrin. 1994. "Political Exclusion, Democratization and Dynamics of Ethnicity in Niger." *Africa Today*, 3rd Quarter:15–39.

Kaplan, Robert. 1994. "The Coming Anarchy." *The Atlantic Monthly*, February:44–54, 58–76.

Ki-Zerbo, Joseph. 1978. *Histoire de l'Afrique Noire: D'Hier à Demain*. Libraire A. Hatier.

Kirk-Greene, A. H. M. 1958. *Adamawa: Past and Present: An (sic) Historical Approach to the Development of a Northern Cameroons Province*. London and New York: Oxford University Press.

Krätli, Saverio. 2007. *Cows Who Choose Domestification: Generation and Management of Domestic Animal Diversity by WoDaaBe Pastoralist (Niger)*. A thesis submitted for the degree of Doctor of Philosophy, Institute of Development Studies, University of Sussex.

Lavie, Smadar. 1990. *The Poetics of Military Occupation: Mzeina Allegories of Bedouin Identity Under Israel and Egyptian Rule*. Berkeley: University of California Press.

Little, Peter D. 1998. "Maasai Identity on the Periphery." *American Anthropologist*, 100(2):444–457.

Little, Peter D., and Michael Painter. 1995. "Discourse, Politics and the Development Process: Reflections on Escobar's "Anthropology and the Development Encounter"." *American Ethnologist*, 22:602–616.

Loftsdóttir, Kristín 2001a. "Birds of the Bush: WoDaaBe Definitions of Society and Nature." *Nordic Journal of African Studies*, 10(3):280–298.

—. 2001b. "Where My Cord Is Buried: WoDaaBe Use and Conceptualization of Land." *Journal of Political Ecology*, 8: 1–24.
http://www.library.arizona.edu/ej/jpe/vol8.htm

—. 2002. "The Place of Birth: WoDaaBe Changing Histories of Origin." *History in Africa*, 29:283–307.

—. 2003. "Never Forgetting? Gender and Racial – Ethnic Identity during Fieldwork." *Social Anthropology*, 10(3):303–317.

—. 2004a. "'This Time It's Different': Globalization, Power and Mobility." *Topographies of Globalization: Politics, Culture, Language*. (eds) Valur Ingimundarson, Kristín Loftsdóttir and Irma Erlingsdóttir. Reykjavík: Háskólaútgáfan, pp. 149–162.

—. 2004b. "When Nomads Lose Cattle: WoDaaBe Negotiations of Ethnicity." *African Sociological Review*, 8(2): 52–76.

—. 2007. "Bounded and Multiple Identities: Ethnic Identities of WoDaaBe and FulBe." *Cahiers d'études africaines*, XLVII 185(1):65–92.

Loutan, L. 1982. "Nutrition et Santé chez un Groupe d'Eleveurs WoDaaBe (Bororo) du Niger." Rapport préliminaire – Discussion Paper. Niger Range and Livestock Project. USAID. République du Niger. Ministéré du Développement Rural.

Lovejoy, Paul E. 1981. "Slavery in the Sokoto Caliphate." *The Ideology of Slavery in Africa*. (ed.) Paul E. Lovejoy. London and Beverly Hills: Sage Publication, pp. 200–243.

Lund, Christian. 1993a. *An Outline of the Political and Adminstrative Landscape in Niger*. Roskilde University. Institute of Geography, Socio-Economic Analysis and Computer Science. Working Paper no. 118.

—. 1993b. *Waiting for the Rural Code: Perspectives on a Land Tenure Reform in Niger*. IIED (International Institute for Environment and Development). Paper no. 44, September.

—. 1997. *Niger: En politisk og økonomisk oversigt*. Copenhagen: The Ministry of Foreign Affairs, DANIDA.

Lutz, Catherine A. and Jane L. Collins. 1993. *Reading National Geographic*. Chicago and London: The University of Chicago Press.

Mabbutt, J. A. and C. Floret (eds). 1980. *Case Studies on Desertification*. Paris: Unesco.

Maliki, Angelo Bonfiglioli. 1981. See under Bonfiglioli.

Marcus, George E., and Michael M. J. Fischer. 1986. *Anthropology as Cultural Critique: An Experimental Moment in the Human Sciences*. Chicago and London: The Unversity of Chicago Press.

Marty, André and Hassane Beidou. 1988. Etude Socio-Economique. Première phase: 21 Septembre–6 Novembre 1988. Entretiens avec les pasteurs et les agro-pasteurs. Ministére de l'Agriculture et de l'Environment. Ministére des Ressources Animales et de l'Hydraulique. Programme Special National – Niger-FIDA-Volet Pastoral. Paris: Institut de Recherches et d'Applications des Méthodes de développement. Unpublished document obtained at the Direction l'Elevage in Tchin-Tabaraden.

Matt, Lisa M. 1994. "Information Management and Development Fund Programming in Niger." Prepared for IRG/ASDG II/ Ministry of Agriculture and Livestock/USAID. November. International Resource Group, Ltd.

Maybury-Lewis, David. 1992. *Millennium: Tribal Wisdom and the Modern World.* New York: Viking Penguin.

Mazumdar, Vina, and Kumud Sharma. 1990. "Sexual Division of Labour and the Subordination of Women: A Reappraisal from India." *Persistent Inequalities: Women and World Development.* (ed.) Irene Tinker. New York and Oxford: Oxford University Press, pp. 185–197.

Meek, C. K. 1925. *The Northern Tribes of Nigeria: An Ethnographic Account of the Northern Provinces of Nigeria together with a Report on the 1921 Decennial Census.* Oxford University Press. London: Humphrey Milford.

Michel, Pierre. 1980. "Sols." *Atlas du Niger.* (eds) Edmund Bernus and Sidikou A. Hamidou. Paris: Editions Jeune Afrique, pp. 18–19.

Miller, Daniel. 1989. "The Limits of Dominance." *Domination and Resistance.* (eds) Daniel Miller, Michael Rowlands and Christopher Tilley. London: Unwin Hyman, pp. 63–79.

Minh-ha, Trinh T. 1984. *Woman, Native, Other. Writing Postcoloniality and Feminism.* Bloomington and Indianapolis: Indiana University Press.

Mohamed Salih, M.A. 1990. Pastoralism and the State in African Arid Lands: An Overview. *Nomadic Peoples.* No. 25–27:7–18.

—. 1991. "Livestock Development or Pastoral Development." *When the Grass Is Gone: Development Intervention in African Arid Lands.* (ed.) P. T.W. Baxter. Seminar Proceedings No. 25. Uppsala: The Nordic Africa Institute.

—. 1995. Pastoral Migration to Small Towns in Africa. *The Migration Experience in Africa.* (eds) Jonathan Baker and Tade Akin Aina. Uppsala: The Nordic Africa Institute, pp. 181–196.

Mohanty, Chandre Telpade, Ann Russo, and Lourdes Torres. 1991. "Introduction: Cartographies of Struggle Third World Women and the Politics of Feminism." *Third World Women and the Politics of Feminism.* (eds) Chandra Telpade Mohanty, Ann Russo, and Lourdes Torres. Bloomington and Indianapolis: Indiana University Press, pp. 1–47.

Moore, Henrietta L. 1988. *Feminism and Anthropology.* Minneapolis: University of Minnesota Press.

—.1994. *A Passion for Difference: Essays in Anthropology and Gender.* Bloomington and Indianapolis: Indiana University Press.

Morel, E. D. 1911. *Nigeria: Its Peoples and Its Problems*. London: Smith, Elder & Co.

Mukhopadhyay, Carol C. and Yolanda T. Moses. 1997. "Reestablishing "Race" in Anthropological Discourse." *American Anthropologist*, 99(3):517–533.

Murphy, Brian K. 2000. "International NGOs and the Challenge of Modernity." *Development in Practice*, 10(3 & 4):330–347.

Nash, June. 2001. "Globalization and the Cultivation of Peripheral Vision." *Anthropology Today*, 17:15–22.

Netting, Robert M. 1986 [1977]. *Cultural Ecology*. Illinois: Waveland Press, Inc.

Newton, Alex. 1992. *West Africa: A Travel Survival Kit*. Hawthorn (Australia): Lonely Planet.

Ngaido, Tidiane. 1993. *Land Use Conflicts in Western Rural Niger: Kollo and Tillabery Arrondissements*. Madison, Wisconsin: Land Tenure Center, University of Wisconsin-Madison.

Nicholson, Sharon. 1984. "Appendix: The Climatology of Sub-Saharan Africa." *Environmental Change in the West African Sahel*. Resource Management for Arid and Semiarid Regions. Advisory Committee on the Sahel Board on Science and Technology for International Affairs National Research Council. Washington, D.C.: National Academic Press.

Nicolaisen, Johannes. 1963. *Ecology and Culture of the Pastoral Tuaregs: With Particular Reference to the Tuareg of Ahaggar and Ayr*. The National Museum of Copenhagen. Denmark: Andelsbogtrykkeriet i Odense.

Nkrumah, Francis K. 1977. Preface. *The Last Africans*. (by) Gert Chesi. Wörgl (Austria): Perlinger-Verlag.

No name. 1983. Cinq études sur la Formation en République du Niger: Etude D: Organisation de la direction du service de l'élevage et des industries animales (DSEIA). Commission des communautés Européennes. République du Niger. Minister du Plan.

Novo, Carmen Martinez. 2007. *Who Defines Indigenous? Identities, Development, Intellectuals and the State in Northern Mexico*. New Brunswick and New Jersey: Rutgers University Press.

Nugent, Stephen. 1990. *Big Mouth: The Amazon Speaks*. London: Fourth Estate.

Nyamnjoh, Francis B. 2007. "'Ever-Diminishing Circles': The Paradoxes of Belonging in Botswana." *Indigenous Experience Today*. (eds) Marisol de la Cadena and Orin Starn. Oxford and New York: Berg, pp. 305–332.

Osborn, Donald W., David J. Dwyer and Joseph I. Donohoe, Jr. 1993. *Lexique Fulfulde (Maasina)–Anglais–Français: Une compilation basée sur racines et tirée de sources existantes suivie de listes en anglais–fulfulde et français–fulfulde.* East Lansing: Editions Michigan State University.

Painter, Thomas M. 1987. "Bringing Land Back In: Changing Strategies to Improve Agricultural Production in the West African Sahel." *Land at Risk in the Third World: Local-Level Perspective.* (eds) Peter D. Little, Michael M. Horowitz, and A. Endre Nyerges. Boulder and London: Westview Press, pp. 144–163.

——. 1991. Approaches to Improving Natural Resource Use for Agriculture in Sahelian West Africa: A Sociological Analysis of the 'Aménagement/Gestion des Terroirs Villageois' Approach and Its Implications for Non-Governmental Organizations. CARE: Agriculture and Natural Resources Technical Report Series. No. 3. Agriculture and Natural Resources Unit, CARE, New York City, NY.

Paris, Patrick. 1997 "Ga'i ngaanyka ou les taureaux de l'alliance: Description ethnographique d'un rituel interlignager chez les Peuls Vod'aab'e du Niger." *Journal des Africanistes,* 97(2)71–100.

Park, Thomas K. 1993. "Ecology and Risk Management: The Case for Common Property." *Risk and Tenure in Arid Lands: The Political Ecology of Development in the Senegal River Basin.* (ed.) Thomas K. Park. Tucson and London: The University of Arizona Press, pp. 293–330.

Parpart, Jane L. and Marianne H. Marchand. 1995. Exploding the Canon: An Introduction/ Conclusion. *Feminism/Postmodernism/Development.* (eds) Marianna H. Marchand and Jane L. Parpart. London and New York: Routledge, pp. 1–22.

Pelletier, Corinne A. and A. Neil Skinner. 1981. *Adamawa Fulfulde: An Introductory Course.* African Studies Program. Madison: University of Wisconsin.

Pletsch, Carl E. 1981. "The Three Worlds or the Division of Social Scientific Labor, circa 1950–1975." *Comparative Studies in Society and History.* 23(4):565–590.

Pollock, Griselda. 1994. "Feminism/Foucault-Surveillance/Sexuality." *Visual Culture: Images and Interpretations.* (eds) Norman Bryson, Michael Ann Holly and Keith Moxey. Hanover and London: Wesleyan University Press, pp. 1–41.

Porter, Dennis. 1994. "Orientalism and Its Problems." *Colonial Discourse and Post-Colonial Theory: A Reader.* (eds) Patrick Williams and Laura Chrisman. New York: Columbia University Press, pp. 150–161.

Porter, Philip W. and Eric S. Sheppard. 1998. *A World of Difference: Society, Nature, Development*. New York and London: The Guilford Press.

Pratt, Mary Louise. 1986. "Fieldwork in Common Places." *Writing Culture: The Poetics and Politics of Ethnography*. (eds) James Clifford and George Marcus. Berkeley: University of California Press, pp. 27-50.

Prior, Julian. 1994. *Pastoral Development Planning*. Oxfam Development Guidelines no. 9. Oxford: Oxfam.

Rabinow, Paul. 1986. "Representations Are Social Facts: Modernity and Post-Modernity in Anthropology." *Writing Culture: The Poetics and Politics of Ethnography*. (eds) James Clifford and George E. Marcus. Berkeley: University of California Press, pp. 234-261.

Rain, David 1999. *Eaters of the Dry Season: Circular Labor Migration in the West African Sahel*. Boulder and London: Westview Press.

Reed, L. N. 1932. "Notes on Some Fulani Tribes and Customs." *Africa*, 5(4):422-454.

Riesman, Paul 1977. *Freedom in Fulani Social Life: An Introspective Ethnography* (Translation by Martha Fuller). London, Chicago: University of Chicago Press.

—. 1984. The Fulani in Development Context: The Relevance of Cultural Traditions for Coping with Change and Crisis. *Life before the Drought*. (ed.) Earl Scott. Boston: Allen & Unwin, pp. 171-183.

Rigby, Peter. 1996. *African Images: Racism and the End of Anthropology*. Oxford: Berg.

Roberts, Pepe. 1981. "'Rural Development' and the Rural Economy in Niger, 1900-75." *Rural Development in Tropical Africa*. (eds) Judith Heyer, Pepe Roberts and Gavin Williams. London and Basingstoke: The Macmillan Press Ltd., pp. 193-221.

Roddick, Anita. 1991. *Body and Soul: Profit with Principles – The Amazing Success Story of Anita Roddick and The Body Shop*. New York: Crown Trade Paperbacks.

Root, Deborah. 1996. *Cannibal Culture: Art, Appropriation, and the Commodification of Difference*. Colorado, Oxford: Westveiw Press, Inc.

Rosaldo, Renato. 1989. *Culture and Truth: The Remaking of Social Analysis*. Boston: Beacon Press.

Roseberry, William. 1994. "Hegemony and the Language of Contention." *Everyday Forms of State Formation: Revolution and the Negotiation of Rule in Modern Mexico*. (eds) Gilbert M. Joseph and Daniel Nugent. Durham and London: Duke University Press, pp. 355-366.

Rossel, Pierre. 1988. "Tourism and Cultural Minorities: Double Marginalisation and Survival Strategies." *Tourism: Manufacturing the Exotic.* (ed.) Pierre Rossel. Copenhagen: IWGIA (International Work Group for Indigenous Affairs), pp. 1–20.

Sa'ad, Hamman Tukur. 1991. "Wuro: The Ephemical Settlement of the Nomadic FulBe." *Studies in Fulfulde Language, Literature and Culture. Proceedings of the 1st– 4th International Conferences on Fulfulde Language, Literature and Culture.* (eds) I. A. Abba, I. Mukoshy and G. Tahir. Centre for the Study of Nigerian Languages, Bayero University. Kano (Nigeria): Triumph Publishing Company (Nig.) Ltd., pp. 207–216.

Sanders, Douglas E. 1977. *The Formation of the World Council of Indigenous People.* IWGIA Document nr. 29. Copenhagen: IWGIA (International Work Group for Indigenous Affairs).

Saugestad, Sidsel. 2001. *The Inconvenient Indigenous: Remote Area Development in Botswana, Donor Assistance, and the First People of the Kalahari.* Uppsala: The Nordic Africa Institute.

Schareika, N. 2003. *Know to Move, Move to Know: Ecological Knowledge among the WoDaaBe of South Eastern Niger.* Rome: FAO.

Scott, Earl. 1984. Introduction: Life and Poverty in the Savanna-Sahel Zones. *Life before the Drought.* (ed.) Earl Scott. London, Sydney: Allen and Unwin, pp. 1–27.

Scott, Michael F. and Brendan Gormley. 1980. "The Animal of Friendship (Habbanaae) in Indigenous Model of Sahelian Pastoral Development in Niger. *Indigenous Knowledge Systems and Development.* (eds) David W. Brokensha, D.M. Warren and Oswald Werner. Washington, D.C.: University Press of America, pp. 92–110.

SDSAP (Subvention au Développement du Secteur Agricole Phase II). 1994. Liste des Projets Ayant un Rapport avec la Gestion des Ressources Naturelles. Niamey, Niger: IRG (International Resource Group)

Shimada, Yoshihito. 1993. "Jihad as Dialectical Movement and Formation of Islamic Identity among the Fulbe." *Unity and Diversity of a People: The Search for Fulbe Identity.* (eds) Paul K. Eguchi and Victor Azarya. Senri Ethnological Studies. No. 35. Osaka [Japan]: National Museum of Ethnology, pp. 87–117.

Sissons, Jeffrey. 2005. *First Peoples: Indigenous Cultures and Their Future.* London: Reaktion Books.

Spitulnik, Debra. 1993. "Anthropology and Mass Media." *Annual Review of Anthropology*, 22:293–315.

Stenning, Derrick J. 1959. *Savannah Nomads: A Study of the WoDaaBe Pastoral Fulani of Western Bornu Province, Northern Region, Nigeria*. London: Oxford University Press.

—. 1964. Cattle Values and Islamic Values in a Pastoral Population. *Islam in Tropical Africa*. (ed.) I. M. Lewis. International African Institute. London: Hutchinson University Library for Africa, pp. 387–400.

Stiglitz, Joseph E. 2002. *Globalization and its discontents*. New York: W. W. Norton & Company.

Stoller, Paul. 1998. Foreword. *Freedom in Fulani Social Life: An Introspective Ethnography*. (by) Paul Riesman. Chicago: University of Chicago, pp. ix–xvi.

Sutter, John W. 1982. "Commercial Strategies, Drought and Monetary Pressure: WoDaaBe Nomads of Tanout Arrondissement, Niger." *Nomadic Peoples*, 11(October):26–60.

Swift, Jeremy and Angelo B. Maliki. n.d. "A Preliminary Evaluation of a Pilot Program to Create Herders' Association in the Pastoral Zone of Central Niger." Unpublished document. Niger Range and Livestock Project.

Swift, Jeremy et al. 1984. *Pastoral Development in Central Niger*. (ed.) Jeremy Swift. Niamey, Niger: USAID.

Tardits, Claude. 1985. "Le Worso." *Journal des Africanistes*, 55(1–2):5–14.

Taussig, Michael. 1993. *Mimesis and Alterity: A Particular History of the Senses*. New York and London: Routledge.

Tedlock, Barbara. 1991. "From Participant Observation to the Observation of Participation: The Emergence of Narrative Ethnography." *Journal of Anthropological Research*, 47(1):69–94.

Terraciano, Annmarie M. 1993. "Access to Resources in the Téra Arrondissement, Niger: Background and Recommendations for Rural Code Reform." Madison, Wisconsin: Land Tenure Center, University of Wisconsin-Madison.

Thébaud, Brigitte. 1995. *Land Tenure, Environmental Degradation and Desertification in Africa: Some Thoughts Based on the Sahelian Example*. IIED (International Institute for Environment and Development) Paper no. 57.

Thomas, David S. G. and Nicholas J. Middleton. 1994. *Desertification: Exploding the Myth*. Chichester: John Wiley & Sons.

Tinker, Irene. 1990. The Making of a Field: Advocates, Practitioners and Scholars. *Persistent Inequalities: Women and World Development*. New York and Oxford: Oxford University Press, pp. 27–53.

Trillo, Richard and Jim Hudges. 1995 [1990]. *West Africa: The Rough Guide*. London: The Rough Guides.

Tsing, Anna. 2000. "The Global Situation." *Cultural Anthropology*, 15:327–360.

Turner, T. S. 1979. "Anthropology and the Politics of Indigenous People Struggles." *Cambridge Anthropology*, 5(1):1–43.

—. 1995a. "The Kayapo Revolt against Extractivism: An Indigenous People's Struggle for Socially Equitable and Ecologically Sustainable Production." *Journal of Latin American Anthropology*. 1(1).

—. 1995b. "Neo-Liberal, Eco-Politics and Indigenous Peoples: The Kayapo, the "Rainforest Harvest," and the Body Shop." *Local Heritage in the Changing Tropics*. (ed.) Greg Dicum. Bulletin series, Yale School of Forestry and Environmental Studies. No 98, pp. 113–123.

Turner, Victor. 1967. *The Forest of Symbols*. Tucson: University of Arizona Press.

Turton, David. 1988. "Anthropology and Development." *Perspectives on Development: Cross-disciplinary themes in Development*. (eds) P. F. Leeson and M. M. Minogue. Manchester and New York: Manchester University Press, pp. 126–159.

Tylor, F. W. 1995 [1932]. *Fulani. Fulani-English Dictionary*. New York: Hippocrene Books.

Udayagiri, Mridula. 1995. "Challenging Modernization: Gender and Development, Postmodern Feminism and Activism." *Feminism/Postmodernism/Development*. (eds) Marianna H. Marchand and Jane L. Parpart. London and New York: Routledge, pp. 159–177.

US Department of State 2007. *Background Note: Niger*. (accessed 14 January 2008) http://www.state.gov/r/pa/ei/bgn/5474.htm

Vansina, Jan. 1990. *Paths in the Rainforest*. Wisconsin: The University of Wisconsin Press.

VerEecke, Cathrine. 1989. "Cultural Construction of Women's Economic Marginality: The Fulbe of Northeastern Nigeria." Working Paper No. 195. Michigan State University.

—. 1991. "Na'i Ngoni Pulaaku: Cattle Values and their Implications for Cultural Change among the FulBe." *Studies in Fulfulde Language, Literature, and Culture*. Proceedings of the 1st–4th International Conference on Fulfulde Language, Literature and Culture. (eds) I. A. Abba, I. Mukoshy, and G. Tahir. Centre for the Study of Nigerian Languages, Bayero University. Kano (Nigeria): Triumph Publishing Company (Nig.) Ltd., pp. 162–186.

—. 1993. "Sub-National Fulbe Identity in Nigeria? Responses to Political Change in Post-Independence Times." *Unity and Diversity of a People: The Search for Fulbe Identity*. (eds) Paul K. Eguchi and Victor Azarya. Senri Ethnological Studies. No. 35. Osaka [Japan]: National Museum of Ethnology, pp. 139–161.

Villiers, Marq de and Sheila Hirtle. 1997. *Into Africa: A Journey through the Ancient Empires*. London: Phoenix Giant.

Virtanen, Tea. 1998. "Ethnicity as Experience: Embodiment of Difference among the Pastoral Fulbe in Cameroon." Paper presented at the conference "Crisis and Culture in Africa: with Special Emphasis on Pastoral Nomads and Farmers in the West African Sahel". Eklundshof, Uppsala, 27–30 March 1998.

Visweswaran, Kamala. 1998. "Race and the Culture of Anthropology." *American Anthropologist*, 100(1):70–83.

von Braun, Joachim and Patrick J. R. Webb. 1989. "The Impact of New Crop Technology on the Agricultural Division of Labor in a West African Setting." *Economic Development and Cultural Change*, 37(3):513–532.

Waldie, Kevin. 1990. "'Cattle and Concrete': Changing Property Rights and Property Interest among the Fula Cattle Herders around Kabala, North East Sierra Leone." *Property, Poverty, and People: Changing Rights in Property and Problems of Pastoral Development*. (eds) P. T. W. Baxter and R. Hogg. Manchester: University of Manchester, pp. 229–239.

Wallerstein, Immanuel. 1974. *The Modern World-System: Capitalist Agriculture and the Origin of the European World Economy in the Sixteenth Century*. New York: Academic.

Werbner, Pina. 2001. "The Limits of Cultural Hybridity: On Ritual Monsters, Poetic Licence and Contested Postcolonial Purifications." *The Journal of the Royal Anthropological Institute*, 7:133–152.

Whitaker, C. S. Jr. 1970. *The Politics of Tradition, Continuity and Change in Northern Nigeria 1946–1966*. Princeton, New Jersey: Princeton University Press

White, Cynthia. 1986. "Food Shortage and Seasonality in WoDaaBe Communities in Niger." *IDS Bulletin*, 17(3):19–25.

—. 1990. "Changing Animal Ownership and Access to Land among the WoDaaBe (Fulani) of Central Niger." *Property, Poverty, and People: Changing Rights in Property and Problems of Pastoral Development*. (eds) P. T. W. Baxter and Richard Hogg. Manchester: University of Manchester, pp. 240–274.

—. 1997. "The Effects of Poverty on Risk Reduction Strategies of Fulani Nomads in Niger." *Nomadic Peoples*, 1(1):90–107.

Williams, Raymond. 1977. *Marxism and Literature.* Oxford, New York: Oxford University Press.
Wilson, Wendy. 1992. "Women in Niger: Socio-Economic Roles in Agro-Pastoral Production, Natural Management and Off-Farm Production." Final Report. Prepared for the GENESYS project, The Futures Group and USAID/Niamey. Office of Women in Development. Bureau for Research and Development. Agency for International Development.
Wilson, Wendy and Asmarom Legesse. 1990. *Nomads' Dialogue: Development instead of Relief: A Meeting of Herders, Farmers and Artisans from East and West Africa held in Ndutu, Tanzania.* Washington: The African Development Foundation.
Wilson-Haffenden, J.R. 1930. *The Red Men of Nigeria: An Account of a Lengthy Residence among the Fulani, or "Red Men", & Other Pagan Tribes of Central Nigeria, with a Description of Their Headhunting, Pastoral & Other Customs, Habits & Religion.* London: Frank Cass & Co. LTD.
Wolf, Eric. 1982. *Europe and the People without History.* Berkeley: University of California Press.
World Bank. 1991. Niger Country Strategy Paper (CESP). November 25, 1991.
World Bank. 1992. Niger Country Strategy Statement. March 20,1992.
World Bank. 1995. Policy Framework Paper (1996-98). Prepared by the Nigerian authorities in collaboration with the staffs of the World Bank and the International Monetary Fund. 25 October 1995.
World Bank. 2003. *Memorandum of the President of the International Development Association to the Executive Directors on a Country Assistance Strategy of the World Bank for the Republic of Niger [Report number 252030].* Niger Country Office/Country Department 13, The World Bank.
Worsley, Peter. 1984. *The Three Worlds: Culture and World Development.* Chicago: The University of Chicago Press.
Worster, Donald. 1977. *Nature's Economy: A History of Ecological Ideas.* Cambridge: Cambridge University Press.
Zinn, Laura. 1991. "Whales, Human Rights, Rain Forests – and the Heady Smell of Profits." *Business Week*, July 15:114–115.
Zubko, Galina V. 1993. "Ethnic and Cultural Characteristics of the Fulbe." *Unity and Diversity of a People: The Search for Fulbe Identity.* (eds) Paul K. Eguchi and Victor Azarya. Senri Ethnological Studies. No. 35. Osaka [Japan]: National Museum of Ethnology, pp. 201-213.

ARCHIVE SOURCES

IRSH (l'Institut de Recherces en Science Humaines)
Bovin, Mette. 1970. Ethno-terms for ethnic groups. Unpublished document.

Centre Culturel Franco-Nigerien – Information Scientifique et Technique (IST)
Wenek, Sophie. n.d. J'ai laqué les ongles des magnifiques Bororodji du Niger. In *Sciences et voyages*, 7–14.

Ministère de l'Agriculture et de l'Elevage (Ministry of Agriculture and Livestock, MAL)
Habou, Akilou, Issoufou Any and Moussa Yacouba. 1990. Code Rural et Pastoralisme: Duxiéme Partie. Situation Actuelle Propositions. République du Niger. Secretariat Permanent du Comité National du Code Rural. République du Niger.

République du Niger. 1960. Reflexions sur les Problèmes de Développement Economique et Social dans la République du Niger.

République du Niger. 1978–1979. Annuaire Statistique. Direction de la Statistique et des Comptes Nationaux. Ministère du Plan.

République du Niger. 1983. Cinq Études sur la Formation en République du Niger: Etude D: Organisation de la direction du service de l'élevage et des industries animales (DSEIA). Commission des Communautés Européennes. République du Niger. Ministère du Plan.

SEDES.1974. Etude de Factibilité de deux projets de ranches Nord Dakoro Nord Goure. Ministère de l'Economie Rurale, de l'Environnement du Climat et d'Aide aux Population. République du Niger. SEDES (Societé d'Etudes pour le Développement Economique & Social).

UNCDF. 1984. Niger: Mission de Planification et de programmation. UNCDF. June 1984.

Ministère du Plan (CIDES Archives)

Mazou, Ibrahim. 1991. Les Politiques d'Élevage au Niger: Évolution Historique. Série Conférences no. 31. Stratégies composantes et politiques alimentaires au Sahel. Centre Sahel: Université Laval. Bibliothèque national du Québec.

Rupp, Mme Marianne. 1976. Observations sur la Situation Générale des Eleveurs après la sécheresse. USAID: Projet de Range Menagement et de l'élevage.

Sidikou, Hamidou Arouna. 1994. Les Associations Pastorales et la Gestion des Ressources Naturelles. Commission des Communautées Européennes. Direction Générale du Développement. Université d'Amsterdam, Faculté des Sciences Environmentales Département de Géographie Humaine. Université Abdou Moumouni de Niamey, Institute de Recherches en Science Humaines Département de Géographie et de l'Aménagement de l'Espace.

Bureau de Coopération Danoise (DANIDA Archives)

Dagois, Franck. 1995. Note Préparatoire pour l'Atelier National Hydraulique de Gestion et de Maintenance des Puits Cimentes. Association Française des Volontaires du Progres.

Guindon-Zador, Evelyne. 1995. L'Evaluation de la Sensibilisation et de la Communication sur l'Environnement: Le Processus de Code Rural au Niger. GreenCom. Environmental Education and Communication Project. U. S. Agency for International Development.

PNUD. 1991. Plan National de Lutte Contre la Désertification: Notes Départementales; Département de Tahoua. République du Niger. Projet PNUD/UNSO NER 90 X 04.

Ministère de l'Hydraulique et de l'Environnement (Ministry of Hydrology and the Environment, MHE)

République du Niger. 1993. Schema Directeur de Mise en Valeur et de Gestion des Ressources en Eau. Niamey. Ministère de l'hydraulique et de l'environnement.

INDEX

The author is referred to as Mariyama. *illus* refers to a photograph or illustration; *n* refers to footnote.

A

agriculture, 26
    crop cultivation, 37–8, 137, 141–2
A'isha, on marriage, 105–6
Akali
    and animal marking, 69–70
    and city life, 191
    and death, 164–5
    and drought, 114–16
    Jumare's accident, 160–4, 166
    and Mariyama, 57, 79, 81, 86–7, 90–2, 121, 124
    migration, 75–7, 123–5
Ali (petrol smuggler), 132–4, 225
Amazon rainforest, 48, 219
Amina (migrant worker), 167–8, 170–7
animals *see* cattle; livestock
anthropology, 14, 227, 228–9
    see also ethnography
archives, 33*n*
arDo (lineage chief), 76
Ardo (WoDaaBe chief), 9–10
artifacts *see* handicrafts

B

Bayre bi Tuka'e, 62
beds, 57*illus*, 64–5
beef production *see* ranches
Bermo (herder), 114–16, 125, 178–9
Body Shop, 52, 198–9
Bonfiglioli, Angelo Maliki, 235
Bovin, Mette, 235
bush life
    contrasted with city life, 139–40
    women's activities, 103, 169
    see also home in the bush
Buuda (migrant laborer), 135
Buuwa, 179, 185–6

C

calabashes, 142, 222*n*
calf rope (*dangol*), 62, 69, 71–2
camels, 68, 75, 77, 80*illus*
cattle
    affection for, 31, 71
    calf rope (*dangol*), 62, 69, 71–2
    cleanliness, 83
    economic and social significance, 67–9, 71
    fodder, 115–16
    herder's stick (*saaruu*), 129
    hired herding, 137, 142*n*
    milking bowl (*birdude*), 72
    origin myth, 62–3
    products for health and beauty, 71
    ranches, 31, 32, 206, 217
    stampede through camp, 82
    taboos, 71–2
    tail hair as body decoration, 71
    see also livestock
cattle-loans (*haBBanaaji*), 72, 73–4
ceeDo (dry/hot season), 60, 114
ceremonies
    and livestock, 72–3
    see also dance ceremonies; festivals
children
    and animals, 68–9
    concept of home, 69
    daily routine, 85, 87–9
city life
    contrast with bush life, 139–40
    koDei (desire/greed), 191–2, 224
    of women, 139, 142, 143, 144, 167–77
    see also migrant laborers; Niamey
civil society, 30
Clifford, James, 66
climate, 26, 58, 114, 117–18
    harmattan wind, 58, 114–15, 117
    see also seasons
clothing
    dance ceremonies, 179, 180*illus*, 181, 185
    of migrant laborers, 129
    for tourists, 149
    traditional WoDaaBe, 144
    turbans, 145, 146, 155, 223
co-operatives, 151–4

cold season (*dabbunde*), 60, 82–3, 90
compliments, 78
Council of Elders, 98–100
cowrie shells, 149
cows *see* cattle
craft products see handicrafts
crop cultivation, 37–8, 137, 141–2
Cultural Survival, 47
culture
    and access to power, 207–8
    see also dance ceremonies; handicrafts; jewelry

D
dabbunde (cold season), 60, 82–3, 90
Dadi (migrant laborer), bush v. city life, 121, 123, 140
daily routine, in the bush, 69n, 85, 87–9
dance ceremonies, 54–5
    audiences, 189, 195
    in the city, 42*illus*, 184
    clothing, 179, 180*illus*, 181, 185
    commercial, 151, 181, 192–8, 193*illus*, 196*illus*
    and ethnicity, 184–90
    geerewol, 53–5, 53*illus*
    and gender, 186–8
    juulde, 184–5, 189–90, 208
    lineage groups, 178–9, 185
    male body decoration, 71
    maleness and beauty, 187–8
    men's, 183
    and sale of artifacts, 151, 195, 198, 212–13
    sexuality in, 54–5
    spectators, 187*illus*
    tourist photographs, 178, 186, 208
    Western spectators, 183, 186, 189
    and women, 182–3, 187, 219
desertification, 39
desire (*koDei*), 191–2, 224, 225–6
development
    criticism of, 20, 27, 29–30, 40–1, 154, 210
    history of, 27–30
    importance to Niger, 26–7

    importance to WoDaaBe, 224–5
    motives, 19–20, 27–30
    and Niger government, 37, 217–18
    pastoral people, 30–3, 204–5
    and power, 216–17
    WoDaaBe view of, 203–7
divorce, 119
djelgul cattle marking, 69–71
Djuri (Bermi's father-in-law), 99–100, 125
donkeys, 68, 122*illus*, 133
Dro, 25*illus*, 184
drought, 32, 36, 37, 114–17
dry season (*ceeDo*), 60, 114
duDal fire, 62–3, 69, 72
Dupire, Marguerite, 101, 193–4, 234

E
eco-indigenism, 46–8, 145, 218, 219
embroidery
    by bush dwellers, 85
    by migrant laborers, 130
    Mariyama takes up, 119–21
    patterns, 168–9
    for tourists, 149–51, 150*illus*, 169
emotions
    affection, 77
    desire (*koDei*), 191–2, 224, 225–6
    munyal (patience), 95–6, 223
    women's emotional control, 111–13, 171
    see also moral values
environmentalism, 46–8, 145, 218, 219
erosion, 58
ethnicity
    and dance ceremonies, 184–7
    Fulani, 93, 98, 158
    and identity, 158–9, 217–18
    WoDaaBe, 18, 92–8, 158–9, 184–7
ethnography, 15–16, 66, 227–31, 232–3

F
family obligations, 61, 121, 138
famine, 157
    see also drought
festivals
    Cure Sallée, 63, 76
    for love and sexuality, 101

INDEX

of new-born baby, 97*illus*
   see also dance ceremonies
fieldwork, 15–16, 229
fire (duDal), 62–3, 69, 72
firewood collection, 83–4, 143
food
   milk (*daniDam*), 91–2
   millet porridge, 78, 107illus
   rules for eating, 78–9
Fulani
   ethnicity, 93, 98, 158
   Hamitic language, 50
   origins of, 52–3
   physical characteristics, 48–9, 51, 52
   pulaaku (social-moral rules), 93–4
   and WoDaaBe, 11–12, 98, 149, 151, 158, 223
Fulfulde language, 11, 72, 79, 95

G
Ganduu, 99–100
gasoline smuggling, 129–36
geerewol ceremony, 53–5, 53illus
gender
   and dance, 186–8
   and lineage groups, 188–9
   segregation, 103
   WoDaaBe viewed as male, 218–19
   see also men; women
Gidado (Akali's brother), 76, 82, 85–6, 114–16
gift exchange, 71
globalization, 19, 202–3
glossary, 6
goats, 68, 124–5, 126*illus*
gonsul migration, 75–7, 81–4, 123–5
groundnut production, 37–8
guards, 134–5, 143, 145–6, 225
guests, in the bush, 64
Guirgui, 104*illus*

H
haBBanaaji (cattle-loans), 72, 73–4
hair braiding, 130, 142, 144, 170, 171–5, 176–7

handicrafts
   adapted for Westerners, 207–8
   co-operatives, 151–4
   overseas dance trips, 151, 195, 198, 212–13
   production, 13, 144–5, 153illus
   selling, 211, 223
   see also clothing; embroidery; jewelry
harmattan wind, 58, 114–15, 117
Hassane (herder), 114
Hausa, 97–8, 157–8, 159
health
   use of cattle products, 71
   see also medicine
herders *see* cattle; livestock; pastoralism
Herskovits, Melville, 67
home in the bush
   beds, 57*illus*, 64–5
   calf rope (*dangol*), 62, 69, 71–2
   daily routine, 69n, 85, 87–9
   description, 57, 57*illus*, 61–3
   duDal fire area, 62–3, 69, 72
   living arrangements, 63–6
   place for guests (*daDDol*), 64
   and the seasons, 126
Hopben, C.E., 234
hospital visit, 160–5

I
Ibonou (herder), 74
Ibrahim, 76, 99–100
identity, 17–18
   see also ethnicity; indigenous people; 'white' Westerners
identity cards, 221
indigenous people
   definition, 44–6
   eco-indigenism, 46–8, 145, 218, 219
   rights, 219–20
   survival, 198–9
   WoDaaBe as, 51, 215–16
Inne (Mariyama's friend), 179, 181–3, 188
international agencies, 26–7

J
jewelry
  making, 145, 149
  selling, 11, 151, 199, 223
Jumare (Akali's sister), 86, 118–19, 120, 160–4, 166
juulde dance ceremony, 184–5, 189–90, 208

K
Kala'i (Akali's father)
  and Mariyama, 11, 226
  migration, 123, 124
  and the WoDaaBe, 9, 59–60, 99–100
Kayapó Indians, 48, 147
kobgal marriage, 72, 107, 170
koDei (desire), 191–2, 224, 225–6
kokke season (first rainfall), 60, 114, 126

L
land, 37–41
languages
  Fulfulde, 11, 52n28, 72, 79, 95
  Hamitic origin of Fulani, 50
  Mariyama's ability, 11, 60, 79, 86
  in Niamey, 157
leso (bed), 57*illus*
lightning, 117–18
lineage chief (*arDo*), 76
lineage groups, 5*illus*, 143, 188–9
  in the cities, 138
  dance ceremonies, 178–9, 185
  women and, 106–7, 188
livestock
  and children, 68–9
  djelgul marking, 69–71
  and famine, 114–16, 137
  health, 33, 116n, 141
  importance for WoDaaBe, 10, 67–74
  ownership patterns, 35–6
  slaughter, 72, 73n
  and social ceremonies, 72–3
  taxation, 33, 34
  watering, 122*illus*
  see also cattle
living arrangements, in the bush, 63–6
Loftsdóttir, Kristín *see* Mariyama

Loutan, L., 235

M
Mama (*kobgal* wife), 170–1, 176
Mariyama
  and Akali, 57, 79, 81, 86–7, 90–2, 121, 124
  in border town, 129–36
  in the bush, 57, 63–6, 81–7, 121, 123
  city accommodation, 16, 210
  city experiences, 167–8, 170–7, 178–84
  and death, 164–6
  as ethnographer, 9, 14, 85–6, 101, 228–31, 232–3
  and food, 78–9
  and Jumare, 160–4, 166, 167
  language abilities, 11, 60, 79, 86
  on migration, 75, 123–4
  pick-up journey, 96
  sadness, 90–2
  travels on foot, 77, 124
  and the weather, 82–3, 117
  as white person, 20, 200–1, 209–10
  WoDaaBe reactions to her, 111, 127–8, 167
  and the women, 111, 119–21, 167
markets, 58, 171
marriage
  breakdown of, 119, 121
  and co-wives, 105–6, 108
  endogamous within lineage, 159, 177
  kobgal (as young children), 72, 107, 170
  teegal (as adults), 72, 106–8, 170
mbodagansi (morality), 93–5, 223
meat production *see* ranches
medicine
  aid, 204
  traditional medicine, 142, 144
men
  and co-wives, 105–6, 108
  and dancing, 71, 183, 187–8
  and girlfriends (*semaru*), 105, 106
  life stages, 103
  and wife-beating, 103, 105–6
  and women, 103, 111–12
  see also marriage

migrant laborers
    clothing, 129
    and dance ceremonies, 189–90
    gasoline smuggling, 129–36
    historical background, 141–3
    living conditions, 130, 134–5
    numbers, 138–9, 143–4, 146
    occupations, 130–2, 144
    and pastoral society, 147
    powerlessness, 9, 10–11, 208–13
    reasons for, 12, 132, 135, 137, 146–7
    and relatives, 130, 137–8
    resiliance, 222
    return home in rainy season, 61, 140–1, 147–8
    send money home, 61–2, 146
    shame, 134, 154–5
    support family in the bush, 132–4
    wish to buy livestock, 132, 135–6, 147–8
    wish to return home, 13, 133, 136, 138, 139–40, 148
migration (*gonsul*), 75–7, 81–4, 123–5
milk (*daniDam*), 91–2
millet
    animal fodder, 115
    porridge, 78, 107*illus*
moral values
    Fulfulde conduct, 95
    mbodagansi (morality), 93–5, 209–10, 223
    munyal (patience), 95–6, 223
    pulaaku, 93–4
    semtuDum (shame), 94–5, 125, 134, 154–5
    women's behaviour, 112
multinational corporations, 217
munyal (patience), 95–6, 223

N
National Geographic, 50, 54
Netting, Robert, 67
NGOs (Non-Governmental Organizations), 30

Niamey
    contrasted with bush life, 139–40
    history and development, 156–7
    Katako market, 171
    Mariyama's accommodation, 16, 210
    women's lives, 167–77
Niger
    and development, 37, 217–18
    economy, 26, 35
    history, 24, 33–4
    land tenure, 39–40
    privatization, 217
    State, 217–18, 221
    Tchin-Tabaraden district, 5*maps*, 58–9, 97
Nigeria, 129–30, 133, 143, 220
night watchmen, 130, 132, 144
    see also security guards
Njunju (herder), 123
Nomads of Niger, 50, 145, 207
Nomads of the Worlds, 50

O
occupations
    city, 130, 143–6, 154–5
    women in the bush, 103, 169
    women in Niamey, 142, 143, 144, 167–77
    see also embroidery; hair braiding; jewelry; security guards
the Other, 20

P
pastoralism, 30–3, 34–5, 36–7, 40, 155–6
patience (*munyal*), 95–6, 223
peanut (groundnut) production, 37–8
petrol smuggling, 129–36
photography, at dance ceremonies, 178, 186, 208
porridge, 78, 107*illus*
power
    agents of power, 216–17
    using culture to gain, 207–8
    WoDaaBe powerlessness, 9, 10–11, 208–13
prostitution, 174–7

pseudonyms, use of, 231
pulaaku (social-moral rules), 93-4

R
race *see* indigenous people; 'white' Westerners
rain
　average rainfall, 26, 58
　kokke season (first rainfall), 60, 114, 126
rainy season (*yaawol*), 60, 75-6
rainbows, 118
Rainforest Foundation, 47
rainforests, 47-8
ranches, 31, 32, 206, 217
Riesman, Paul, 235
rope selling, 155

S
saga (table), 57*illus*
Sahel, 58
sales
　artifacts at dance ceremonies, 151, 195, 198, 212-13
　handicrafts, 155, 211, 223
　jewelry, 11, 151, 199, 223
　rope, 155
　tea, 144, 146, 155
Samari, 210
seasons, 58, 60
　ceeDo (dry/hot), 60, 114
　dabbunde (cold), 60, 82-3, 90
　kokke (first rainfall), 60, 114, 126
　yaawol (rainy), 60, 75-6
security guards, 134-5, 143, 145-6, 225
sexuality, dance ceremonies, 54-5
shame (*semtuDum*), 94-5, 125, 134, 154-5
sheep, 68
silver *see* jewelry
Sollare
　befriends Mariyama, 77-8
　daily routine, 85, 87-9
　dance trip, 195
　desires, 225
　and embroidery, 120
　view of 'aid projects', 205
Stenning, Derrick, 234-5

storms, 117-18
subject positions, 214-15
suudu (house), 61
Swift, Jeremy, 235
swords, 145

T
table (*saga*), 57*illus*
taboos
　cattle, 71-2
　duDal fire, 62, 72
　migration movements, 83, 125
tattoos, 158, 223n
taxation, livestock, 33.34
Tchin-Tabaraden district, 5*maps*, 58-9, 97
tea selling, 144, 146, 155
teegal marriage, 72, 106-8, 170
tents, 117
theft, WoDaaBe fear being accused of, 210
Third World, 43-4
thunderstorms, 117-18
tourism, 145, 149-52, 207, 212, 220-1, 223, 224
　see also dance ceremonies; handicrafts
traditional medicine, 142, 144
transportation, 38*illus*, 75, 80*illus*, 96, 222n
Tuaregs, 145, 158-9
turbans, 145, 146, 155, 223

U
United Nations, 46, 219
United States, 28, 29, 51
uranium, 24, 26

V
vegetation, 58-9

W
water
　in the bush, 75-6, 83, 85, 126-7
　calabashes, 142, 222n
　city water carriers, 144, 155
　for livestock, 122*illus*
　well construction projects, 204
weather *see* climate
wells, construction projects, 204

White, Cynthia, 235
'white' Westerners, 20-2, 153-4, 201,
    208-11, 224-5
Wilson, Wendy, 235
wind, 58, 114-15, 117
WoDaaBe
  ethnic identity, 18, 92-8, 158-9, 184-7
  and Fulani, 11-12, 98, 149, 151, 158, 223
  and the future, 155-6, 222-4
  indigenous people, 51, 215-16
  lineage organization 5*illus*
  and livestock, 10, 67-74
  marginalization, 12
  media representation, 13, 42-3,
    50-5, 207-8
  and Nigerien nationality, 221
  numbers, 11*n*
  origins, 52-3, 62-3, 159n
  patrilocality, 61
  physical characteristics, 48-9, 51, 52,
    223*n*
  powerlessness, 9, 10-11, 208-13
  and questioning, 86-7
  research on, 16-17, 16-22, 234-5
  subject positions, 215-21
  and Westerners, 15, 153-4, 210-11,
    224

women
  boofiiDo period, 102-3, 108-10
  breasts, 110
  bush activities, 103, 169
  and cattle-loans, 73-4
  city occupations, 142, 143, 144, 167-77
  and co-wives, 105-6, 108
  dance ceremonies, 182-3, 187, 219
  emotional control, 111-13, 171
  hair color, 71
  and husband's girlfriends (*semaru*),
    105, 106
  life stages, 102-3, 108-10
  menstruation, 103
  sexual freedom, 101-2
  status, 219
  travel abroad, 144
  wife-beating, 103, 105-6
  see also embroidery
World Bank, 51, 219-20
wuro (home), 57*illus*, 61-3

Y
yaawol season (rainy), 60, 75-6

Z
Zerma language, 157